D1604239

Virginia at War, 1863

VIRGINIA
AT WAR
1863

Edited by William C. Davis
and James I. Robertson Jr.
for the Virginia Center for Civil War Studies

THE UNIVERSITY PRESS OF KENTUCKY

Scholarly publisher for the Commonwealth,
serving Bellarmine University, Berea College, Centre
College of Kentucky, Eastern Kentucky University,
The Filson Historical Society, Georgetown College,
Kentucky Historical Society, Kentucky State University,
Morehead State University, Murray State University,
Northern Kentucky University, Transylvania University,
University of Kentucky, University of Louisville,
and Western Kentucky University.
All rights reserved.

Editorial and Sales Offices: The University Press of Kentucky
663 South Limestone Street, Lexington, Kentucky 40508-4008
www.kentuckypress.com

ISBN 978-0-8131-2510-7

Manufactured in the United States of America.

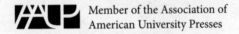 Member of the Association of
American University Presses

A Book Club Edition

Contents

Preface

After all the activity of 1862 on the battlefields, the year that followed in some ways seemed like a return to 1861 for Virginians. There was but one major battle on their soil, though it cost them one of their two great heroes of the conflict. Other actions were minor by comparison, and the greatest battlefield effort of the year for Virginian armies took place in the North, at Gettysburg. Perhaps it is well that it was so, for by 1863 the pressures of the conflict, not just in the Old Dominion but all across the Confederacy, were turning other aspects of life in the state into battlegrounds of their own.

Consequently, this third volume of the series Virginia at War looks more inward, at what the war was doing to the people and their institutions by the midpoint of the conflict. From the outset, the approach of this series has been to provide only a broad outline of military operations of each year for reference and context, but otherwise to stay off the battlefield to examine the war experience in its political, social, economic, and even psychological aspects. In this respect 1863 is a particularly rich year for study, for by then the war was stamping its impress upon virtually everything in the average Virginian's daily life. It interrupted the education of youth, disrupted the affairs of the church and challenged the faith of every flock, provided opportunities never before available to some of Virginia's slaves, and pitted families against one another in miniature echoes of the war itself. It made Virginians look for new occupations to take their minds from the uncertainty and anxiety of what was happening at the front, and come to terms with what was happening among their brothers-turned-enemies in the North.

Preceded by the epic activity of 1862 and half a dozen major battles, and soon to be followed by the grueling military campaigning of 1864, the year 1863 itself was oddly a rather quiet year militarily for the Old Dominion. Only one major battle would be fought on its soil, though that one, Chancellorsville, would be the greatest victory of the Army of Northern Virginia's career. Other than some inconclusive, might-have-been operations in the late fall, the big battlefield moments for Virginians after Chancellorsville would come on another state's soil, in the North, in Pennsylvania. Yet it was still a season of considerable minor activity in southwest Virginia and in the southeast as well, in the always important Shenandoah Valley. The year's land operations are ably outlined here by A. Wilson Greene, the author of one of the finest books yet written on a portion of the Petersburg campaign of 1864–1865. Greene is a distinguished public historian who spent many years with the National Park Service before becoming president of the Association for the Preservation of Civil War Sites (now the Civil War Preservation Trust). For more than a decade now he has been director of Pamplin Historical Park near Petersburg, Virginia, one of the nation's most innovative Civil War interpretive sites.

War spares no one, but its impact on youth, especially during the Civil War, has largely gone unstudied until recent years. Whether the field armies were active or not, the mere existence of a war, and the hardships and shortages that maintaining large standing armies imposed on the civilian population, dictated that every category of civilian felt the war deeply. None felt it more than Virginia's children who, though youth may have kept them happily unaware of just what was going on beyond their home orbit, could not help but notice the absence of fathers and brothers, the disappearance of schoolteachers, the scarcity of treats and even staples from their dinner tables, and the anxious and often anguished looks on their parents' faces. By 1863 that shortage and hardship had finally come into virtually every home, for two years of war, the incredible casualties of Antietam, Chancellorsville, and especially Gettysburg, plus the expanding reach of army impressment officers taking food and livestock from civilian barns and pastures, meant that everyone felt the pinch now, even the youngest. Meanwhile, the closed schools, the shortage of books and learning materials, the funerals of fathers killed in action, all brought the battlefield to the hearth. James Marten takes a penetrating look at the wartime experience of the Old Dominion's children in all its ramifications. In many ways it was no different than that of children in other states north and south, but Virginia was still a special case because so much of it was occupied territory from early in the war, and because it hosted more fighting than any other state: for its youth, the war was always on the doorstep. Marten is the author of *The Children's Civil War* as well as several other distinguished works, including *Children and War: A Historical Anthology* and *Texas Divided: Loyalty and Dissent in the Lone Star State,*

1856–1874. He is professor of history and chair of the history department at Marquette University.

Ironically, even while a major segment of Virginia's youth was seeing its education suffer by 1863 due to the war's demands, there was one other, until then largely forgotten, group of youths whose educational opportunities began to expand dramatically, thanks directly to the war. Having undertaken to secure freedom for slaves, Northern philanthropists and social reformers realized that the next thing after freedom must be education, which had been virtually banned in the Southern states after various slave uprisings made slave owners fearful that an educated servile population would be better equipped to conspire to revolt. The Protestant churches were the first to address the challenge, though they would soon be followed by other humanitarian groups and eventually by the Union government via the Freedmen's Bureau. In 1862 the first missionaries from the North arrived in southeastern Virginia, now securely under Union occupation, to begin teaching fundamentals to the thousands of escaped Virginian slaves who had come there as soon as Union military forces established a foothold, but it would be in the following year that the educational mission to the freedpeople really took hold, and with it one of the foundations of the ill-starred programs later carried on during Reconstruction. Benjamin H. Trask provides an insightful exploration of these early, fumbling—though well-intentioned—efforts. Trask earned his bachelor's and master's degrees in education and history at Virginia Tech, and a second master's in library science from the University of North Carolina. He spent many years as a communications officer for the United States Marines and is author of three histories of Virginia Confederate regiments, as well as editor of the Confederate memoirs of William H. Stewart and William C. Corsan. He is currently a teacher and historical consultant in Williamsburg, Virginia.

It is a truism that civil wars are always the most bloody and destructive, because they often continue and exacerbate old prewar political, social, and family feuds under the legitimizing guise of warfare. They also originate new feuds that outlast the wars themselves, and certainly the Civil War did both. What was probably America's most celebrated family feud of all saw its origins in the mountains of western Virginia, the legendary Hatfield-McCoy feud, which really took hold in 1863 but would last the rest of the war and then carry on well into the next century. It was appropriate that such feuds grew out of the mountains, where remoteness tended to exaggerate the family's importance as a social, economic, and protective unit. Moreover, in the thinly settled mountain regions of the South the war was always most bitter because of the deep divisions of sympathies, whereby pro-Confederate mountaineers were often pitted against former neighbors who sided with the Union. For Virginians this was exaggerated even more by the split between Virginia and the new—and scarcely legitimate—Union state of West Virginia. No one has studied the origins of the Hatfield-McCoy feud more thoroughly than James M. Prichard, whose essay brings to light much new material never before examined. He is an Ohio native who took his undergraduate and master's degrees at Wright State University. For more than twenty years he has been supervisor of the Research Room at the Kentucky State Archives in Frankfort, and he is also adjunct professor of history at Kentucky State University. Long involved with studies on the Underground Railroad, he is also coauthor of a history of the Confederate Tenth Kentucky Cavalry. He is currently at work on a book dealing with a mass slave escape attempt in Kentucky in 1848.

In such a volatile wartime environment, with friendly and invading armies both eroding the traditional security of home and community, with former slaves starting to run free, with children cut loose from parental control, and the war often coming down to the most local and personal level as family was pitted against family, the church was often the last remaining institution of social control and stability. Yet war disrupts the work of gods as well as that of men. Contrary to wartime propaganda, neither Union nor Confederate soldiers targeted enemy churches for wanton vandalism or disruption, but still it occasionally happened. Pastors went to war with the troops, leaving laymen behind to try to continue ministering to an increasingly frightened and insecure flock. The growing losses at the front presented civilians at home with ever-greater challenges to their faith as Virginians wondered if God were really on their side, and if he was, how he could allow their sons and husbands and fathers to keep dying in ever-increasing numbers. How were people to maintain faith in a loving supreme being in the midst of a nightmare that a just God seemingly would not allow to happen? By the midpoint of the war, pressure on faith reached its greatest force, testing both the temporal and the spiritual reserves of Virginians as they had never been tried before. David Rolfs examines the ordeal of the Old Dominion's churches and their congregations, and the changes that the conflict wrought on both. Rolfs earned his doctorate at Florida State University and is currently an instructor of history at Maclay College Preparatory School in Tallahassee. His doctoral dissertation dealing with the religious experience of Civil War soldiers will soon be published.

Besides the church, Virginian civilians turned to many other pastimes to fill their idle hours in the absence of so many of their prewar entertainments. One new, mostly middle-class, hobby that had come on the scene shortly before the war was the keeping of scrapbooks. The war and scrapbook keeping, in fact, came at just the right time for each other. The result was that thousands of civilians—and even a few soldiers—began keeping their own highly personalized record or archive of their war experience in the blank pages of almanacs or store ledgers, or in purpose-made scrapbooks themselves. Many—indeed probably most—started in 1861, but it was the events of 1863 in Virginia that would provide more content for scrapbooks than any other year of the war. Coeditor of this series William C. Davis examines the social phenomenon of scrapbooking in Virginia during the war and what it produced, much of it of lasting historical importance to this day. Davis, director of programs for the Virginia Center for Civil War Studies, is a Missouri native who for many years was editor, then publisher, of *Civil War Times* and numerous other magazines. He is author or editor of more than fifty books on the Civil War and southern history.

One thing very few Virginians included in their scrapbooks was a newspaper copy of Abraham Lincoln's Gettysburg Address. Not only was Lincoln himself the devil incarnate to many Confederates, but any reminder of Gettysburg and the devastating losses in Lee's army only served to keep alive the horror of the casualty lists and the shock of defeat. Yet the manner in which Virginians did learn what little they heard of Lincoln's epic speech is revealing of how civilians in the Old Dominion received and interpreted much of their news from the world outside their communities. Jared Peatman provides an insightful examination of what Virginians knew of the events of November 19, 1863, at Gettysburg and how they learned it. Peatman received his bachelor's degree from Gettysburg College and his master's degree in 2006 from Virginia Tech, where he helped develop a forthcoming Civil War newspaper index Web site while a graduate assistant for the Virginia Center for Civil War Studies. He is currently working on his doctorate at Texas A&M University.

As in the previous two volumes of this series, one contemporary voice continues to speak for Virginians and their wartime experience, Judith

Brockenbrough McGuire. This first annotated edition of her famous *Diary of a Southern Refugee during the War* continues in the mold of the previous two installments. Once again, because the balance of coverage in the diary is not equal for every year, the portion contained in this volume does not strictly relate only to 1863. Rather, it begins with September 2, 1862, and concludes with the entry of May 28, 1863, when McGuire is jubilant over recent good news from Vicksburg, Mississippi, and saddened by the recent casualties at Chancellorsville. As previously, this installment is edited by James I. Robertson Jr., coeditor of this series. Robertson, director of the Virginia Center for Civil War Studies, is one of the deans of Civil War historians. He served as executive director of the United States Civil War Centennial Commission, and is author or editor of more than thirty distinguished works, including the multi-prize-winning *Stonewall Jackson*. He is Alumni Distinguished Professor of History at Virginia Tech, where he has been on the faculty for nearly forty years.

The editors continue to express their gratitude not only to the contributors to this volume, but most especially to the family of William E. Jamerson of Appomattox, Virginia, for its generous support of this project as it now passes its midpoint. They should also like to thank once more the staff of the University Press of Kentucky, particularly director Stephen M. Wrinn and editor Joyce Harrison, for the high editorial and production standards they continue to maintain, as well as for their commitment to this series. We look forward to working with them all again as the final two volumes come to fruition.

Virginia at War, 1863

Land Operations in Virginia in 1863

High-water Mark and Beginning of the Ebb

A. Wilson Greene

The Union army of the Potomac awakened on New Year's Day 1863 in a bad mood. Their cheerless, mud-soaked camps in southern Stafford County contributed to their foul humor, but memories of December's fiasco at Fredericksburg explained most of their discontent. "The recent battle was only a murder, for which [army commander] . . . A. E. Burnside [is] responsible," wrote one Michigan survivor of the slaughter on the far side of the Rappahannock. South of the river, the Army of Northern Virginia basked in the praise of its beloved commander, Gen. Robert E. Lee, who had just the night before lauded the "fortitude, valor, and devotion" of his soldiers while acknowledging their great victory.[1]

Maj. Gen. Ambrose E. Burnside, the genial but now discredited Union commander, determined to spare his army a winter of humiliation and despair. Overcoming the political machinations of scheming and disloyal subordinates and the grave doubts of President Abraham Lincoln and his military brain trust in Washington, Burnside gained permission to launch a new offensive in January. He planned to march secretly up the left bank of the Rappahannock and cross at Banks's Ford, four miles above Fredericksburg and beyond the strongest portions of Lee's river defenses. Feints orchestrated farther upstream and below the city would keep Lee guessing long enough to allow Burnside to maneuver the main body of his army across the river to Spotsylvania County. From there, the Federals could move on Lee's dangling left flank and compel the Confederates either to fight at a disadvantage or to retreat southward, closer to their capital at Richmond. The movement would begin on January 20.

The plan was not without merit and might have succeeded—had it not been January. A fierce nor'easter, laden with a cold rain that turned Stafford County into a sea of boot-gripping mire, stopped the Army of the Potomac in its tracks. Whatever confidence the soldiers—and the country—had retained in Burnside after the Fredericksburg debacle washed away with the topsoil that drained into the roiling Rappahannock. Burnside's tenure as army commander concluded on January 25, when Lincoln named one of his primary detractors, Maj. Gen. Joseph Hooker, to replace him.[2]

Hooker, a boastful man whose ego far exceeded his ethics, took immediate steps to improve the army's fighting trim. Although known as "Fighting Joe," Hooker demonstrated a firm grasp of organizational principles and army administration. He improved camp sanitation and rations, granted furloughs to the dispirited men, established a Bureau of Military Information to gather intelligence, and instituted a corps badge system, which provided the troops with unit esprit de corps while making it easier to identify malingerers. He also reconfigured the army, adding a separate cavalry corps, the first step toward revolutionizing the usefulness of that combat arm.[3]

Lee and his army struggled with different administrative challenges, primarily the fundamental need for supplies. Central Virginia already endured a deteriorating economy, and providing enough food for the soldiers and fodder for the horses and mules during the winter months proved difficult. "The Yankees say that we have a new gen'l in command of our army & say his name is *General Starvation* & I think for once they are about right," wrote a Georgia soldier. "We generally draw rations for three days at a time & eat them up in two, & do without untill we draw again."[4]

General Lee and the Confederate War Department looked covetously at southeastern Virginia and neighboring North Carolina, where huge volumes of grain, preserved meat, and livestock lay ripe for the taking from the Tidewater's occupying bluecoats. In February, Lee detached his "old war horse," Lt. Gen. James Longstreet, along with two veteran infantry divisions to mount a campaign aimed at collecting those supplies. Lee would remain on the defensive around Fredericksburg, but he warned Longstreet that should Hooker cross the Rappahannock, Longstreet must hurry north to meet the foe.

Hooker spent the season honing his army—"the finest on the planet," he pronounced it—and allowing his new cavalry corps to flex its muscles. The Federal horsemen broke the calm of the waning winter on March 17 with a bold operation twenty-five miles up the Rappahannock to Kelly's Ford. In the war's largest all-cavalry battle to date, the Union horsemen encountered the Virginia troopers of Brig. Gen. Fitzhugh Lee, the Confederate commander's nephew. After spirited combat, the Yankees withdrew with the honors, although the outnumbered Virginians had given as well as they took. Maj. John Pelham, the renowned young Confederate artillerist who had garnered Lee's praise at Fredericksburg, fell mortally wounded at Kelly's Ford, plunging both Virginia and Pelham's native Alabama into mourning.[5]

A month later, Longstreet's forces launched their campaign toward Suffolk in southeastern Virginia. Their operation drew little blood, and the Confederates managed to extract more than one million pounds of bacon and other needed edibles from Virginia and Tarheel farms. But while Longstreet gathered rations, Lee and Stonewall Jackson were left to cope with Hooker's spring offensive.[6]

Ironically, Hooker's plan borrowed liberally from the premise of Burnside's infamous "Mud March." As Burnside did in January, Hooker would bait the Confederates with feigned offensives both opposite Fredericksburg and a few miles downstream. Mesmerizing Lee and Jackson with this show of force, Hooker's main body would sneak well upriver—to the scene of the recent cavalry battle at Kelly's Ford—and there cross the Rappahannock beyond the Confederate river defenses. Four Federal infantry corps would rendezvous at a rural intersection dominated by the red brick Chancellor house—endowed with the pretentious name of Chancellorsville—ten miles west of Fredericksburg. Hooker would send his cavalry corps on an even wider sweep to the west, where it would eventually cut Lee's communications with Richmond. If all went as planned, Lee's army, trapped between superior forces at Fredericksburg and Chancellorsville, would flee south, be slowed by the cavalry, and then face destruction from the blue wave that would engulf it in pursuit. "May God have mercy on General Lee," Hooker intoned, "for I will have none." Hooker's confidence was not without substance. With Longstreet absent in southeastern Virginia, Lee's 60,000 soldiers faced odds of more than two to one.[7]

Information about the Federal movements gradually arrived at Lee's headquarters near Fredericksburg, but deciphering what it all meant puzzled the Confederate high command. Were the Yankees intending to attack below Fredericksburg? Was the flanking movement to the west, reported by cavalry chief J. E. B. "Jeb" Stuart, a lunge toward the railroad junction at Gordonsville, a diversion toward the Shenandoah Valley, or the business end of a giant strategic pincers? On the night of April 29, Lee sent one division west to watch the gathering enemy.

By the next evening, he determined that Hooker's flanking movement represented the true threat. Lee ordered one of Jackson's divisions, reinforced by a brigade, to remain on the high ground overlooking Fredericksburg while the bulk of Stonewall's force marched west through the night to assume a blocking position east of Chancellorsville. This would be but the first of a series of gambles executed by Lee and Jackson during five days of maneuver and combat that would demonstrate that inspired generalship could trump superior firepower.[8]

Jackson arrived at an important intersection six miles west of Fredericksburg on the morning of May 1. The division that preceded him had begun to dig earthworks covering both the Orange Plank Road and Orange Turnpike leading from Chancellorsville toward Fredericksburg. Told by Lee only to make preparations to repulse the enemy, Stonewall instructed the soldiers to lay down their shovels and pick up their rifles. Jackson would attack.

The Federals had unwisely halted their advance on April 30 to consolidate their forces (the first of Hooker's many mistakes in this campaign), but by the morning of May 1 the Union commander had assembled more than 65,000 men in the Chancellorsville area; Jackson had fewer than 20,000 on the ground. Hooker expected the Confederates to "ingloriously fly" when confronted with the reality of their situation, but instead he found himself the target of a bold and aggressive offensive. Jackson's audacity drained the conviction from Fighting Joe's swagger. The Northerners slowly retired to Chancellorsville, where Hooker ordered his army to assume defensive positions, squandering the advantages gained by his successful marching. Thus handed the initiative, General Lee joined Jackson at an obscure country crossroads, and the two great Virginians pondered their next move.[9]

Chancellorsville occupied the eastern margins of what residents called "the Wilderness of Spotsylvania." This area of some eighty square miles contained quantities of iron ore that at once limited the fertility of the soil and gave birth to a modest smelting industry. Old furnaces dotted the landscape, now entangled by second- and third-growth scrub oak and pine, the by-product of several generations of charcoal making. Roads were scarce, as were clearings and homesteads. The open ground around Chancellorsville provided one of the few places in the Wilderness where contending armies might see their foes. In this Virginia jungle, Lee and Jackson first had to locate their opponent.

Scouts penetrated the darkness of that chilly night, eventually returning to the commanders' little bivouac with the news that the Yankees had created a strong perimeter guarding the Chancellorsville crossroads. No practical means existed of attacking them in their lair. Then Jeb Stuart dashed into the camp with important information. Hooker had failed to anchor his right flank on any natural or artificial obstacle. In the parlance of the time, Hooker's flank was "in the air." Lee and Jackson immediately appreciated this potential weakness, but they still faced the problem of exploiting it. More scouts, guided by local citizens and aided by Jackson's chaplain, who knew the area well, identified a series of hidden charcoal roads that might provide an avenue to pounce on Hooker's exposed flank.

The two generals sat on abandoned hardtack boxes around a modest campfire. "What do you propose to do?" asked Lee, knowing full well that both men had the same plan in mind. "Go around here," came Jackson's response, as he pointed to the twelve-mile hike outlined by the scouts. "What do you propose to make this movement with?" countered Lee. "With my whole corps," Jackson replied. Jackson's audacity momentarily surprised even the bold Lee. Stonewall's proposal possessed the virtue of providing enough punch to do serious harm to Hooker's vulnerable army—assuming he could march his men to their attack points without being detected and in time to exploit their opportunity. But while Jackson marched, Lee would be left with only 13,000 men to bemuse Hooker. Should the Union commander regain his vigor, or even detect the nature of his divided enemy, the Army of Northern Virginia could face destruction.[10]

Lee assented without further hesitation. The two officers spoke briefly on the morning of May 2, and then Jackson led his 30,000 troops into the green maze of the Wilderness. It was the last time Virginia's two greatest soldiers would meet.[11]

Jackson's flanking march began about 7:00 A.M. on May 2 and would continue all day. Stonewall took precise steps to maintain discipline and to keep his ranks closed as the men negotiated narrow roads that snaked through the thick foliage. Despite all of these precautions, the Federals discovered Jackson's movement within an hour after it commenced. Lookouts located in trees atop high ground called Hazel Grove spotted the gray column as it passed a clearing about a mile to the south. Quickly, word of this ominous development spread through the Union high command. Hooker authorized his gunners to fire at the marching Confederates, and he sent warnings to his right flank commander, Maj. Gen. Oliver O. Howard, to be on the alert for a possible Confederate offensive. Jackson diverted his men away from the clearing, detached a few troops as a rear guard facing Hazel Grove, and continued his mission.

Hooker, however, developed a change of heart. By noon he had convinced himself that the Confederates were in the process of retreating, not maneuvering for an attack. After all, this was the outcome he had anticipated all along. Eventually he ordered a large portion of his army to sally forward from Hazel Grove and gobble up the Confederate rear guard around Catharine Furnace. By then Stonewall was in place and ready to strike.

Jackson's flank attack ranks among the most famous of all Civil War offensives. He arrayed his brigades on both sides of the Orange Turnpike and at about 5:00 P.M. signaled the advance. General Howard had done little to heed Hooker's morning warning, and, in fact, had been assured that the Confederates were in retreat. The troops once in his immediate support were now around Catharine Furnace among the Union units scooping up Jackson's rear guard. Howard stood truly isolated, and Jackson's assault caught the Federal corps completely by surprise. The Northerners put up a better fight than is usually acknowledged, but by nightfall Howard's entire corps had been routed, and Jackson's advance forces halted less than one mile west of Hooker's headquarters at Chancellorsville.[12]

Not content with the day's remarkable accomplishments, General Jackson sought to deliver a knockout blow. He ordered fresh troops, who had arrived too late to be involved in the flank attack, to make their way to the front lines in preparation for a night assault. While they moved into position, Jackson and a small party of staff officers, couriers, and scouts plunged into the inky darkness of the Wilderness to determine the precise condition and location of the Union lines. As Jackson's mounted party returned from its reconnaissance, a regiment of North Carolina infantry mistook it for the enemy. First a few ragged shots and then a determined volley pierced the air. Jackson fell wounded, struck by three balls fired, tragically, by his own men.

Aides removed the wounded general to a field hospital. After midnight a surgeon amputated his left arm. His senior division commander, Maj. Gen. A. P. Hill, had also been wounded, so Stuart took command of Jackson's corps. "Any victory is a dear one that deprives us of the services of General Jackson, even for a short time," said Lee. The Confederate commander realized that despite Stonewall's commendable achievement on May 2, the Army of Northern Virginia still faced dire peril. Hooker had received fresh levies during the night, and his reinforced Goliath stood firmly between the separated wings of Lee's outnumbered forces. If he wished to avoid the possibility of piecemeal destruction, Lee must immediately unite the two segments of his army.[13]

The high ground at Hazel Grove held the key. If Stuart could capture the clearing there, Lee's divisions could link and move against Hooker's center at Chancellorsville. Stuart vowed to try. Then Hooker made it easy for him. Wishing to shorten his defensive lines, the Union commander unwisely ordered his units on Hazel Grove to fall back one-half mile to another clearing called Fairview. Lee and Stuart made their connection and then turned to attack.

The fighting between Hazel Grove and Fairview on the morning of May 3 proved to be the bloodiest of the year on Virginia soil. Stuart sent wave after wave of determined troops against the Union position, only to have the brave Northerners repulse them each time. Hooker, however, seemed to have lost control of the fighting and failed to send fresh ammunition to his beleaguered men at Fairview. When a Confederate artillery shell struck the Chancellor house, sending part of a pillar crashing into the Union commander and rendering him temporarily unconscious, the Army of the Potomac became literally leaderless. The Confederates eventually overwhelmed the blue-clad defenders at Fairview and formed to attack a hard knot of Union soldiers at Chancellorsville, which provided a rear guard for the now-retreating Federals. They, too, disappeared into the Wilderness by late morning, and General Lee rode into the burning clearing at Chancellorsville experiencing his finest moment as a soldier. "It must have been from such a scene that men in ancient times rose to the dignity of gods," thought a staff officer.[14]

Events at Fredericksburg cut short the Confederate celebration. Word arrived that a portion of Hooker's army had overpowered the thin Confederate defenses behind the city and were even now marching west toward Lee's rear. Ever the gambler, Lee divided his army yet again, sending all but 25,000 of his men to deal with this new threat. The Confederates stopped the Union advance at Salem Church on the afternoon of May 3, and then drove the Federals back across the Rappahannock River at Banks's Ford the following day.

Lee then intended to unite his army and attack Hooker north of Chancellorsville, but rain on May 5 slowed his plans. That night, Hooker abandoned his final line of defense (one too strong for Lee to have hoped to capture) and crossed the river in defeat. The battle of Chancellorsville, "Lee's greatest victory," had come to an end.

American history knows few engagements more illustrative of what an outnumbered army can accomplish if boldly led. Hooker lost more than 17,300 men between May 1 and May 5, and his army returned to Stafford County as thoroughly whipped as it had been in December. Yet unlike the battle of Fredericksburg, Chancellorsville had serious consequences for Lee.[15]

The Army of Northern Virginia suffered more than 13,000 losses, a far greater percentage of its strength than represented by Hooker's casualties. The most important of those losses was Thomas Jackson. Physicians fully expected Stonewall to recover from his wounds. As a precaution against capture, however, Lee ordered Jackson moved to a place of safety, convenient to the railroad to Richmond, where Stonewall could recuperate before regaining the field. On May 4 the stricken general endured a twenty-seven-mile wagon ride to a plantation in Caroline County. Six days later Jackson died there, a victim of pneumonia. General Lee, the Army of Northern Virginia, and the Confederate cause would never replace him.[16]

For the Confederates, Jackson's death (along with the loss of so many less renowned soldiers) seemed, at the time, the only repercussion of the Chancellorsville campaign. In hindsight, Lee's victory paved the way for another Confederate tragedy in the summer of 1863. Lee had long subscribed to the strategic vision of bringing the war to the North, despite his misadventure in Maryland the previous year. President Jefferson Davis hesitated to adopt that risky approach, but after the improbable victory at Chancellorsville, who could deny that Lee's army would be invincible on the attack? After reorganizing his divisions into three infantry corps, Lee laid plans for his second major campaign across the Potomac.

The Army of Northern Virginia would use the Blue Ridge Mountains as its shield during the movement north. One by one, Lee's corps would slip up the south bank of the Rappahannock, cross the mountains, and enter the Shenandoah Valley. Lee had no particular destination in mind, although railroads, rich farms, and industrial facilities in Pennsylvania provided attractive objectives. The Confederate commander also hoped that by removing the war from the Old Dominion, he could resupply his troops on Northern soil, allow Virginia farmers a respite from combat to plant and harvest their crops, and defeat the inevitable Union effort to drive them back across the Potomac.[17]

Jeb Stuart had concentrated his cavalry corps in Culpeper County, thirty miles northwest of Fredericksburg, in position to screen Lee's infantry as it headed toward the Potomac. Lee arrived near Brandy Station on June 8 and watched approvingly as Stuart, "the personification of grace and gallantry combined," conducted a review of his superb horsemen. The next day Stuart was to ride north and use his renowned skills as a cavalryman to block the gaps in the Blue Ridge to keep Hooker from interfering with Lee's march down the Valley. The largest cavalry battle fought on American soil would cancel those plans.[18]

Hooker's mounted forces had discovered Stuart's concentration a few days before Lee's grand review. Worried that the Confederate troopers meant mischief, Hooker ordered his own cavalry, under Brig. Gen. Alfred Pleasonton, to attack Stuart in his camps and destroy his ability to conduct a raid. Dividing his troopers into three wings, Pleasonton converged on Stuart's bivouacs on June 9.

The resulting battle of Brandy Station engaged some 20,000 mounted troops. Stuart had been caught completely by surprise, despite the failure of Pleasonton's envelopment to unfold as crisply as he had diagrammed. The first Union attack struck at dawn, the Federal horsemen crossing the Rappahannock at Beverly Ford and pounding toward little St. James Church and the dominating terrain beyond, called Fleetwood Hill. While Stuart's men poured everything they had against this Federal column, another of the Union wings appeared at last from the south, aiming for the rear of Fleetwood Hill, held at this time by one lone piece of Confederate horse artillery.

The moment of crisis had arrived. Stuart's veteran cavalry galloped over the crest of Fleetwood Hill from the north as Union horsemen, led by an English soldier of fortune named Sir Percy Wyndham, appeared on the ridge from the southwest. The landscape turned crimson with the blood of thundering horses and their reckless riders, "an indescribable clashing and slashing, banging and yelling," as one trooper recalled it. Sabers whirred and pistols exploded at point-blank range as blue and gray waves pulsed back and forth over the smoke-enshrouded hilltop. Both sides launched reinforcements into the fight. By 4:30, the worst of the combat had passed, and Pleasonton, satisfied that he had sufficiently disrupted any imminent plans Stuart might have for an offensive, slowly withdrew across the Rappahannock.[19]

Nearly 1,400 troopers became casualties at Brandy Station. Never again would anyone sarcastically inquire, "Whoever saw a dead cavalryman?" The vaunted Jeb Stuart held the field at the end of the day, but his ego had been as badly bruised as his command. "Our victory was near akin to defeat," thought the Prince George County fire-eater Edmund Ruffin, "& but for the desperate bravery of our troops, the result must have been a most disastrous defeat." The Virginia press took Stuart to task for the delinquency that led to his surprise, and Stuart felt the weight of a compromised reputation.[20]

The battle of Brandy Station delayed Stuart's ride to the north, but Lee did not wait for his cavalry to recover. By June 13, Lt. Gen. Richard S. Ewell's Second Corps, 19,000 strong, approached the outskirts of Winchester in the lower Shenandoah Valley, held by a Union garrison of nearly 7,000 men commanded by Maj. Gen. Robert H. Milroy. The Washington brass had urged Milroy to abandon his advanced position at Winchester, but the stubborn Hoosier had confidence in his position, anchored by three strong forts west and north of town.

Ewell divided his corps, and after some skirmishing prepared to attack the Federals on several fronts. A late afternoon assault on June 14 captured one of Milroy's forts, and the Union commander, finally appreciating his precarious position, ordered a full-scale retreat north toward Harpers Ferry. Ewell had anticipated Milroy's move and placed a blocking force across the road near Stephenson's Depot. The Federals struck the Confederate column at dawn on June 15, desperately trying to cut their way through what had now become a murderous trap.

It was no use. Ewell's forces controlled every avenue of escape, and the bluecoats had no choice but to hoist a white flag. Although Milroy managed to get away, some 3,300 of his men were not so lucky. "This battle of Winchester . . . was one of the most perfect pieces of work the Army of Northern Virginia ever did," thought one Virginia cannoneer. Ewell lost fewer than 300 soldiers in what would prove to be the highlight of this Virginian's military career.[21]

By this time, Lee's entire army was on the move, including Stuart's humbled horsemen. Hooker's Army of the Potomac had also started north, following the footprint of the Bull Run Mountains, a low range separated from the Blue Ridge to the west by the Loudon Valley. Here, Stuart would have to block Pleasonton's probes and prevent the Yankee cavalry from discovering and interfering with Lee's infantry as it padded toward the Potomac.

Three small but intense cavalry clashes resulted. The first occurred on June 17 near Aldie. During four hours of vicious fighting, Federals led by Brig. Gen. Judson Kilpatrick tested Virginia regiments under Col. Thomas T. Munford. One Massachusetts unit lost 198 out of 294 men during the engagement, but Union reinforcements arriving near sunset forced the Confederates back. Kilpatrick suffered more than 300 casualties during the fight, almost three times as many as the Confederates. Meanwhile, a few miles to the west, a lone Union regiment under Col. Alfred Duffié had reached Middleburg, forcing Stuart to abandon his headquarters and the social events he had planned for the evening. Stuart directed a brigade to descend on the isolated Federals, and by next morning only four officers and twenty-seven Union troopers had managed to escape.

The now-cautious Pleasonton advanced toward Middleburg from Aldie on June 18, and Stuart withdrew to a strong elevation west of town, setting the stage for another blood-soaked day on June 19. In temperatures that approached one hundred degrees, Union horsemen assaulted from the east and the north, finally forcing the tenacious Confederates to retire westward.

A welcome downpour on June 20 ended a drought in the Loudon Valley and allowed Stuart to consolidate his brigades. The Confederate commander hoped to rest his men on Sunday, June 21, but Pleasonton, under pressure to penetrate Stuart's screen, would not allow it. Reinforced by infantry, Pleasonton rode forward, encountering the Confederates in a running battle near the village of Upperville. Stuart seemingly took advantage of every rise in the ground and each stone wall east of the mountains. The Union wave gradually enveloped each of Stuart's stands, and eventually the Confederates retired to Ashby's Gap in the Blue Ridge. "There the sun ... setting behind the mountains made a glorious ending to a day filled with the ... excitement of battle," wrote a Federal trooper. But Pleasonton, although tactically victorious at Aldie, Middleburg, and Upperville, had failed to reach the mountains, and Lee's army was already splashing across the Potomac unhindered and undiscovered. For his part, Stuart had regained a measure of the bravado compromised at Brandy Station and in a few days would set out to recoup every ounce of his prestige.[22]

Less than four weeks later, the Army of Northern Virginia returned to the Old Dominion, diminished in more than merely prestige. Between July 1 and July 3, near Gettysburg, Pennsylvania, Lee's men suffered about 28,000 casualties during the culmination of a campaign that had started so ominously at Brandy Station. The Army of the Potomac, now commanded by Maj. Gen. George G. Meade, had pursued the Confederates to the banks of the Potomac in Maryland, but could not prevent their escape into Virginia. Gettysburg had battered both armies beyond the ability to take the offensive. Many weeks would be required before the primary Virginia armies would be able to mount a new campaign.[23]

While Lee and Meade rested, the largest armies in the western theater moved toward a collision near the strategic rail junction at Chattanooga, Tennessee. Lt. Gen. James Longstreet, Lee's senior corps commander, argued for the detachment of his divisions to the west to repulse the Union army aiming for Chattanooga. The War Department agreed, and by September 8 most of Longstreet's corps was on the move. Traveling by rail through Richmond, Petersburg, and down the East Coast, Longstreet's veterans arrived in time to tip the scales at the sanguinary battle of Chickamauga on September 20.

Longstreet's transfer to the west triggered a series of actions that would define military strategy in Virginia for the rest of the year. Their defeat at Chickamauga prompted the Federals to undertake a bold troop transfer of their own, sending two full corps by rail from bivouacs in northern Virginia through six states, until they arrived in the Alabama hill country west of Chattanooga. Fighting Joe Hooker earned a second chance as the force's commander, ironically including the corps that had been routed at Chancellorsville.[24]

Now it was Lee's turn to act. Wishing to prevent the detachment of any more of Meade's units, "Marse Robert" began a new campaign on October 9. The gray commander hoped to interpose the Army of Northern Virginia between Meade and the Union supply base at Centreville in Fairfax County. He crossed the Rapidan River (the de facto boundary between Union and Confederate Virginia at this stage of the war) and marched rapidly to achieve his objective. Meade, however, guessed Lee's intentions and quickly abandoned his camps, withdrawing ahead of the advancing Confederates. On October 14 the armies clashed near a whistle stop on the Orange & Alexandria Railroad named Bristoe Station.

Lt. Gen. A. P. Hill, smelling blood, launched his afternoon attack at Bristoe against what he thought was the tail end of a retreating Federal army. Instead, Hill's divisions encountered Federal troops in their front and on their right flank, strongly posted behind the railroad embankment. Hill, with a reputation for impetuous action, did not hesitate. Changing front to attack the Yankees behind the tracks, Hill's brigades charged across open ground. Bravery could not compensate for Hill's miscalculation and the power of Northern lead. In a short, furious fight, one of Hill's divisions lost 1,361 men, while the entire Federal army suffered less than half that many casualties. The Federals made good their escape, and the Bristoe campaign came to an end. The next day Hill conducted General Lee across the battle-field, attempting to explain why the affair had gone so badly. "Well, well, General, bury these poor men and let us say no more about it," replied the somber commander.[25]

Lee canceled his offensive and led his army back to the south bank of the Rappahannock River, where he expected to remain on the defensive until Longstreet returned from his still-active campaign in east Tennessee. Part of Lee's river defense plan included maintaining a bridgehead on the north side of the river at Rappahannock Station (modern Remington). The Confederates in two forts there could threaten any Federal attempt to cross downstream at vulnerable Kelly's Ford.

Stalemate did the Union cause no good. The Lincoln administration had been anxious to bring Lee to bay since the Confederates slipped across the Potomac after Gettysburg, and on November 7 (one day after the battle of Droop Mountain, the largest engagement fought in the new state of West Virginia), Meade made his move to cross the Rappahannock. Predictably, he targeted both Kelly's Ford and Rappahannock Station. While the Northern-ers negotiated Kelly's Ford with comparatively little problem, as expected, their victory over two veteran brigades at Rappahannock Station caught the Confederates by surprise. The Federals rushed into the works and quickly killed, wounded, or captured some 80 percent of the defenders. For the second time in three weeks, the Army of Northern Virginia had suffered a devastating loss. Lee quickly regrouped and ordered his forces to withdraw, once again using the Rapidan River as nature's moat. Not since Chancellorsville (and, perhaps not coincidentally, the death of Stonewall Jackson), had the Army of Northern Virginia been victorious.[26]

The worsening autumn weather allowed one final campaign in 1863. With the Confederates dug in behind the Rapidan, Meade probed for a weakness. He commanded 80,000 men, Lee just 50,000. Combined with the element of surprise, Meade's superior numbers and his army's recent history suggested that a decisive victory lay within his grasp.

Several unguarded fords beyond Lee's right held the key to a possible end to the standoff. If they could move rapidly, the Federals might gain the Confederate rear before Lee could react. Meade scheduled the advance to begin on November 24. But, much as had happened to Burnside in the year's first Federal offensive, a punishing storm turned the roads to a russet clay soup, delaying Meade's advance by forty-eight hours. Good Confederate scouting, an incompetent Federal corps commander, and the execrable roads conspired to rob Meade of the element of surprise. The Confederates quickly shifted to meet the Federal flanking force, colliding with the Yankees at Payne's Farm on November 27. More rain followed, as Meade maneuvered Maj. Gen. Gouverneur K. Warren's troops (the victors at Bristoe Station) into position to attack an exposed Confederate flank. Warren needed longer than expected to get into position, and Meade delayed the attack until dawn of November 30.

That night the mercury plummeted to below zero, and the soldiers spent what was, for many of them, their most uncomfortable night of the war. Despite these brutal conditions, A. P. Hill responded to the Union initiative and put his corps into hastily dug works—presaging the army's skillful reliance on field fortifications for the rest of the war—eliminating what had been a vulnerable position. Warren crawled ahead on his hands and knees to reconnoiter this new Confederate line the next morning, and opted to cancel the assault. A disappointed Meade reluctantly, but courageously, validated Warren's decision and ordered the army back across the Rapidan the next day. By December 3, the entire Army of the Potomac had gained the right bank and began to go into winter camp. Fighting in Virginia in 1863 had come to an end.[27]

Meade fully expected to be removed from command, believing that his failure to attack at Mine Run had doomed his career. Although the Army of the Potomac had neutralized Lee's offensive at Bristoe Station and forced its way across the Rappahannock in early November, at year's end Meade's soldiers were just thirty miles west and no closer to victory than when they had started the year. But the removal orders never came. Federal forces led by Maj. Gen. Ulysses S. Grant had lifted the siege of Chattanooga days before the aborted assault at Mine Run. Burnside's new army had turned back Longstreet's offensive at Knoxville, Tennessee. Under these promising circumstances, Lincoln saw no need to sack the victor of Gettysburg, although the president would have a plan in mind to change commanders in Virginia.

Jefferson Davis also pondered command changes. With Gen. Braxton Bragg now fully discredited following his bungling management of events at Chattanooga, the president considered sending Robert E. Lee to the West to redeem the Confederacy's fortunes. Lee tactfully deflected Davis's inquiries and, to the great delight of the Army of Northern Virginia, remained in command in Orange County along the south bank of the Rapidan River. The Confederates, like their blue-clad counterparts in Culpeper County, erected humble winter quarters and prepared to endure the war's third winter.[28]

On balance, 1863 had been a disappointing year for General Lee, whose personal health suffered, with symptoms of the heart ailment that would lead to his death seven years later. The spring had started with such grand promise at Chancellorsville, a victory marred more than he could know by the loss of the great Jackson. For a second time, the tidal wave of Southern independence crested in defeat north of the Potomac, and just as during the previous year, the Army of Northern Virginia limped back into the Old Dominion, its regiments shattered but its pride and esprit de corps intact.[29]

But something had been lost in 1863 that, unlike the previous year, would never be regained. The Union cavalry, grotesquely inferior to Jeb Stuart's troopers during the first half of the war, gained parity with the Virginia cavalier. Brandy Station demonstrated how much the Union horsemen had improved. Lee's infantry, still a potent weapon on the defense, could no longer force its will on the Army of the Potomac. At Hazel Grove, Fairview, and a Pennsylvania hilltop called Cemetery Ridge, some of the best and bravest of Lee's soldiers made their last charge. The war would continue. There was no end in sight. But when a small, cigar-smoking man in a rumpled blue uniform arrived in Virginia the following spring, the deadly chess game would enter a new dimension.

Notes

1. Eugene Carter, quoted in Gary W. Gallagher, ed. *The Fredericksburg Campaign: Decision on the Rappahannock* (Chapel Hill: University of North Carolina Press, 1995), 177; Lee, quoted in Daniel E. Sutherland, *Fredericksburg and Chancellorsville: The Dare Mark Campaign* (Lincoln: University of Nebraska Press, 1998), 83.

2. For an analysis of the Mud March and its impact on Union morale, see A. Wilson Greene, "Morale, Maneuver, and Mud: The Army of the Potomac, December 16, 1862–January 26, 1863," in Gallagher, *The Fredericksburg Campaign,* 171–227.

3. For background on Hooker and his administrative improvements to the army, see Ernest B. Furgurson, *Chancellorsville, 1863: The Souls of the Brave* (New York: Knopf, 1992), 20–35.

4. Sergeant W. R. Montgomery, quoted in Stephen W. Sears, *Chancellorsville* (Boston: Houghton Mifflin, 1996), 36.

5. For a detailed description of the battle of Kelly's Ford, see John Bigelow Jr., *The Campaign of Chancellorsville: A Strategic and Tactical Study* (New Haven: Yale University Press, 1910), 89–105.

6. For the Suffolk campaign, see Steven A. Cormier, *The Siege of Suffolk: The Forgotten Campaign, April 11–May 4, 1863* (Lynchburg, Va.: H. E. Howard, 1989).

7. Hooker, quoted in Bigelow, *Campaign of Chancellorsville,* 108.

8. A good review of Confederate strategy at this point in the campaign is Douglas Southall Freeman, *Lee's Lieutenants: A Study in Command,* 3 vols. (New York: C. Scribner's Sons, 1942–1944), 2:522–28.

9. See Sears, *Chancellorsville,* 172–224.

10. Frank E. Vandiver, *Mighty Stonewall* (New York: McGraw-Hill, 1957), 467–68.

11. For an account of Lee and Jackson's final meeting, see Lenoir Chambers, *Stonewall Jackson* (New York: Morrow, 1959), 2:379–86.

12. For Jackson's flank march and attack, see Sutherland, *Fredericksburg and Chancellorsville,* 148–56.

13. For Jackson's wounding and its consequences, see Freeman, *Lee's Lieutenants,* 2:563–83 (which also contains the quote from Lee); and Robert K. Krick, "The Smoothbore Volley That Doomed the Confederacy," in Gary W. Gallagher, ed., *Chancellorsville: The Battle and Its Aftermath* (Chapel Hill: University of North Carolina Press, 1996).

14. Charles Marshall, quoted in Sears, *Chancellorsville,* 250. The fighting on May 3 claimed about 17,200 men: 8,800 Confederates and 8,400 Federals. See Bigelow, *Campaign of Chancellorsville,* 378.

15. For a thoughtful analysis of the significance of the battle of Chancellorsville, see Sears, *Chancellorsville,* 431–49.

16. Jackson's final days are poignantly described in James I. Robertson Jr., *Stonewall Jackson: The Man, the Soldier, the Legend* (New York: Macmillan, 1997), 737–62.

17. For the decision to move north, see Stephen W. Sears, *Gettysburg* (Boston: Houghton Mifflin, 2003), 1–17.

18. For Lee's review of the cavalry, see Freeman, *Lee's Lieutenants,* 3:4–5.

19. Noble D. Preston, quoted in Eric J. Wittenberg, *The Union Cavalry Comes of Age: Hartwood Church to Brandy Station, 1863* (Washington, D.C.: Brassey's, 2003), 286. Wittenberg's account of the battle of Brandy Station may be found on pp. 245–317.

20. Ruffin, quoted in *The Diary of Edmund Ruffin,* ed. William Kauffman Scarborough, 3 vols. (Baton Rouge: Louisiana State University Press, 1972–1989), 3:9.

21. Robert Stiles, quoted in *Four Years under Marse Robert* (New York: Neale, 1903), 92. For a brief monograph on the battle, see Charles S. Grunder and Brandon H. Beck, *The Second Battle of Winchester, June 12–15, 1863* (Lynchburg, Va.: H .E. Howard, 1989).

22. David McM. Gregg, quoted in Robert F. O'Neill Jr., *The Cavalry Battles of Aldie, Middleburg and Upperville, June 10–27, 1863* (Lynchburg, Va.: H. E. Howard, 1993), 148.

23. For Lee's retreat into Virginia, see Kent Masterson Brown, *Retreat from Gettysburg: Lee, Logistics, and the Pennsylvania Campaign* (Chapel Hill: University of North Carolina Press, 2005).

24. For the shifting of troops from Virginia to the Chattanooga area, see Steven E. Woodworth, *Six Armies in Tennessee: The Chickamauga and Chattanooga Campaigns* (Lincoln: University of Nebraska Press, 1998).

25. Lee, quoted in William D. Henderson, *The Road to Bristoe Station: Campaigning with Lee and Meade, August 1–October 20, 1863* (Lynchburg, Va.: H. E. Howard, 1987), 193.

26. For an account of the battle of Rappahannock Station, see Freeman, *Lee's Lieutenants,* 3:264–69.

27. The Mine Run campaign is discussed in Jeffry D. Wert, *The Sword of Lincoln: The Army of the Potomac* (New York: Simon and Schuster, 2005), 320–22.

28. For consideration of command changes in both armies, see ibid., 322; and Emory M. Thomas, *Robert E. Lee: A Biography* (New York: Norton, 1995), 312–13.

29. For a discussion of Lee's health in 1863, see Thomas, *Robert E. Lee,* 278–79.

Days of Misery and Uncertainty

Childhood in Wartime Virginia

James Marten

In early 1863 ten-year-old John Steele and his twelve-year-old sister Sarah began keeping a joint diary of daily life in the no-man's-land between the Union and Confederate forces in northern Virginia. Their brief entries, which they kept up through Christmas, reveal the mundane events and terrible trials many Virginia children experienced in the war's middle year.

John and Sarah wrote sparingly of their young lives, despite family tragedies—the deaths of their father and little sister, for instance—mostly chronicling their household chores. But the war inevitably intervened, and the terse entries also reported the comings and goings of Union and Confederate armies. Soldiers from both sides frequently stayed in their house or stopped for meals, while thousands of Federal prisoners marched past on their way to camps in the South. Their farm was the site of a small skirmish during which a Confederate officer collapsed and died in their front yard. Like many boys his age, John participated in "battle class" at school—probably military drill led by his teacher—and, more typical to modern sensibilities, at least, "playing soldier" with other boys. When Christmas finally came, there was little holiday cheer for the Steele children. They ate cake, fried doughnuts, and pies brought by Federal soldiers and managed to scrounge together the makings for eggnog, which they shared with a passing Confederate officer. And on Christmas Day they attended a community or church exhibition of some sort. But apparently they received no presents, which, even in the 1860s, was a customary part of a child's Christmas.[1]

The Steele children's diary narrates a conflict that overran the lives of most Confederate civilians. Virginia children shared with girls and boys throughout the Confederacy a set of experiences rarely endured by American children: the danger of coming under artillery and small-arms fire, occupation by an enemy army, the tightened belts and straightened circumstances brought on by the collapsing wartime economy, and heightened responsibilities due to absent fathers and older brothers. Some children became refugees; most longed both for Confederate victory and for an end to the fighting. And many filled parts of their days with pastimes and play that mimicked the adult version of the war raging around them, which reflected their insistence that even the youngest Rebels could display their patriotism. These changes and incidents occurred throughout the war, of course, but for youngsters in Virginia, 1863 marked the year in which the war truly came to affect every facet of their lives.[2]

In 1863 the Civil War swept away the peaceful lives of fourteen-year-old Sue Chancellor and her family. Soldiers had come and gone from her family's home—the imposing brick house that had at one time served as an inn on the Plank Road between Fredericksburg and up-country Virginia—throughout the first two years of the war, but that romantic and exciting phase of the war ended when Gen. Joseph Hooker's Army of the Potomac opened the 1863 campaigning season by plunging into the Wilderness west of Fredericksburg. Gen. Robert E. Lee wheeled the Army of Northern Virginia to face the invaders and sent Gen. Thomas "Stonewall" Jackson's corps to the west, beyond the Yankees' right flank. About that time, Union forces took over the Chancellor home, which became the center of the first of the bloody battles of the war's third summer.

From early in the war, Confederate pickets had often dined with the Chancellors, enjoying the sisters' piano playing and teaching them card games. One of the officers who visited was Gen. J. E. B. Stuart, who, in his typically chivalrous way, presented Sue's sister Fannie with a gold dollar. Yankees also came by from time to time. Sue wrote that they would "come in a sweeping gallop up the big road with swords and sabres clashing," while servants hid meat under the front steps and Sue would "run and hide and pray . . . more and harder than ever in my life, before or since." As a result of these frequent visits, the Chancellors may have thought themselves accustomed to war.[3]

But the true impact of war would arrive with the opening shots of the battle that would bear the family's name. Sue's account of the Battle of Chancellorsville begins with the arrival of Gen. George G. Meade and his staff, who established Gen. Joseph Hooker's headquarters in the house. The

Chancellor women and girls could not, of course, know of the thousands of troops converging on their crossroads clearing, but they saw "couriers coming and going" and sensed that the Yankee officers "were very well satisfied with their position and seemed to be very confident of victory" (141). Sue and her family and friends "got through Thursday and Friday as best we could" (141–42). As the shooting came closer on Saturday—the day of Jackson's famous march across the Union front—the civilians took shelter in the basement. "There was firing, fighting, and bringing in the wounded all that day," Sue reported, and then, on Saturday afternoon, Jackson launched his attack on the Union flank (143).

Wounded Yankees streamed into the Chancellor house, where surgeons hastily established a field hospital and turned the piano into an amputating table. As Jackson's corps crushed the Federal right, things got even worse. "Such cannonading on all sides, such shrieks and groans, such commotion of all kinds!" Sue exclaimed. "We thought that we were frightened before, but this was far beyond everything, and it kept up until long after dark" (143). After a very long night, the fighting began again. The house soon caught fire, forcing the Chancellors to flee.

A Union staff officer led the terrified band of women and children out of the cellar. They saw amputated limbs spilling from an open window and rows of dead bodies covered with canvas littering the yard. "The woods around the house were a sheet of fire," wrote Sue, "the air was filled with shot and shell; horses were running, rearing, and screaming; the men were amass with confusion, moaning, cursing, and praying" (143). Ducking "missiles of death" and stepping over "the bleeding bodies of the dead and wounded," the Chancellors joined the retreating Union troops (144). "At our last look," she recalled, "our old home was completely enveloped in flames" (144). Helped, even befriended, by other Union officers, a kind chaplain, and a friendly drummer boy, the Chancellors sat out the rest of the war in Charlottesville, where Sue attended school and Mrs. Chancellor worked in a hospital.

The year 1863 brought to Sue Chancellor nearly the entire spectrum of experiences that Virginia children would face during the Civil War: their peaceful lives interrupted by invaders and defenders, the danger of living near battlefields, the loss of property, and long-term absences from their homes. Relatively few Virginia children actually suffered the complete destruction of their homes, but most were affected one way or another by the war. And most insisted on incorporating the war into their own lives.

Of all the challenges facing children, the least common but most dramatic was, of course, coming under fire. Children in Harpers Ferry, for instance, frequently faced the sharp end of war, especially during the contest's first two years. Eight-year-old Annie P. Marmion of Harpers Ferry was forced to live in such a way; she recalled that "the great objects in life were to procure something to eat and to keep yourself out of light by day and your lamps . . . hidden by night" so as not to draw the fire of Union pickets.[4]

In the contested areas of Virginia, where Union and Confederate troops jockeyed to occupy ground and to have access to civilians' livestock and grain bins, skirmishes could break out at any time. Some children were drawn to the excitement; others were terrified. The children of Cornelia Peake McDonald—who left one of the most useful accounts of the wartime experiences of a Virginia family—witnessed two fights near their home at Winchester. One occurred in 1862, when her two oldest sons successfully begged to be allowed to investigate a battle being fought nearby. Cornelia almost immediately regretted her decision, and with distant gunfire reminding her of the peril her sons may have wandered into, she waited restlessly for their return until after dark. The boys finally came home, "very grave and sad looking." To their mother, "they seemed not like the same boys . . . though there was no sign of fright or of excitement, they were very grave and sorrowful." It was no wonder. While the boys were sitting on a fence watching the fighting, a human head rolled by. The fighting was much closer a year later, when, during the run-up to the Gettysburg campaign, Confederate troops crushed a smaller Union contingent near Staunton, where the McDonalds had moved a short time earlier. At first Cornelia even let the little ones play in the yard. She calmly wrote that they "seemed to forget the shells," turning the battlefield into a playground. As passing Confederate soldiers limped past their yard or collapsed to rest for a moment, the children were "running and catching the men as they passed, saying, 'I take you prisoner.'" But the Union troops were soon routed. Men streamed onto the McDonald porch and inside until wounded, demoralized, and frightened Yankees occupied every foot of floor space in the house.[5]

Aside from the terrifying and exciting occasions when civilians were caught in skirmishes or full-scale battles, the war had many other previously unimaginable effects on the lives of Virginia children. Throughout the state, as in other parts of the hard-pressed Confederacy, schools closed when funds dried up or teachers went into the army, children took over farm chores or plantation management for absent fathers, and girls and young women rushed to obtain jobs in factories or government agencies.

Teenaged Virginians were often forced to grow up quickly. Benny Fleet's experiences on Green Mount plantation in King and Queen County were typical. By the middle year of the war, the seventeen-year-old was, for all practical purposes, running the plantation, and his journal for the summer and fall of 1863 is sprinkled with references to managing slaves and crops. In fact, by late 1861, although he still managed to go to school—when it was in session—Benny had begun assuming more and more responsibility after his older brother, Fred, departed for the army. Adding to his burden was his father's drinking. Fairly early in the war, Benny had "the painful duty" of informing Fred that their father had "commenced drinking, & has been in quite a big frolic." In between bouts of drinking, the elder Fleet, who was a physician as well as a planter, was often away on business or with the local militia. As Benny matter-of-factly wrote Fred, he was "in charge," with the authority to "give orders without Pa's knowing anything about it." In addition to joining the local home guard company in June, Benny also made a major trip to Richmond with a wagonload of corn, peas, chickens, and eggs; he visited friends in the camp of the Twenty-sixth Virginia and sold his produce the next day.[6]

Young women and girls also had to step out of customary roles. Members of yeoman families replaced brothers and fathers in the fields, while members of slave-owning households whose bondspeople ran away gradually took on household duties and did without personal servants. A sampling of letters written in 1863 to Secretary of the Treasury Christopher Memminger by women and girls pleading for government jobs indicates the desperate straits and new responsibilities faced by young women living in Richmond. Some were widows with small children; others were teenagers who had to support themselves. One widow with three children under the age of five, a refugee from south of Richmond, wrote that "at the present prices for all articles of necessity, you may well imagine with what anxiety I look at my little helpless babies . . . and wonder how I shall provide for them." Fifteen-year-old Hattie Hilby, an orphan, needed a job because the relative with whom she lived was married to a low-paid private. In her third letter to Memminger requesting work, she assured him that "it is urgent necessity, alone that compels me again to trouble you." Another fifteen-year-old orphan, whose older brother was in the army, needed work to provide for her younger sister and brother "and perhaps to continue them at school."[7]

Such genteel labor was not available to all young Confederate females. Many found work in uniform and munitions factories. One of the largest was the Confederate Laboratory on Brown's Island in Richmond. By late winter 1863, more than 300 females, mainly between the ages of twelve and twenty, were on the workforce. In mid-March an explosion tore through the factory, killing three dozen workers and injuring thirty more, many of them children. Although the exact number of young victims is unknown, a War Department official reported that "most of them were little indigent girls." A newspaper account described families streaming toward the wreckage after the explosion. "The most heartrending lamentations and cries issued from the ruins" as rescue workers pulled the killed and injured from the smoking rubble. "Mothers rushed wildly about, throwing themselves upon the corpses of the dead and persons of the wounded." Children "clamored" into ambulances, "crying bitterly in their search after sisters and brothers."[8]

Such tragedies turned children into casualties of war. But even in the midst of war, children could sometimes still be children. Even Benny Fleet, the hardworking head of Green Mount plantation, found time during the busy year of 1863 for the sort of activities in which a young Virginia gentleman was expected to partake. He played cards with his pretty cousins, relished a "candy stew" at a co-ed school party (where they also played something called "Dodge the Devil"), went hunting, and early in the year hugely enjoyed attending a "negro marriage," where he stayed up late "watching the darkies play" and gorged himself on possum, cake, and pudding. During the early winter lull in farm work and in war news, he took up his normal studies at Aberdeen Academy, working especially hard on Latin and French. One night he recorded in his diary: "My mind has been very clear tonight, have read 40 lines in Horace in about 40 minutes." He continued his affectionate and newsy correspondence with his brother, Fred; Benny kept him up-to-date on the goings-on in the family and the community, while Fred described his adventures on the battlefield and in camp.[9]

But 1863 was also a time of growing uncertainty for the Fleet family and frustration for Benny. Increasing rumors of incursions by Yankee raiders were sometimes true, and Benny took part in efforts to recapture slaves who left with the Northerners. Early in the year he casually reported that he and other boys had elected several classmates to lead the company they formed at school. In March, just before the campaign season began, Benny reported to Fred that a friend had gone off to serve in the army as a wagon master. "I can't help envying him a little," he wrote, "& I wish I was in the Service of my Country. How badly I will feel after our independence is achieved to think that I did nothing to gain our liberty, & persons pointing a sneering finger at me will say, 'that fellow did nothing to gain his independence & now he is enjoying it as much as I do, who have fought, bled, & almost died for my country.'" Later in the summer, no doubt inspired by the big battles being fought throughout the country, and a little jealous of Fred, he wrote in a letter to his brother that "I have been very anxious to go in the Army this summer, but Pa is so opposed to it that I won't go." He wanted to join Col. John S. Mosby's partisan rangers or sign on with the Confederate commerce raiders the *Alabama* or the *Florida*. Benny's mother wrote separately to Fred that "Brother has seemed very restless lately about going in the army, but I told him if it had been intended for him to go he would have been born sooner." At the end of 1863 the teenager, still yearning to be a soldier, took time out from the now-frequent drilling sessions with his home guard company to visit Fred in camp for a few days.[10]

From time to time he got his chance to go out with the home guards. Sometimes he acted as an "advance scout" for squads checking out reports of marauding Yankees. One of the more dramatic incidents occurred in late June, when a skirmish broke out between a raiding party and the home guards. Benny missed the actual fight, and no one was hurt, but they returned home "pretty tired." They learned later that the Union forces amounted to more than 2,000 men, against whom the 100 home guards "couldn't do anything." A day or two later word went around that the "Yankees have sworn vengeance against us, the home guard, that they had hung 2 & said they meant to hang everyone of us."[11]

Sometimes the haphazard drilling and fruitless scouting expeditions made the activities of home guard units—filled as they often were with boys too young to go into the army—seem like boys' clubs. Benny Fleet and his friends would, of course, have scoffed at the notion they were only "playing." In any event, Virginia children did often mimic the women and men they had watched deal with various wartime situations. One day, "playing ladies" with a little friend, Nannie Belle Maury complained, "I don't feel very well this morning. All my niggers have run away and left me." On another occasion, her mother overheard her declare, "[U]pon my word an' honour,

Sir, there are no letters and papers in this trunk at all"—the exact words the elder Maury had spoken to a Federal guard on the way out of Fredericksburg some weeks before.[12]

Such play was not, of course, restricted to 1863. The diary of one Virginia mother shows how even the youngest children insisted on incorporating the war into their play. "Almost their entire set of plays have reference to a state of war," wrote Margaret Junkin Preston. Five-year-old George staged marches and battles with paper soldiers, built hospitals with blocks and corncobs, made ambulances with chairs, and administered pills to his rag dolls. "He gets sticks and hobbles about," reported his mother, "saying that he lost a leg at the Second battle of Manassas; tells wonderful stories of how he cut off Yankees' heads, bayoneted them, &c." From time to time he announced that his "furlough is out and he must go to his regiment again." Her three-year-old "also kills 'Lankees,' as he calls them, and can talk war lingo almost as well as George. . . . They can tell all about pickets, cavalry, cannon, ambulances, &c." On another occasion, her children and their little friends interrupted a paper-doll dance when imaginary Yankees suddenly appeared and the paper soldiers had to dash off to fight them. Mrs. Preston seemed resigned to the fact that "the thought of war is never out of our minds. If it could be, our children would bring it back by their plays!"[13]

Pastimes that were innocent in peacetime gained a political edge whenever Yankees came on the scene. Winchester boys taunted Federal officers by throwing snowballs at them in the early winter of 1863; one incident led to the arrest and imprisonment for several hours of a fifteen-year-old. That same boy—Cornelia Peake McDonald's son Harry—and his younger brother nearly got into even worse trouble a few weeks after the snowball incident, when a squad of bluecoats raced to their backyard after they heard an explosion. It was caused by the boys' miniature homemade cannon, which they had made from eight-inch lengths of old gun barrels. Their mother complained in her diary that "I have to be constantly on the watch for fear of my boys doing something to provoke the persecution of the Yankees."[14]

The desire to be a part of the great military adventure that surrounded them came naturally to Virginia youngsters, who embraced their state's military tradition. Many formed their own militia companies and learned how to drill and perform the manual of arms. Sometimes they formed shadow companies to the units formed by their fathers and brothers. A few of the young soldiers were girls. The sons and daughters of Rev. William Ward grabbed broomsticks and fire pokers and learned the rudiments of drill. "We could shoulder arms, carry arms, right-about face, guide right, and guide left, right wheel, left wheel, march, double-quick" and "keep step beautifully," wrote his daughter Evelyn. Whenever the Ward children drilled, so did the little slaves, who served as privates to the white "officers."[15]

As Evelyn's story suggests, black children were also eager participants in the conflict. Booker T. Washington, who was only nine when the war ended, recalled listening to his master's family talk about the war as he fanned the flies away from the table during mealtime. He "absorbed a good deal" of war news and reported it to his elders back in the quarters. As a result, in the little slave community on his farm and on plantations throughout the state, "every success of the Federal armies and every defeat of the Confederate forces was watched with the keenest and most intense interest."[16]

The war upon which so much depended for young Afro-Virginians affected their lives in many ways. As white belts tightened due to shortages of food, so, too, did slaves' diets suffer (although Washington suggested that, because slaves were already used to plain and rather rough rations, they suffered less than whites). As white children found the presence of Union and Confederate troops to be both exciting and dangerous, so, too, did black children face new threats posed by the armed men infesting parts of Virginia. They learned to fear the beefed-up slave patrols as well as deserters from either army, who, according to Washington, would cut off the ears of any "Negro boy" they found in the woods.[17]

Tensions also arose out of the rough "play" that developed, perhaps inevitably, out of the mock battles fought by boys' companies. The innocent patriotism of the early days of the war gave way by 1863 to somewhat less wholesome forms of military play. The boys' companies of Wytheville, Virginia, called themselves the "Baconsoles" and the "Pinchguts," and blasted away at one another with "cannons" made of sawed-off musket barrels. When they captured "enemies," like guards in the infamous prison camps of both the North and the South, they rifled their pockets. In Richmond, recalled a Virginian who had lived in the capital during the war, the boys formed "as many clans as the seven hills" on which the city was built. "They had all caught the fighting spirit, just like the new soldier boys." Their re-created battles were fought with rocks and had to be broken up by policemen.[18]

The rowdy behavior of these boys suggests that the stresses of war contributed to a breakdown of social order, at least in urban areas. Observers reported gangs of Richmond boys committing minor crimes, carelessly firing guns, bullying smaller children and African American refugees, and injuring innocent bystanders. Richmond authorities contended with gangs of "incipient blackguards" who vandalized houses and public buildings, as well as bands of "very mischievous urchins" who made a practice of robbing younger children.[19]

Some of this social disorder came to a head in the early spring of 1863 during the famous "bread riot" in Richmond. Although descriptions of the rioters—or protesters, depending on one's point of view—and of their motivations vary widely, the incident that began as a protest over the high price and low availability of food soon turned into an attack on stores in Richmond's commercial district. Despite the conflicting views of the purpose and worthiness of the rioters, it appears that a number of adolescent boys were among the looters. One observer reported seeing one "come out of a store with a hat full of money."[20]

Another category of experience that some Virginia children experienced more deeply in 1863 was the temporary or even permanent loss of their homes. Well-to-do families who came in harm's way had the resources or family connections to travel to havens far from the fighting. Taking a few possessions and, in some cases, a few slaves, they became refugees for a few weeks or even for years. At the other end of the economic spectrum was Cornelia Peake McDonald, who, with her nine children—all under the age of fourteen when the war began—was forced from her Winchester home in May 1863 when Union forces occupied their house for use as a hospital. She packed up her kids and what belongings she could muster and, determining to, as a twentieth-century playwright would later say, "rely on the kindness of strangers," set up her new household in Lexington, Virginia, where she knew a colony of refugees had been established. The McDonalds had a hard time finding a suitable place to live; most decent houses were taken and some landlords would not accept children. They eventually landed in a hotel, where they scraped by on handouts and a small income from the older boys' chopping wood and their mother's sewing. When she referred to this time as "dark days of misery and uncertainty," she was speaking for thousands of other displaced Virginians. The McDonalds would never again live in Winchester. Mr. McDonald eventually died, and Cordelia moved to Louisville, Kentucky, several years after the war.[21]

The McDonalds were among thousands of Virginian refugees, including the 10,000 or so former slaves who crowded into the Union-occupied southeastern counties of the state and the many others who flowed to occupied havens in northern Virginia, where hundreds ended up in Freedman's Village, a contraband camp in what is now Arlington National Cemetery. Hundreds of children were among these black refugees. Many were able to attend school for the first time in their lives.[22]

The serious "refugeeing" of white Virginians began late in 1862, when the women and children of Fredericksburg fled after their town was bombarded and then occupied by Union forces. Richmond was a magnet for these and other refugees, and the population of the capital city grew from fewer than 40,000 to more than 100,000 during the war. They competed for scarce jobs and even scarcer resources. One resident of the city wrote late in 1862 that "a portion of the people look like vagabonds," wearing "dingy and dilapidated" clothes and looking "gaunt and pale with hunger." In a letter to a government official pleading for a job, one of those refugees, the widow of an army chaplain, reported that she had thus far been unable to find affordable lodgings or any kind of work. "I do not know what will become of us unless some kind friend will lend a helping hand." As a refugee, she was "a stranger here & do not know to whom to apply." She had "struggled hard to support myself & children," but the "vile Yankees cross my path at every step."[23]

The problems that faced children in Richmond can be traced in the diary of John B. Jones, author of the famous *A Rebel War Clerk's Diary*. Acerbic and self-important, Jones was nevertheless a thorough reporter and careful observer of the social and political life of Richmond. And since he was the doting father of an adult son who worked with him in the Confederate government and of several teenagers, his diary records the pressures the war exerted on urban children.

Late in 1862, he reported a diet of liver and rice several times a week. "We cannot afford anything better; others do not live so well." The high demand and higher prices did not abate in 1863. A couple of months later, Jones summarized the severity of the food situation in the city with a story told by one of his daughters. While working in the kitchen, she was confronted by "a young rat [that] came out of its hole and seemed to beg for something to eat; she held out some bread, which it ate from her hand, and seemed grateful. Several others soon followed, and were tame as kittens." Perhaps, Jones reflected, "we shall have to eat them!" His frequent references to food—or the lack of it—indicate the extent to which he worried about the health of his family. He reported having lost twenty pounds himself, and in July 1863 he described his wife and children as "emaciated to some extent." A few months later he commented several times on the family cat staggering about the house due to hunger.[24]

To make matters worse, the early winter of 1863 saw an outbreak of smallpox in Richmond, and white flags marking the homes with quarantined patients popped up in many neighborhoods. By the end of 1863, Jones's usual cheerfulness, even in the face of hardship, had dwindled. On December 25 he described "a sad Christmas; cold, and threatening snow. My two youngest children, however, have decked the parlor with evergreens, crosses, stars, etc." They even erected a Christmas tree, but because candy cost $8 a pound, it went undecorated. The customary holiday shooting off of pistols and firecrackers was nearly unheard in the city on this third Christmas of the war.[25]

Despite the catastrophic decline in the family's standard of living, the Jones children, at least according to their father, remained committed to the Confederate cause. Early in the year, Jones had reported that his children were "more enthusiastic for independence than ever. Daily I hear them say they would gladly embrace death rather than the rule of the Yankee." That may have been wishful thinking, but it certainly reflected a common belief among Virginian parents as they justified the sacrifices forced upon their children.[26]

Despite the appalling events of 1863, the worst was still to come for many Virginia children. Indeed, Benny Fleet did not long survive 1863. Not long before he planned to leave home to join Mosby's rangers, he and two friends conducted an ad hoc scout of a column of Yankee cavalry that had entered King and Queen County. The bluecoats spotted the teenagers and, when the latter fled, fired on them. Benny, still seventeen, was mortally wounded; his body was found in nearby woods the next day.[27]

Of course, the conditions that had developed in 1863 worsened in 1864, as Union armies pressed into the Shenandoah Valley and besieged Petersburg and Richmond. Prices for basic necessities soared in the capital, hunger and disease stalked white and black children alike, and more Virginia youngsters found themselves in the path of advancing Union armies. A Petersburg girl named Ann Banister described her family's sacrifices in a postwar memoir: her father was killed and her sixteen-year-old brother died of disease while serving with the home guard; two other brothers fought with Lee. The Banister home was near the front lines, so for the last year of the war they were forced to live in a two-room basement in a different part of town. Ann described both the horrifying explosion on July 30 at "the Crater" that shattered their windows and her brother Blair's visit home the night after the battle, clothes stained with blood from the hand-to-hand fighting. By the fall of 1864, children in the neighborhood could identify the kinds of shells they spotted soaring overhead, while young and old alike would, at night, "go out . . . to watch the mortar shells. They were like arches of fire, and very beautiful."[28]

Jane Friend, whose father was in a Virginia regiment and whose Petersburg home was destroyed during the war, recalled long afterward her wartime belief that for a cousin who had lost a husband and a neighbor who had lost a son, the worst was over. "They had no more sickening dread of news from the front. Their boy was past suffering, and his suffering, if at all, had been short."[29]

"These were sad reasonings for a child of ten years," she wistfully stated in her reminiscences, "but war is transforming. At thirteen, when it closed, I was a full-fledged woman." Many other Virginia children could have said the same thing about the way in which the war became a dramatic and exciting, but often tragic and frightening, intrusion on their childhoods.[30]

Notes

1. "Diary of John Magill Steele and Sarah Eliza Steele," April 3, June 11, 1863, in Garland A. Quarles et al., eds., *Diaries, Letters, and Recollections of the War between the States* (Winchester, Va.: Winchester-Frederick County Historical Society, 1955), 69, 75.

2. General accounts of children during the Civil War include Emmy E. Werner, *Reluctant Witnesses: Children's Voices from the Civil War* (Boulder, Colo.: Westview, 1998), which emphasizes the experiences of underage soldiers; and James Marten, *The Children's Civil War* (Chapel Hill: University of North Carolina Press, 1998), which emphasizes the home front.

3. Sue M. Chancellor, "Personal Recollections of the Battle of Chancellorsville," *Register of the Kentucky Historical Society* 66 (April 1968), 139. Subsequent page references to this work will be given parenthetically in the text.

4. Annie P. Marmion, *Under Fire: An Experience in the Civil War* (n.p., 1959), 7, 16.

5. Cornelia Peake McDonald, *A Woman's Civil War: A Diary, with Reminiscences of the War from March 1862,* ed. Minrose C. Gwin (Madison: University of Wisconsin Press, 1992), 158–59. The most complete account of life in the occupied South appears in Stephen V. Ash, *When the Yankees Came: Conflict and Chaos in the Occupied South, 1861–1865* (Chapel Hill: University of North Carolina Press, 1995).

6. Betsy Fleet and John D. P. Fuller, eds., *Green Mount: A Virginia Plantation Family during the Civil War: Being the Journal of Benjamin Robert Fleet and Letters of His Family* (Lexington: University of Kentucky Press, 1962), 90, 77.

7. M. L. Clarke to Christopher Memminger, March 5, 1863, Hattie S. Hilby to Memminger, September 17, 1863, and Mary Rankin to Memminger, n.d., Civil War Papers, box 4, American Antiquarian Society, Worcester, Massachusetts. For women's roles in the home-front economy, see LeeAnn Whites, *The Civil War as a Crisis in Gender: Augusta, Georgia, 1860–1890* (Athens: University of Georgia Press, 1995), esp. 15–95.

8. John B. Jones, *A Rebel War Clerk's Diary,* ed. Earl Schenck Miers (New York: Sagamore, 1958), 175; *Richmond Examiner,* March 13, 1863.

9. Fleet and Fuller, *Green Mount,* 218, 198, 230.

10. Ibid., 211, 252, 253.

11. Ibid., 247.

12. Betty Herndon Maury, *The Confederate Diary of Betty Herndon Maury, 1861–1863,* ed. Alice Maury Parmalee (Washington: Privately printed, 1938), 89.

13. Elizabeth Preston Allan, *The Life and Letters of Margaret Junkin Preston* (Boston: Houghton Mifflin, 1903), 158–59, 179.

14. McDonald, *A Woman's Civil War,* 133.

15. Evelyn D. Ward, *The Children of Bladensfield* (New York: Viking, 1978), 32. Daniel E. Sutherland describes one such boys' company in *Seasons of War: The Ordeal of a Confederate Community, 1861–1865* (New York: Free Press, 1995), 38.

16. Booker T. Washington, *Up from Slavery: An Autobiography* (New York: Doubleday, Page, 1901), 6–7.

17. Ibid., 5. Little has been written specifically about slave children during the war. A still-useful account is Peter W. Bardaglio, "The Children of Jubilee: African American Childhood in Wartime," in Catherine Clinton and Nina Silber, eds., *Divided Houses: Gender and the Civil War* (New York: Oxford University Press, 1992), 213–29.

18. B. H. Wilkins, *"War Boy": A True Story of the Civil War and Re-construction Days* (Tullahoma, Tenn.: Wilson Brothers, 1990), 41–42.

19. *Richmond Examiner,* January 21, November 6, 1862, April 21, 1863, January 20, 22, 1864.

20. Jones, *A Rebel War Clerk's Diary,* 183. A balanced account of the incident is provided in Ernest B. Furgurson, *Ashes of Glory: Richmond at War* (New York: Knopf, 1996), 193–96.

21. McDonald, *A Woman's Civil War,* 191.

22. Felix James, "The Establishment of Freedman's Village in Arlington, Virginia," *Negro History Bulletin* 33 (1970): 90–93. See also Robert Francis Engs, *Freedom's First Generation: Black Hampton, Virginia, 1861–1890* (Philadelphia: University of Pennsylvania Press, 1979).

23. Jones, *A Rebel War Clerk's Diary,* 126; F. C. Jones to "My Dear Major," Civil War Papers, American Antiquarian Society.

24. Jones, *A Rebel War Clerk's Diary,* 137, 164, 258, 351, 358.

25. Ibid., 320.

26. Ibid., 176.

27. Fleet and Fuller, *Green Mount,* 316.

28. Ann Banister, "Incidents in the Life of a Civil War Child," Harrison Henry Cocke Papers, Southern Historical Collection, University of North Carolina, Chapel Hill.

29. Jane Minge Friend Dangerfield Recollections, White Hill Plantation Books, p. 37, Southern Historical Collection.

30. Ibid.

"A gift from God"

Missionary Teachers and Freedpeople in Southeastern Virginia

Benjamin H. Trask

Jane Pyatt of Portsmouth recalled in an interview: "When I was growing up, although I was a slave, I had everything a person could wish for except an education. I can't write or spell, but strange as it sounds I can read anything I wish. Sometimes I believe my ability to read is a gift from God." The octogenarian also remarked: "By listening to my mistress talk, I learned how to use a lots of words correctly. Although it was against the law to teach a slave, my mistress taught me my alphabets." The interviewer Thelma Dunston emphasized that "on listening to Mrs. Pyatt talk, one would think she was an educated woman. She has no difficulty at all in expressing her thoughts. Her memory is excellent."[1]

For slaves not as lucky as Pyatt was, the Civil War created opportunities for literacy. During the conflict one of the areas where slaves first obtained a classroom education was southeastern Virginia.[2] The opportunity to learn arose because the region was in flux. Specifically, the Union navy evacuated the Gosport Navy Yard in Portsmouth. At the same time, to the north, the Union army held fast to Fort Monroe at Old Point Comfort near Hampton on the tip of the Virginia Peninsula and to Fort Calhoun (later renamed Fort Wool) in Hampton Roads. In the spring of 1862, when Federal troops moved up the peninsula and into northeastern North Carolina, Confederate forces abandoned Norfolk and Portsmouth. Even before the defenders retreated, however, slaves found freedom at Fort Monroe thanks to the maneuverings of Maj. Gen. Benjamin F. Butler.

In the spring of 1861, Butler implemented an innovative policy that freed slaves before the Emancipation Proclamation was conceptualized.

His tactic unshackled the slaves without changing their status as property, thereby avoiding the complex issue of manumission. Because these laborers belonged to Rebels and were deployed to assist their masters in the treasonous cause, Butler dubbed them "contrabands-of-war" and refused to return slaves to their masters.[3] Massachusetts soldier Edward V. Pierce recalled that the news spread by "the mysterious spiritual telegraph which runs through the slave population," and the slaves flocked to the fort in desperate straits, emboldened by the whispers of freedom.[4]

Butler, the critical protector of these local runaways, was a Massachusetts lawyer and Democratic politician-turned-volunteer general. Although the general was inept in battle and corrupt as an administrator, Abraham Lincoln kept him in uniform because of his considerable influence as a recruiter. In the summer of 1861, the general assured merchant and abolitionist Lewis Tappan that "I shall continue to receive and protect all the negroes especially the women and children who come to me."[5] Butler later departed the Old Dominion for Louisiana but returned in the fall of 1863 as departmental commander. During both tours of duty in Virginia, he championed the rights of African Americans.[6]

The contrabands reached the fort with few possessions and in poor physical condition. There was an immediate reaction in the Northeast and Midwest to this situation. Religious and abolitionist leaders sent ministers, supervisors, observers, and teachers as well as material assistance. Various groups, such as the National Freedman's Relief Association of New York, the Pennsylvania Freedman's Relief Association of Philadelphia, the American Freedman's Union Commission, the American Union Commission, and the Friends' Association of Philadelphia for the Relief of Colored Freedman, moved to comfort the contrabands. Like-minded groups merged, while difference continued to divide other organizations.[7]

The groups that operated in southeastern Virginia included the New England Freedman's Aid Society and the Baptist and African Methodist Episcopal churches. The American Missionary Association (AMA), however, was the most active organization to operate in the area. Abolitionists, many from the Congregationalist Church, originally formed the AMA in 1846 with the intent of giving aid to the slaves who revolted and took their ship to gain freedom. The AMA later evolved into an international outreach organization that operated from Hawaii to West Africa.[8]

In May 1862, Union major general John Wool, a veteran of the War of

1812, captured Norfolk. After Wool left that spring, he was replaced by Maj. Gen. John A. Dix. Like Butler, Dix was a War Democrat, but he showed only a moderate concern for the contrabands.[9] As the Peninsula campaign raged, Dix faced a dilemma. Capt. Charles B. Wilder, the superintendent of contrabands and an AMA associate, relayed that black refugees had been transported to Hampton. In his frantic dispatch, Wilder informed his senior that "we are overrun with contrabands. . . . What shall be done with them? Capt. Elliot has a Bargeload of women & children utterly destitute & most brutally treated."[10]

As Dix contended with his departmental responsibilities, Brig. Gen. Egbert L. Viele, who directly oversaw affairs in Norfolk and Portsmouth, found that one of his most pressing problems was accommodating the destitute of both races. In a communication that sounded much like Wilder's dispatch, Viele informed Dix: "We are . . . holding here in custody about 20,000 people; we must either let them feed themselves or we must feed them."[11] The civilians suffered because the Union blockade cut the shipping trade, and local farmers did not bring produce to market. Authorities shifted the contrabands to camps at Fort Norfolk, nearby farms, and Craney Island, on the west bank of the mouth of the Elizabeth River. In this sea of uncertainty, rumors spread that parents were to be separated from their children and shipped to Cuba as slaves. Despite these obstacles, by mid-1862 an educational foundation took shape.[12]

Long before Union troops retook Norfolk, free black adults had sought educational opportunities for their offspring. Around 1823, in Princess Anne County, Johnson Hodges, a farmer and folk-remedy doctor, sent his children to a school taught by a poor white woman. One of Hodges's children, Willis Augustus Hodges, recalled: "This woman taught us to read, etc. I was between 7 and 8 when I began to go to school, and continued for several months, which is all the schooling I have ever had." After young Hodges left Virginia for New York, he made the most of his limited education by founding the short-lived newspaper the *Ram's Horn*. Remarkably, the radical abolitionist John Brown was a contributor.[13]

Antebellum African Americans such as Jane Pyatt considered an education a godsend and a means to their salvation. In that same spirit before the arrival of missionaries, Portsmouth slave and caulker George Teamoh recalled: "I did not know one of the twenty six letters which make up the English alphabet. Yet, such [was] the confidence I had in the Supreme Being,

I considered nothing too difficult for His wisdom to Master." With that faith, the young Teamoh listened to children sing alphabet songs, made flash cards, found a primer, and learned from whites via popular music scores.[14]

After the liberation of Norfolk and Portsmouth in the spring of 1862, free blacks began teaching in their homes and churches before relocating to school buildings. Mary Jane Wilson of Portsmouth recalled that she "didn't get any teachings when I was a slave. When I was free, I went to school. The first school I went to was held in a church."[15] While missionary associations debated the issue of separation of church and state, black church leaders gave that little thought. Churches became schoolhouses, and schoolhouses became houses of worship.[16] These efforts continued, and free blacks held regular charity meetings with the aim of helping contrabands.[17]

From Villa Margaret in Hampton, Rev. Lewis C. Lockwood of the AMA prepared to expand his teaching responsibilities into Norfolk. The creekside villa was the summer home of former president and slave owner John Tyler. The AMA used the home as a base of operations from the Virginia Peninsula to northeastern North Carolina. The hostility of local whites made Norfolk one of the more challenging sectors in which to start schools. Nonetheless, within six month modest educational inroads had been made.[18]

At the close of 1862, Union lieutenant A. B. Lawrence evaluated the condition of a newly formed community of more than 700 North Carolina contrabands who had reached Suffolk. The lieutenant described the seventy log cabins in two settlements as "very neat" and "comfortable," built by the contrabands with the assistance of soldiers of "more acknowledged intelligence." The army's quartermaster and commissary sections hired the former slaves as laborers, mechanics, and clerks. Despite these improvements, Lawrence reported a "lack of proper clothing, there being no means or opportunity of supplying themselves except at the expenses of their abandoned masters or Mistresses wardrobe." Even when struggling to find food and work, the contrabands still desired an education. Lawrence observed: "But few are able to read or write at all, all being very desirous to learn & make rapid progress under instruction—It is not at all uncommon to find them at their leisure pouring [sic] over books carried by them in their pockets—obtained in various ways."[19]

With the year 1863 approaching, former slaves in southeastern Virginia orchestrated a jubilee to celebrate freedom at a local church.[20] In response, Rev. Overton Bernard of Portsmouth fumed that the "the slaves seduced from their homes have flocked in town, idle impudent and thievish dreaming of freedom by first of January."[21] In antebellum Norfolk, on the first day of the year, some masters allowed slaves to negotiate for their annual services. Sister Harrison of Portsmouth remembered: "It was on that day that the specially favored or hired out slaves went to a place called the hiring grounds to hire their labors out for the year. . . . The Hirin' Grounds was always lively."[22] The first day of 1863, however, was like no other. It was on that occasion that the Emancipation Proclamation went into effect across much of the Confederacy, and about 5,000 contrabands in Norfolk heralded the day. Chloe Tyler Whittle, a nineteen-year-old white Norfolkian, reported that "they have had a grand procession. True to negro character they have made a great deal of noise—their cheers resounded through the air. . . . They went down to Gen. Viele's—he made them a speech calling them 'My friends.'"[23]

This joyous outburst by the contrabands may have caused former U.S. congressman John S. Millson of Norfolk to share his views with his old friend Richard Parker. About a fortnight after the parade, Millson concluded that "whatever may have been our impressions formerly, the experiences of this unhappy war, have to certainly assure us, that our slaves are not indifferent to the chances of freedom." Parker was the judge at Harpers Ferry during the trial and execution of the revolutionary abolitionist John Brown. No doubt he, too, reflected on the past.[24]

Interestingly, the Emancipation Proclamation specifically excluded "Princess Anne, and Norfolk, including the cities of Norfolk and Portsmouth."[25] The document stated that these locales were "for the present left precisely as if this proclamation were not issued." African American John Oliver, a carpenter turned teacher and a native of Petersburg, lamented to an official in the AMA: "Lincoln leaves us as we were before his proclamation of freedom. . . . Whether this place is a modern Sodom not to be saved under the blessing of Abraham , . . I do not know."[26] Despite this formal exclusion, hundreds of the slaves who had reached Norfolk were not returned to their masters. Furthermore, the Federals showed only modest interest in returning slaves. When Butler returned to the department, he issued a sweeping response that stymied any attempts to place runaways back into bondage.[27]

The same wave that brought contrabands to the region also carried missionary teachers. The educators were an extension of the abolitionist campaign and the American Protestant evangelical movement. Consequently, the rigid zeal to educate was fortified with a desire to inculcate former slaves with Victorian moral values. The missionaries not only saw to the necessities of life, they stressed the importance of legally documented marriages, good citizenship, domestic skills, formalized religious services, table manners, and economic productivity. Many of the instructors had prior teaching experience and at least some college education.[28] Nevertheless, this challenge was fraught with surprises and frustration. The teachers included idealists both black and white who hoped to educate and bring spiritual awareness to freedpeople of all ages. From 1862 to 1870 more than fifty teachers instructed black students in and around Norfolk and Portsmouth. The majority of them were white women from New England, along with Pennsylvanians and New Yorkers. A few hailed from that hotbed of abolitionism, Oberlin, Ohio. The number of married and unmarried women appeared to be fairly equal, and some men and women made the trip south with family members.[29]

The quality of the teachers varied despite a screening process. The AMA granted a certificate of commission and paid for traveling expenses, room, board, rations, and a salary of $4 to $10 a month. One applicant initially balked at the modest pay, retorting that her annual shoe bill alone was $50. Assisting in this daunting educational undertaking were supportive spouses, soldiers, local blacks, monitors, and volunteers. Even Sarah Butler, the former actress and general's wife, taught Sunday school.[30]

Divergent views on slave values reveal how the missionaries interpreted African American religious practices. Consider the open-ended conclusions of Dr. LeBaron Russell of the New England Freedman's Aid Society. Russell went on fact-finding missions for state and government officials.[31] While in Hampton, he noted: "I have just come back from one of their evening meetings, which was very interesting. The service began with a strange & wild chant which seemed as if it came from Africa itself then a prayer by one of them full of feeling & devotion—so full that it at times overpowered the voice of the speaker & caused his hearers to groan & shout in sympathy."[32]

In contrast, Lucy Chase, a Quaker teacher on Craney Island, was not as understanding as Russell. She noted:

> At one of their prayer-meetings, which we attended, last night, we
> saw a painful exhibition of their barbarism. Their religious feeling
> is purely emotional; void of principle, and of not practical utility.
> The Dr [Orlando Brown] says they will rise from prayer and lie or
> steal, if the way opens therefore. The brother who knelt in prayer

had the friendly sing-song. His sentences were incoherent, and aimless—"ohuh Lorder! This afternoonugh, hear our prayerer!" . . . They must know what is right! In order to worship aright the God of right.

And so, for the contrabands seeking assistance and literacy, the missionaries attempted to reshape the former slaves between this hammer of righteousness and the anvil of understanding.[33]

Fatefully, the path of these two humanitarians with such opposing first impressions on contraband worship practices crisscrossed during the war. It was Russell who gave Lucy Chase and her sister Sarah their commissions to leave their comfortable home in Worcester, Massachusetts. He later visited the contraband camps along the seaboard. Lucy Chase and Russell corresponded about their endeavors. Chase had her hoard of eager students, and Russell did his best to dispatch assistance and provide her with details of his other, related activities along the coast. In spite of their conflicting impressions, they were both dedicated to the cause of helping the contrabands.[34]

Missionary women such as the Chases rarely moved around the region without an escort because the white residents deeply resented the teachers. Verbal abuse or shunning whites sympathetic to the Union became the norm. A Federal surgeon's wife had a church door locked in her face when she tried to enter. One Chase sister who simply asked for directions was greeted by a woman resident with "vinegar pouts and vinegar glances."[35] Other teachers were denied lodging by local whites and lived with free black families, an arrangement the white teachers noted but appear not to have resented. Therefore, the missionaries considered it a coup and even a sign from God when they rented the house of former mayor William W. Lamb without his knowledge of their intention to teach blacks in the community.[36]

The aforementioned Dr. Orlando Brown, former surgeon of the Eighteenth Massachusetts, was one of many dedicated and innovative New Englanders in Virginia at this time. He was the government official in charge of the contrabands around Norfolk, under a department sometimes called the Office of the Assistant Quartermaster Superintendent of Contrabands or the Bureau of Negro Affairs. Described as tall and handsome but somewhat awkward, Brown nevertheless moved with a certain grace from his faith in his cause. Like many officials, he was accompanied by his proactive wife and children.[37]

One of the isolated locations that required Brown's attention was the contraband camp on Craney Island. Early in the war, free blacks and slaves had constructed batteries for the Confederates on the twelve-acre crescent. A year later, in the shadow of the charred hulk of the CSS *Virginia,* the isle harbored former slaves. Brown, his wife, W. O. King of the AMA, and Lucy and Sarah Chase supervised the distribution of supplies to contrabands and responded to their collective cry for learning. The abandoned stronghold became living quarters for about 2,000 former slaves. Most of the refugees hailed from eastern Virginia and North Carolina, but others originated in Tennessee, South Carolina, and Kentucky. Among the group close to the Chase sisters were "pretty, and neat girls" who had once belonged to the Washington and Custis families.[38] Their skill with a needle and thread was matched by their eagerness for an education. By harnessing the collective sewing talents of the women, Brown hoped to earn an army contract to provide clothing, thus helping to make the contrabands self-sufficient and proving that, with the proper guidance, freedpeople could contribute to the economy.[39]

Once on the island, the Chase sisters requested assistance from the Quakers in New York for the construction of a meeting- and schoolhouse and asked for a thousand writing slates (in the meantime, five slates would have to suffice). Before help and supplies arrived, classes remained quite an undertaking. Up to the task, the Chase sisters blended the sewing circles with alphabet lessons and Bible readings. They posted letters on the walls for the entire circle to study to keep "heads and fingers busy." Sarah converted an attic into a classroom and taught fifty children at once. Lucy created a schoolroom in a barracks. She divided her students into groups of three reading levels, tailoring her questions to each level and making sure that the class was lively and interesting. Students were also asked to copy letters on one of the few slates available; the letters they were given were from their own names in order to pique interest in the drill. During this exercise, the students became excited trying to outperform one another. It was then, Sarah claimed, that she must "outscream the screamiest."[40]

The teachers were also responsible for the distribution of clothing, shoes, cloth, bedding, and blankets. In this melee of humanity on the island they found it difficult to determine who was getting his or her first blanket and who was after more than this meager share. Rag-covered contrabands pestered the teachers for these items, but they were just as likely to request not clothing but private instruction in reading, often asking, "[W]ill you be so kind, Miss, as to make me a copy of a b c?" At times the students begged for lessons. Lucy Chase described her notable female students as "greedy learners."[41]

The teachers discovered "a number" of contrabands who had "learned to read in slavery." Freedpeople taught others and turned to the white teachers to improve their own skills. One of these student teachers was described by Lucy Chase as a "very bright woman" who recognized that she had learned to read in "a broken manner." The woman taught reading to a large number of students but hoped to better understand scripture.[42] Many slaves were skeptical of their masters' interpretation of Christianity, especially with regard to an ideal of submissive servants. Therefore, literacy was critical for those who wished to read the Holy Book to form their own interpretations.[43] Jane Washington, another "good reader" who learned to read when she was young with her owner's children, taught the children in camp to read. Despite their acknowledged shortcomings, the contrabands took pride in the skills that they did possess. An elderly man responded to an inquiry about his literacy level, claiming proudly, "I can stumble along right smart."[44]

By spring the teachers were instructing students in a newly built school-house. The teachers on the island still awaited the arrival of blackboards, but they did have primers. For adult learners a school was not necessary. The gangs that toiled gathering wood, burying the dead, and building shelters came home tired. Pushing on, these exhausted workers rested in doorways and around fires at dusk to study books, with children peering over their shoulders. By August the number of contrabands on the island had been cut in half, and in the fall the schoolhouse was dismantled, as most of the islanders had departed.[45]

As they broke camp, the contrabands engaged in an activity that high-lights both their resourcefulness and their desperate living conditions. Cooks lit their fires as gangs pried up the floorboards and hunters went after hundreds of rats with a vengeance. The rodents were so numerous that the dogs in the camp had made no effort to pursue them. The contrabands assured Lucy Chase that, skinned and roasted, the rodents tasted like chicken. The rats had fattened themselves on rations, and when it came time to get even, the contrabands supped on their tormentors.[46]

But the rodents could not impede the desire for an education. As the gangs carried the floor planking down to the wharf, men, women, and children needled their comrades into spelling contests. Drawing from their environment, the contestants spelled "board," "house," and "every." The spelling bee continued into the night as bystanders at the evening dance continued to prod one another with orthographic challenges. After all of the laboring and festivities, authorities finished redistributing the island's residents to other camps and farms.[47]

Freedpeople and teachers from the island found conditions different in Norfolk. John Oliver had taught on the peninsula before venturing to the city. Taking a break from his studies for the ministry in Boston, he headed south. Oliver returned home in the fall of 1862 and began a second tour of teaching in Virginia. The opposition to his efforts to open a school in Norfolk, however, was so strong that Oliver decided to transfer to Portsmouth. In January 1863 he established a school in a black Methodist church for former North Carolina slaves. Within a few days the school attracted 130 students, and Oliver then opened a Sabbath school in the same church as the number of students rose. Following his success, he considered returning to Norfolk to try again to establish a school. At the close of February Oliver left his Portsmouth school in the hands of instructors Harriet Taylor and Rev. Gorham Greely, also of the AMA.[48]

Taylor and Greely immediately ran into trouble with their students. The boys created discipline problems for Taylor, and they were quick to take advantage of the reverend's poor hearing. Greely soon requested a return to his pastoral duties. Taylor became ill and could assist only with evening classes. She expected that the AMA would send another male teacher to share the undertaking. Instead, Miss Susan Drummond arrived, and she preferred to instruct the younger pupils.[49] Wilder concluded that it would be best to close the boys' department until "a suitable efficient Teacher" could be found and meanwhile to avoid white teachers "with little or no gumption or experience."[50]

Overcoming troublesome students and the opposition from whites, missionaries started schools in Norfolk. Rev. William. L. Coan transitioned from being a collector of supplies in Boston to an instructor. By late spring Coan reported that there were more than 1,400 students in various educational endeavors, including day and evening schools. The classes averaged fifty students, but attendance varied greatly. The number of students in and around Norfolk grew in the summer as Confederate divisions appeared in the outskirts of Suffolk. Coan soon became a leader among the teachers, and his school was a model for inspectors.[51] But success only brought more tension. Coan noted: "I am now in charge of one of the day schools, assisting in the evening school and am also in charge of a singing school. . . . Every thing looks well now. *Secech* shows its cloven foot in many ways our scholars are stopped on the streets, bricks flung at and against them, *books* occasionally taken from them."[52]

A summer census indicated there were almost 19,000 blacks living in Nansemond, Princess Anne, and Norfolk counties. The breakdown divided into 4,961 slaves, 4,140 free blacks, and 9,882 contrabands. This tally included 11,694 permanent residents and 7,289 transients.[53] Some of the schools closed in the heat of the summer, but with the coming of fall education once again became a priority. Rev. "Professor" William H. Woodbury, a friend of Captain Brown, arrived to supervise the teachers. Like the instructors, he promoted Victorian values and self-reliance.[54] W. O. King moved from Craney Island to Portsmouth, where he taught "a colored regiment" and "partly supplied it with books."[55]

Black students found learning opportunities in singing classes, sewing circles, night schools, lessons for black soldiers, and Sabbath schools. With hundreds of students, the teachers of the AMA were constantly requesting a replenishment of school supplies and textbooks. These items included testaments, singing books, slates, crayons, paper for blackboards, geography texts, primers, spellers, readers, arithmetic and picture lesson books, as well as maps of the world and the war. Similarly, the sewing classes required yards of calico, dozens of needles, and spools of thread.[56]

An alternative to urban settlements was the relocation of blacks to farms and plantations. In some instances the personal property and real estate had been abandoned, but in other cases the owners were evicted. This separation of the races was designed to make the contrabands productive, relieve the overcrowded cities, and allow students and instructors to interact without harassment. Sometimes called "government farms," they served a variety of purposes: clearing centers, schools, dairies, and market and subsistence farms. By the close of 1863, there were about nineteen government farms. The cautious Viele was transferred to New York in the fall, and missionary administrators sought to establish more schools in town. The resettlement of agricultural estates, however, continued throughout the war. This practice elevated the expectation among black farmers that they might keep the land they cultivated.[57]

The most noteworthy converted estate was Henry A. Wise's Rolleston plantation in Princess Anne County. As governor, Wise had pushed for the swift capture and prosecution of John Brown. He was an influential secession delegate who led the Commonwealth out of the Union, and during the war the newly commissioned Brigadier General Wise raised a legion. Consequently, Federal authorities were quick to transform his estate into a platform for guiding former slaves into citizenship. The AMA and Free Will Baptist Association established schools on the plantation. By December 1863, Rev. W. S. Bell of the AMA boasted that "the School keeps increasing day after day, until it has outgrown the dimensions of our room." Amid all this activity the resident teachers did not miss the significance of their surroundings. They rode in the former governor's carriages and hung a likeness of John Brown in the parlor.[58]

A few of Wise's former slaves remained on the property, and others returned to Rolleston to take advantage of this new arrangement. Not only were the contrabands supposed to be productive, but they were also expected to learn table manners. Educator Thomas P. Jackson pondered: "How can I teach decent habits to people to whom I have neither knife, fork or plate or spoon to give, that they may learn to eat." Later Jackson remarked that "I will have them eat at a table (which I made yesterday) . . . to improve their habits of eating."[59] Outside of etiquette classes, the sixty-one settlers produced 100 barrels of potatoes and more than 2,000 bushels of corn. Willis Hodges, the free black activist whose father paid a white teacher for his meager education, returned to Princess Anne County during the war. After spending time in Wise's parlor and musing about his old acquaintance John Brown, Hodges knelt under a chestnut tree in the moonlight and prayed.[60]

In December 1863 abolitionist Francis W. Bird provided testimony to the American Freedman's Inquiry Commission, making this observation about the levels of instruction north and south of the James River: "The schools in both districts are represented to be in a very flourishing condition. I visited only those in Norfolk, and am entirely safe in saying from my own experience in the management of schools and from the testimony of teachers that they have been at least as great and under similar discouraging circumstances."[61] All told, there were eighty-three missionaries and teachers aided by nineteen assistants in the Commonwealth, with major operations in Arlington, Hampton, Yorktown, Norfolk, and Portsmouth.[62]

Just before Bird gave his testimony, Butler returned to Virginia. The general's arrival polarized the department. The local pro-Confederate *Daily Times* bemoaned that "Butler . . . is now appointed over us. You can never know the mental anxiety . . . under which our people continually exist." In stark contrast, the New York–based *Freedman's Advocate* gushed that the general "does more to elevate the unfortunate colored race than any man in this country." Wilder also sang Butler's praises to the AMA, extolling his "hearty sincerity & integrity."[63] Butler's well-known views soon became policy, when he declared in General Order No. 46: "Religious, benevolent, and humane persons have come into this department for the charitable purpose of giving to the negroes secular and religious instructions; and this, too, without any adequate pay or material reward. It is therefore ordered, That every officer and soldier shall treat all such persons with the utmost respect; shall aid them by all proper means in their laudable avocations; and that transportation be furnished them whenever it may be necessary in pursuit of their business."[64]

Butler made fellow Massachusetts lawyer Lt. Col. Josiah B. Kinsman the superintendent of Negro affairs within the vast department. Dr. Brown continued to serve as the district supervisor for Norfolk vicinity, while Woodbury was the superintendent of education. By the close of 1863, determined educators met the challenge of teaching in town, and Coan located a school with four classes on Church Street.[65]

In December Lucy Chase wrote to the readers of the *Liberator* that "John Brown's daughter, led by the on-marching soul of her father, has come to Norfolk to join us on doing her father's work." The daughter in question was probably Anne Brown Adams. In a later edition of the *Liberator* she is described as "a lady of about twenty summers."[66] Anne Brown had accompanied her father to Harpers Ferry in 1859, and her presence as a housekeeper at the Kennedy House served as cover for her father's mission of sparking an armed slave insurrection.[67] Incredibly, after the war, Lucy Chase met Henry Wise in Charleston, South Carolina. The former governor asked Chase if John Brown's daughter had taught children in his home. Chase did not record her response to the inquiry.[68]

The scope of educational endeavors grew during Butler's tenure, as did the contrasts with antebellum Norfolk. The *Freedman* reported that a Norfolk slave owner had sold a man to pay his taxes for a schoolhouse, but "now, the brothers and sisters of that slave attend school in that very house."[69] However, unless the taxpayer was greatly in arrears with his taxes, this levied obligation would have been a few dollars and not enough to justify selling a valuable slave. Likewise, the use of the residences of John Tyler and Henry Wise was often cited to demonstrate that a revolution had occurred with the education of former slaves. The missionaries would have been even more gleeful to learn that Tyler had presented academic medals to the students of Hampton Academy before the war. And Wise was an education reformer who supported the free education of white children, with the expectation that an educated populace was necessary for a strong republic.[70]

The missionaries who ventured into southeastern Virginia did more than establish schools. They did their best to protect contrabands from antagonistic Federal soldiers and Confederate sympathizers. Along with moralizing came literacy, food, clothing, and shelter. In addition, the missionary associations tapped their political connections and supported the creation of the Bureau of Freedman, Refugees, and Abandoned Lands (Freedman's Bureau), which formalized the ties between the Federal government and the associations through Reconstruction. The efforts of like-minded missionary workers and supporting associations that surfaced in southeastern Virginia and elsewhere continued after the establishment of the troubled Freedman's Bureau under Maj. Gen. Oliver O. Howard. Supervisors such as Wilder, Brown, and Woodbury remained in Virginia and coordinated their efforts with the bureau.[71]

On the classroom level, the interaction between teachers and students was not always a one-way exchange. Truly enriching classes generate personal growth for all. For example, Lucy Chase, the same young woman who arrived in Norfolk with the steely determination to make sure that her charges understood the true meaning of religion, soon fell under the influence of the contrabands and demonstrated that she was able to evolve as a person. Nine months after her arrival, she acknowledged that even without her guidance, "some of them show, unmistakably, that their souls are blessed."[72] With this revelation, the teacher learned from her pupils that there was more than one path to salvation. Undoubtedly, Chase was not the only educator who learned from her students.

One black student who benefited from these exchanges was Mary Jane Wilson. Born into slavery, she began her education with missionary teachers. She later attended Chestnut Street Academy, and in 1874 graduated from Hampton Institute. Wilson opened a school in her home and noted that after "two years my class grew so fast and large that my father built a school for me in our back yard." Some of her students became teachers. Wilson recalled: "I had my graduation exercises in the Emanuel A.M.E. Church. Those were my happiest days."[73] Her success was only part of the story.

Like Wilson, thousands of eager African Americans received a rudimentary education despite the turbulent environment. Beyond 1863, the seeds sown by Butler and the AMA grew, despite major obstacles. None of this would have been possible, however, without the intense desire of freedpeople to obtain an education. Those seeking an education learned despite hostile Federals, Confederate sympathizers, familial upheaval, poverty, disruptive rumors, and constant displacement. Furthermore, the desire for literacy was apparent even before the basic necessities were obtained, before the Federals and the AMA provided shelter, clothing, or food. Instinctively, former slaves understood that what their masters had kept from them while in chains was a critical component to becoming spiritually complete and full-fledged American citizens.

Notes

1. Charles L. Perdue Jr. et al., eds., *Weevils in the Wheat: Interviews with Virginia Ex-Slaves* (Charlottesville: University Press of Virginia, 1992), 234.

2. This essay covers southeastern Virginia. It is defined as the former counties of Norfolk, Nansemond, and Princess Anne, which contained the town of Suffolk and the cities of Norfolk and Portsmouth. Most of Norfolk County is now the city of Chesapeake. Princess Anne County became the city of Virginia Beach, and Nansemond County is the expanded city of Suffolk. Today, residents call the region "Tidewater" or "Southside," but they were not designators used during the Civil War.

3. Armistead L. Robinson, *Bitter Fruits of Bondage: The Demise of Slavery and the Collapse of the Confederacy, 1861–1865* (Charlottesville: University of Virginia Press, 2005), 173–78; Silvana R. Siddali, *From Property to Person: Slavery and the Confiscation Acts, 1861–1862* (Baton Rouge: Louisiana State University Press, 2005), 52–53; and Ira Berlin et al., eds., *Free at Last: A Documentary History of Slavery, Freedom, and the Civil War* (New York: New Press, 1992), 9–10.

4. Edward V. Pierce, "The Contrabands at Fortress Monroe," *Atlantic Monthly,* November 1861, 627, 628 (quotation).

5. Benjamin F. Butler to Lewis Tappan, August 10, 1861 (HI-4336), American Missionary Association Archives, Armistead Research Center, Dillard University, New Orleans (hereafter cited as AMAA).

6. John D. Winters, *The Civil War in Louisiana* (Baton Rouge: Louisiana State University Press, 1991), 125–48.

7. Robert H. Bremner, *The Public Good: Philanthropy and Welfare in the Civil War Era* (New York: Knopf, 1980), 98–110; and Henry Lee Swint, *The Northern Teacher in the South, 1862–1870* (New York: Octagon, 1967), 10, 19.

8. Joe M. Richardson, *Christian Reconstruction: The American Missionary Association and Southern Blacks, 1861–1890* (Athens: University of Georgia Press, 1986), 4; Robert C. Morris, *Reading, 'Riting, and Reconstruction: The Education of Freedmen in the South, 1861–1870* (Chicago: University of Chicago Press, 1981), 3–13; Clarence E. Walker, *A Rock in a Weary Land: The African Methodist Episcopal Church during the Civil War and Reconstruction* (Baton Rouge: Louisiana State University Press, 1982), 54–55; and Ronald E. Butchart, *Northern Schools, Southern Blacks, and Reconstruction: Freedmen's Education, 1862–1875* (Westport, Conn.: Greenwood, 1980), 77–81.

9. W. O. King to S. S. Jocelyn, January 7, 1863 (HI-4636), AMAA; Ludwell H. Johnson III, "Blockade or Trade Monopoly? John A. Dix and the Union Occupation of Norfolk," *Virginia Magazine of History and Biography* 93 (January 1985): 56–58.

10. C. B. Wilder to Maj. Gen. Dix, July 2, 1862, John A. Dix Papers, Special Collections, Butler Library, Columbia University, New York.

11. United States War Department, *War of the Rebellion: A Compilation of Official Records of the Union and Confederate Armies* (Washington, D.C.: Government Printing Office, 1880–1901), series I, vol. 18, 384 (hereafter cited as *OR*).

12. Robert Francis Engs, *Freedom's First Generation: Black Hampton, Virginia, 1861–1890* (Philadelphia: University of Pennsylvania Press, 1979), 52; and Ervin L. Jordan Jr., *Black Confederates and Afro-Yankees in Civil War Virginia* (Charlottesville: University Press of Virginia, 1995), 86.

13. Willard B. Gatewood, ed., *Free Man of Color: The Autobiography of Willis Augustus Hodges* (Knoxville: University of Tennessee Press, 1982), lxvii, 8 (quotation).

14. George Teamoh, *God Made Man, Man Made the Slave: The Autobiography of George Teamoh,* ed. F. M. Boney, Richard L. Hume, and Rafia Zafar (Macon, Ga.: Mercer University Press, 1990), 69–73 (quotation p. 71).

15. Perdue et al., *Weevils in the Wheat,* 330.

16. For those missionaries who supported the unification of literacy and

religious instruction there was a practical architectural fusion. Harriet Beecher Stowe, author of *Uncle Tom's Cabin*, and her sister Catherine E. Beecher offered the plans for a "small church, a school-house, and a comfortable family dwelling [that] may be united in one building, and for a very moderate sum" in their domestic guide. Catherine E. Beecher and Harriet Beecher Stowe, *American Woman's Home; or, Principles of Domestic Science* (1869; repr., Hartford, Conn.: Stowe-Day Foundation, 1985), 453–61 (quotation p. 455).

17. John Oliver to S. S. Jocelyn, January 14, 1863 (HI-4637), AMAA; Engs, *Freedom's First Generation*, 52; and Henry Lee Swint, ed., *Dear Ones at Home: Letters from Contraband Camps* (Nashville: Vanderbilt University Press, 1966), 84.

18. Sing-Nan Fen, "Notes on the Education of Negroes at Norfolk and Portsmouth, Virginia, during the Civil War," *Phylon* 28 (Summer 1967): 197–99; and Engs, *Freedom's First Generation*, 52.

19. A. B. Lawrence to Dr. L. B. Russell, December 11, 1862, LeBaron B. Russell Collection, Pilgrim Society, Plymouth, Massachusetts. Lawrence may have been describing the same settlement near Suffolk known as Union Town. By the spring of 1863, there was a school at the colony with about 130 young students. Two of the teachers were former slaves. Cpl. Charles R. Sikes of the First New York Mounted Rifles helped to establish the school and made arrangements with Wilder to obtain textbooks. W. O. King to S. S. Jocelyn, April 11, 1863 (HI-4212), AMAA.

20. *OR*, series I, vol. 18, 501, 502; and John Oliver to S. S. Jocelyn, January 14, 1863 (HI-4637), AMAA.

21. Diary of Rev. Overton Bernard, December 31, 1862, December 25, 1862 (quotation), Overton and Jesse Bernard Diaries #62, Southern Historical Collection, University of North Carolina, Chapel Hill.

22. Perdue et al., *Weevils in the Wheat*, 135.

23. Chloe Tyler Whittle Diary, July 30–September 27, 1863 (quotation January 1, 1863), box 1, Whittle-Green Papers, Special Collections, Swem Library, College of William and Mary, Williamsburg, Virginia.

24. John S. Millson to Judge [Parker], January 16, 1863 (typescript copy), J. S. Millson Collection, Small Special Collections Library, University of Virginia, Charlottesville; Craig M. Simpson, *A Good Southerner: The Life of Henry A. Wise of Virginia* (Chapel Hill: University of North Carolina Press, 1985), 205, 287.

25. "Emancipation Proclamation," in *the New York Public Library Desk Reference* (New York: New York Public Library and Strongsong, 1989), 718.

26. Clara Merritt DeBoer, *His Truth Is Marching On: African Americans Who Taught the Freedmen for the American Missionary Association, 1861–1877*

(New York: Garland, 1995), 32–37; John Oliver to S. S. Jocelyn, January 14, 1863 (HI-4637), AMAA.

27. Brian Steel Wills, *The War Hits Home: The Civil War in Southeastern Virginia* (Charlottesville: University Press of Virginia, 2001), 99–97, 199–200; Benjamin F. Butler, *Private and Official Correspondence of Gen. Benjamin F. Butler, during the Period of the Civil War,* 5 vols. (Norwood, Mass.: Plimpton, 1917), 3:156.

28. DeBoer, *His Truth Is Marching On,* 37–49; Charles C. Cole Jr., *The Social Ideas of the Northern Evangelists, 1826–1860* (New York: Octagon, 1966), 221–31; Richard D. Brown, *The Strength of a People: The Idea of an Informed Citizenry in America, 1650–1870* (Chapel Hill: University of North Carolina Press, 1996), 190–91; and Bertram Wyatt-Brown, *Yankee Saints and Southern Sinners* (Baton Rouge: Louisiana State University Press, 1985), 73–75.

29. *New York Freedman's Advocate,* February 1864, 6; and Swint, *Northern Teacher,* 35–69, 175–200.

30. George N. Greene to S. S. Jocelyn, July 21, 1863 (HI-4869), certificate of commission of Harriet B. Greely, November 17, 1863 (HI-5115), letter of agreement between AMA and Harriett B. Greely, November 17, 1863 (HI-5116), AMAA; and Steven F. Perrine, "Benjamin Butler and the Bureau of Negro Affairs in Tidewater, Virginia, 1861–1865," (master's thesis, Old Dominion University, Norfolk, Va., 1975), 124.

31. Swint, *Dear Ones at Home,* 51, 85; and Swint, *Northern Teacher,* 15, 163.

32. L. B. R. to Lucia [Lucia Jane Russell], May 29, [1862?] (typescript copy), Russell Collection, Pilgrim Society.

33. Swint, *Dear Ones at Home,* 21–22.

34. Ibid., 5n, 51n, 62, 85–86.

35. Ibid., 35–36 (quotation p. 35).

36. John Oliver to S. S. Jocelyn, February 28, 1863 (HI-4664), G. Greely to S. S. Jocelyn, March 2, 1863 (HI-4669), George N. Greene to Br. Jocelyn, May 27, 1863 (HI-4795), AMAA.

37. Perrine, "Benjamin Butler and the Bureau of Negro Affairs," 44; Swint, *Dear Ones at Home,* 22, 43; and E. Allen Richardson, "Architects of a Benevolent Empire: The Relationship between the American Missionary Association and the Freedman's Bureau in Virginia, 1865–1872," in Paul A. Cimbala and Randall M. Miller, eds., *The Freedmen's Bureau and Reconstruction: Reconsiderations* (New York: Fordham University Press, 1999), 126.

38. Swint, *Dear Ones at Home,* 20–21 (quotation p. 20). The women who had belonged to the Custis family may have among the almost two hundred slaves freed by George W. P. Custis. At the close of 1862, Gen. Robert E. Lee,

the executor of the will, signed the deed of manumission. To examine a copy of the deed, see Jordan, *Black Confederates and Afro-Yankees,* 324–25.

39. James H. Brewer, *The Confederate Negro: Virginia's Craftsmen and Military Laborers, 1861–1865* (Durham, N.C.: Duke University Press, 1969), 131; W. O. King to S. S. Jocelyn, January 7, 1863 (HI-4636), AMAA; and Perrine, "Benjamin Butler and the Bureau of Negro Affairs," 45.

40. Swint, *Dear Ones at Home,* 21, 29 (quotation), 41, 56, 62, 63 (quotation), 64.

41. W. O. King to S. S. Jocelyn, March 17, 1863 (HI-4685), AMAA; and Swint, *Dear Ones at Home,* 23 (quotation), 56 (quotation), 62.

42. Swint, *Dear Ones at Home,* 39 (quotations), 62, 63 (quotations).

43. Cheryl J. Sanders, "African Americans, the Bible, and Spiritual Formation," in Vincent L. Wimbush, ed., *African Americans and the Bible: Sacred Texts and Social Textures* (New York: Continuum, 2000), 591.

44. W. O. King to S. S. Jocelyn, January 7, 1863 (HI-4636), AMAA; and Swint, *Dear Ones at Home,* 63, 56.

45. W. O. King to S. S. Jocelyn, January 7, 1863 (HI-4636), W. O. King to S. S. Jocelyn, March 17, 1863 (HI-4685), W. O. King to S. S. Jocelyn, August 4, 1863 (HI-4903), and W. O. King to S. S. Jocelyn, September 30, 1863 (HI-5035), AMAA; and Swint, *Dear Ones at Home,* 61.

46. W. O. King to S. S. Jocelyn, September 2, 1863 (HI-4960), AMAA; and Swint, *Dear Ones at Home,* 90.

47. Swint, *Dear Ones at Home,* 90.

48. John Oliver to S. S. Jocelyn, January 14, 1863 (HI-4637), January 26, 1863 (HI-4641), February 5, 1863 (HI-4648), February 23, 1863 (HI-4664), AMAA; DeBoer, *His Truth Is Marching On,* 32–37; and Richardson, *Christian Reconstruction,* 11.

49. G. Greely to S. S. Jocelyn, March 2, 1863 (HI-4669), March 4, 1863 (HI-4672), March 11, 1863 (HI-4681), Harriett Taylor to S. S. Jocelyn, March 23, 1863 (HI-4692), Harriet Taylor to S. S. Jocelyn, April 28, 1863 (HI-4745), AMAA; and DeBoer, *His Truth Is Marching On,* 37.

50. C. B. Wilder to Brethren, March 6, 1863 (HI-4675), AMAA.

51. W. L. Coan to Bro. Jocelyn, May 12, 1863 (HI-4773), W. Graham Taylor to Father Jocelyn, July 24, 1863 (HI-4878), AMAA; and Perrine, "Benjamin Butler and the Bureau of Negro Affairs," 124–25.

52. William L. Coan to Brother Whipple, May 7, 1863 (HI-4759), AMAA (all quotations).

53. Ira Berlin et al., eds., *The Destruction of Slavery,* Freedom: A Documentary History of Emancipation, 1861–1867 (New York: Cambridge University Press, 1985), series I, vol. 1, 91.

54. [William Woodbury] to S. S. Jocelyn, August 26, 1863 (HI-4943), AMAA; Richardson, "Architects of a Benevolent Empire," 128; and Perrine, "Benjamin Butler and the Bureau of Negro Affairs," 123–24.

55. W. O. King to S. S. Jocelyn, October 24, 1863 (HI-5075), AMAA.

56. G. N. Greene to [AMA Headquarters], May 6, 1863 (HI-4755), W. L. Coan to Brother Whiting, October 10, 1863 (HI-5049), Harriet Taylor to Prof. Woodbury, December 10, 1863 (HI-5169), AMAA.

57. Berlin et al., *Free at Last,* 278; and Swint, *Dear Ones at Home,* 38, 50–54, 70–71.

58. Simpson, *A Good Southerner,* 287–89; W. S. Bell to S. S. Jocelyn, November 19, 1863 (HI-5121), W. S. Bell to S. S. Jocelyn, December 9, 1863 (HI-5166), AMAA.

59. Thomas P. Jackson to George Whipple, March 28, 1863 (HI-4701), Thomas P. Jackson to George Whipple, April 7, 1863 (HI-4712), AMAA.

60. Berlin et al., *Free at Last,* 283–84; and Gatewood, *Free Man of Color,* lvi.

61. Berlin et al., *Free at Last,* 284–85.

62. *Boston Freedman,* January 1864, 4.

63. *Norfolk Daily Times,* December 7, 1863; *New York Freedman's Advocate,* February 1864, 8; and C. B. Wilder to Rev. Mr. Whipple, December 31, 1863 (HI-5201), AMAA.

64. *OR,* series III, vol. 3, 1144.

65. Ibid., 1139–44; *New York Freedman's Advocate,* February 1864, 6; and Perrine, "Benjamin Butler and the Bureau of Negro Affairs," 124–26.

66. *Boston Liberator,* January 29 and March 25, 1864.

67. Louis Ruchames, ed., *John Brown: The Making of a Revolutionary* (New York: Grosset and Dunlap, 1969), 60, 190, 231, 234.

68. Swint, *Dear Ones at Home,* 211.

69. *Boston Freedman,* February 1864, 8.

70. Margaret Munford Sinclair, *In and around Hampton: America's Oldest Continuous English Speaking Settlement* (Hampton?: n.p., 1957), 22–23; and Brown, *The Strength of a People,* 154.

71. William T. Anderson, "The Freedmen's Bureau and Negro Education in Virginia," *North Carolina Historical Review* 29 (January 1952): 64–67; William S. McFeely, *Yankee Stepfather: General O. O. Howard and the Freedmen* (New York: Norton, 1970), 67; Richardson, *Christian Reconstruction,* 14; and Richardson, "Architects of a Benevolent Empire," 128.

72. Swint, *Dear Ones at Home,* 91.

73. Perdue et al., *Weevils in the Wheat,* 331.

The Devil at Large

Anse Hatfield's War

James M. Prichard

Far from Richmond and the Shenandoah Valley, Virginia's mountainous western border was a thinly guarded frontier by the late summer of 1863. Indeed, virtually all of the Confederate forces in east Tennessee and southwestern Virginia had been ordered south that August to reinforce Braxton Bragg's hard-pressed Army of Tennessee. The abandonment of east Tennessee permitted Union major general Ambrose Burnside's forces to sweep through the region and seize both Knoxville and Cumberland Gap. By early September, Burnside's advancing forces posed a serious threat to Confederate control of the mountainous region between the vital East Tennessee & Virginia Railroad and the Kentucky border.[1]

Maj. Gen. Sam Jones, the Confederate commander of the Department of Western Virginia, worked feverishly to gather a force to defend the Virginia-Tennessee line. However, some of his units, composed largely of mountaineers raised along the rugged Kentucky-Virginia frontier, were reluctant to abandon the border. Desertions plagued the Forty-fifth Virginia Infantry Battalion when that unit was ordered from Saltville to the Tennessee line. Although the exact date of his desertion is not known, 1st Lt. William Anderson Hatfield of Company B left the battalion without authorization sometime after August 31, 1863.[2] For Hatfield and other mountain Rebels, the real war, *their* war, had always been near their homes on the remote, isolated Virginia border. Better known as "Devil Anse" to friend and foe alike, "Captain" Hatfield returned to his native Tug River Valley to resume the merciless guerrilla warfare he had waged since the beginning of the conflict.

Winding through the rugged Cumberlands toward the Ohio, the Big Sandy River and Tug Fork, one of its main tributaries, became the western border of the Confederacy when a referendum in Virginia on May 23, 1861, approved secession. Kentucky's singular policy of neutrality forestalled bloodshed on the border during the first summer of the war, but the state's subsequent declaration of support for the Union made the region the scene of armed conflict by the fall of 1861. Men who had once been friends, neighbors, or kinsmen became armed enemies virtually overnight.

As Union and Confederate forces fought for control of the region during the winter of 1861–1862, local partisans on both sides unleashed the full horrors of civil war. Federal volunteers from outside the region were shocked by the merciless nature of the war on the border, including Col. James A. Garfield who, in late December, assumed command of Union forces in eastern Kentucky. Following the battle of Middle Creek, Garfield issued a proclamation to the "Citizens of the Sandy Valley" on January 16, 1862, that announced the restoration of Federal control in the region. In a private letter written nearly a month later, the future president revealed that his proclamation was "[d]esigned to effect one purpose—to weed out from the war here the infernal devil that has made this valley a home of fiends, and converted this war into a black hole in which to murder any man that any soldier from envy, lust or revenge, hated. . . . If these people are ever to live together again in peace I think the reconciliation ought to be begun while the army is here."[3]

Garfield's efforts had little effect, however, and in March 1862 one of his subordinates, Capt. Charles Henry of Ohio, left a stark description of the state of affairs on the border: "[M]en who for years were neighbors now hunt each other with guns among the interminable hills. Long after the war is closed . . . men will bear here the old grudge toward each other, the bitter gall of hatred will still course their veins, the feudal flames will yet be unquenched; I can see no brighter future for them. A simple declaration of peace . . . will never do the thing effectual for these simples. . . . They reduce the war to too horrid an individuality to say quits and be good friends now."[4]

In reality, the conflict in western Virginia was no more savage than the war in Missouri or any other part of the nation's borderland. The people of the Big Sandy Valley, whose homes were located on the border of warring nations, experienced civil war in its worst form. Civil government ceased to exist, and any order or protection offered by the military rarely, if ever, reached the more remote parts. The isolated hills and valleys along the Kentucky-Virginia border became a desolate killing ground where civilians lived in constant terror of marauding irregular bands, or small parties of conventional Union or Confederate raiders who killed, burned, or plundered under the guise of military authority. Unlike Garfield's Ohioans, the mountaineers on both sides went to war with the full knowledge that their homes were often left at the mercy of the enemy. Not surprisingly, desertions plagued both Union and Confederate units from the borderland as the war progressed. Faced with fighting on distant battlefields in a national cause or deserting to defend their homes, many of these men chose the latter. They swelled the ranks of the numerous guerrilla bands that, in the words of one mountaineer, caused the "awfulest times that ever was."[5]

The foremost Confederate partisans along Virginia's western border were Col. Vincent A. Witcher and William S. "Rebel Bill" Smith. During the fall of 1864, Smith's small battalion of "Border Rangers" won complete control of the Virginia side of Sandy—from the head of the Tug to the Ohio River. However, the mountains swarmed with long-forgotten guerrilla chieftains, who often terrorized several counties with a mere handful of men. It was one of these many "captains" who is best known today. A resident of Logan County, western Virginia, William Anderson Hatfield was a terror to Unionists of the Tug River Valley. Although he was only a minor guerrilla chieftain, Hatfield would later win lasting notoriety as the leader of one of the warring factions in the celebrated Hatfield-McCoy feud.

In fact, traditional accounts of the feud depict that notorious postwar bloodletting as a resurgence of the "border warfare" that began between gray-clad Hatfields and pro-Union McCoys in 1861. Recent studies revise this long-held belief, finding many members of the McCoy clan who supported the Confederacy, including Randolph McCoy, Devil Anse's legendary rival during the feud. Indeed, Hatfield family traditions remember McCoy actually riding with Devil Anse during the first part of the war.[6] Nevertheless, the war remains a major factor in understanding both Devil Anse and the feud. Captain Hatfield's wartime exploits unquestionably enhanced his postwar prestige and notoriety in the region. Furthermore, the most ardent supporters of Randolph McCoy were many of Hatfield's old Union foes in Pike County, Kentucky.[7] Certainly Devil Anse's Confederate service is an important element in the story of that famed postwar feud, yet, with the exception of his alleged role in the 1865 killing of Asa Harmon McCoy, Randolph's Unionist brother, Hatfield's wartime exploits have remained largely unknown.[8]

The outbreak of the war found William Anderson Hatfield leaving home to start his own family. Sometime after his marriage to Levicy Chafin on April 18, 1861, the twenty-one-year-old farmer established their first-time home on Tug River, just opposite the mouth of Peter Creek in Pike County, Kentucky.[9] The site of present-day Delorme, this corner of Logan County was owned by the heirs of Jacob Cline Sr., and young Hatfield probably worked for the Clines as a tenant farmer.[10] When war came, the majority of Logan County residents rallied to the Confederate cause, and by late summer of 1861 several companies of the 129th Regiment of Militia were on active duty. While tradition has Hatfield joining this local command a week after his marriage, it is likely that he did not see active service until the winter of 1861–1862.[11]

When Kentucky formally entered the war in the fall of 1861, the first clashes in the Big Sandy Valley ignited the flames of border warfare. Capt. Vincent A. Witcher, a young attorney from Wayne County, Virginia, led a company of Rebel cavalry that terrorized Tug Valley Unionists during the first winter of the war. Indeed, one of Garfield's Ohio volunteers reported that a large party of Pike County Unionists arrived at headquarters seeking arms and ammunition to drive Witcher's company from the region.[12] The Union men of Peter Creek organized for local defense, and on February 12, 1862, Asa Harmon McCoy enlisted as a private in Captain Cline's company of Kentucky Home Guards.[13]

Although the majority of Tug Valley residents, including his older brother Randolph, supported the Confederate cause, Harmon McCoy, like many of his Peter Creek neighbors, fought for the Union. The son-in-law of the late Jacob Cline, one of the wealthiest men in the region, McCoy further cemented his ties to the clan by fighting side by side with his brothers-in-law, William Trigg and Peter Cline, during the first year of the war. Ironically, the man fated to become one of the last war casualties in the vicinity nearly became one of the first. Shortly after his enlistment, on February 16, McCoy fell gravely wounded in an isolated skirmish "near Sandy River."[14] Tradition credits Anse Hatfield himself with the near-fatal shot.[15] Contemporary records reveal that Hatfield's uncle James Vance, who commanded the Hatfield forces in the bloody night attack on Randolph McCoy's home in 1888, was in arms in early 1862. However, virtually nothing is known of Anse's activities during this initial wave of border fighting. Nevertheless, he undoubtedly experienced his first taste of guerrilla warfare during this period of the conflict.[16]

Union control of the Sandy Valley brought a lull in the fighting through-out the spring and early summer of 1862. However, the withdrawal of Federal forces from Pikeville in late June paved the way for a resurgence of border warfare that was waged with grim ferocity by both sides. According to a report in the *Lynchburg Virginian,* Pike County was the scene of "bitter fighting" by early July.[17] Rebel cavalry plundered Pikeville itself on August 2, and four days later Union home guards engaged another band of Rebels, probably Witcher's command, on Peter Creek. According to the *Louisville Journal,* more than nine Tug Valley Unionists were killed in the fighting. However, the Unionists killed "a considerable number of guerrillas" before being forced to retreat.[18] Subsequent reports indicate that by late August the fighting had degenerated to a mutual war of extermination. On September 9, 1862, the *Journal* boasted that the "union Home Guards on Tug Fork of Sandy have rid the country of several well-known and active secession sympathizers." The report concludes that the "Home Guards are said to have sworn vengeance against the rebel sympathizers and have determined to shoot them wherever they may find them."[19]

It was during this period of renewed violence that Anse Hatfield volunteered for active duty in the Virginia State Line. Authorized by the Virginia legislature on May 15, 1862, the State Line was organized by Maj. Gen. John B. Floyd solely for the defense of western Virginia. Although his role in the loss of Fort Donelson had tarnished his military reputation, Floyd remained extremely popular in western Virginia, where hundreds of mountaineers flocked to his standard.[20] Fifty-one-year-old Ephraim Hatfield, Anse's father, promptly enlisted in Col. Henry M. Beckley's First Virginia State Line. In addition to Anse, two other sons, Ellison and Elias, joined the same regiment. The younger Hatfields followed the example of hundreds of men who seized the opportunity to avoid three years in the regular army by serving twelve months on local defense.[21] While his father and brothers served in the ranks, Anse was commissioned a first lieutenant of infantry on September 20, 1862. The young officer was subsequently assigned to duty in Company G of the Second Virginia State Line. Hatfield was probably pres-ent when his regiment marched down the Tug and routed a force of Union home guards at Warfield in Lawrence (now Martin) County, Kentucky, on October 12, 1862.[22]

Headquartered in Logan County, Floyd's command operated on the border throughout the fall and winter of 1862. During this period he frequently sent small detachments into Kentucky to seize horses and livestock from local Unionists. He also attempted to break up the numerous bands of pro-Union irregulars still operating in the Tug Valley. Micajah Woods, a young officer on Floyd's staff, was appalled by the nature of this border warfare. In a letter to his parents he observed:

> No person reared in the full light of our Eastern Virginia civiliza-
> tion can form a remote conception of the condition of the counties
> through which we passed and their inhabitants. To subdue the
> people, the houses of the greater portion of the Southern men have
> been committed to flames, and their families thrown out into the
> dreary world, homeless, destitute, and penniless. Neighbor against
> neighbor—the roads are waylaid, and in many communities the
> men have not slept in their own houses for months past, but have
> pursued a course of life termed "laying out" in the gorges of the
> mountains waiting for opportunities to slay some solitary or per-
> sonal opponent.[23]

Like other "outsiders," Woods was convinced that mountaineers were incapable of fighting in a "civilized" manner. "Language fails me," he wrote, "in expressing my intense disgust and abhorrence of the main body of the population of this region—ignorant, filthy, malignant and semi-savage in their nature." He concluded that "the war has called forth their worst passions."[24] While Wood's observations about mountaineers are deplorable, he accurately depicts the brutal nature of the fighting in late 1862. It was during this phase of the conflict that Anse Hatfield gained notoriety as a man of blood. A skilled hunter and marksman before the war, he seemed to regard his enemies as human prey—to be stalked, cornered, and killed. The Union men of Peter Creek soon came to regard him as a determined, deadly foe.[25]

One of the most noted home guard chieftains operating on the Tug was Capt. William Francis Jr. of Pike County. A prominent local official in the Peter Creek community, Francis, who owned more than 1,300 acres on the left fork of the stream, was operating a store on the Tug when the war broke out.[26] Sometime in the late summer of 1862 he organized a company of fifty-seven men that included three of Anse's Kentucky cousins, James, Joseph, and Thompson Hatfield. Francis also operated with another company of fifty-one men recruited in the same area by Capt. Uriah Runyon. This company included Jacob and Peter Cline; their brother-in-law, Asa Harmon McCoy; and his cousin, Pleasant McCoy. The great Confederate invasion of Kentucky that fall, which forced the Federals to completely abandon the Big Sandy Valley, totally isolated these home guard units. Driven down the Tug sometime in September, Francis and Runyon formally attached their companies to one of the few Union regiments still operating in the region—the 167th Militia of Wayne County, western Virginia.[27]

Although based far downriver, the Tug Home Guards apparently led forays into Pike and Logan counties during the fall of 1862. It was probably during this period that Anse Hatfield allegedly claimed two of his first victims. Supposedly, Hatfield discovered Reuben Dotson "gathering paw paws on Peter Creek" and "deliberately shot him down."[28] Then, according to the only account of Hatfield's war career by a contemporary—and a hostile one at that—"Hatfield went to Datson [*sic*] stripped him of his pants saw the wound and remarked to Datson dam you that will do you." Hatfield then supposedly left Dotson, who was permanently disabled by the wound and eventually died from its lingering effects.[29] In fact, Dotson did die in 1886, and significantly he was also the brother-in-law of Moses Coleman, another of Hatfield's alleged victims.[30] Daniel Webster Cunningham, author of that account of Hatfield's wartime activities, went on to say that "about the same time Datson [was wounded], Ans [*sic*] Hatfield shot Moses Coleman in like manner to Datson." Like Dotson, Coleman was permanently disabled by his wound. "Coleman is still living," Cunningham said in the 1890s, "but dieing everyday from the effects of the wound received of Hatfield."[31]

While both Dotson and Coleman survived their wounds, Hatfield allegedly killed other Union men during this period of the conflict. According to Cunningham: "In Pike County Kentucky opposite the home of Ans Hatfield lived Charley Mounts. Mr. Mounts was a Union man at home. Ans slipped upon him [and] shot him [dead] the ball passing through his heart. Mounts was making sorghum molasses [and] his head went into the furnace of fire. No one was present but two of his children, and they succeeded in getting him out of the fire."[32] In fact, however, John C. and Hiram Sansom, members of Capt. John Buchanan's company of Beckley's First Virginia State Line, were actually indicted for the "murder" of Charles Mounts after the war. They testified that Buchanan's company was stationed in Logan County, western Virginia, in October 1862 when they were ordered to scout Peter Creek in

Pike County, and that "while going up said creek the party were fired into by a party of Home Guards from the bushes. The Rebel party took to the bushes and a regular bushwhacking fight took place . . . in which Charles Mounts was unfortunately killed dead." Several Pike County citizens also testified that "Mounts was a Home Guard and was killed as stated."[33] A first cousin of Peter, Perry, and Jacob Cline Jr., Mounts was living in Logan County when the war broke out. The prosperous farmer and miller was one of twelve members of the Mounts clan enrolled in Captain Runyon's company.[34] Despite the fact that he was past fifty, Mounts was unquestionably an armed enemy at the time of his death. While it is certainly possible that Hatfield fired the fatal shot during the skirmish, he clearly did not murder a man who was peacefully making molasses. Postwar exaggeration and animosity would credit Hatfield with several such fictitious crimes, as if his actual excesses were not enough for posterity.

A major raid into Kentucky apparently set the stage for the next act of violence linked to Devil Anse. On December 3, 1862, Col. John N. Clarkson led a sizeable force of State Line cavalry across the Tug. The following day he attacked and captured a large convoy of Union supply boats near Prestonsburg, Kentucky. During the return march to Virginia, the command swept through Pike County, capturing more than twenty-five Unionists.[35] Among those taken prisoner was Asa Harmon McCoy, who was captured at his Peter Creek residence on or about December 5. McCoy, still suffering from the effects of his old chest wound, remained a prisoner in Richmond for the rest of the winter. Exchanged in the spring of 1863, he was admitted to the U.S. General Hospital in Annapolis on April 6, where a surgeon recommended that he be discharged from active service. He was accordingly sent home on May 18, 1863.[36]

The prisoners taken with McCoy also included one Enoch Cassidy, a former member of Captain Runyon's Home Guards, who had recently enlisted in the Thirty-ninth Kentucky Mounted Infantry. While he did not specify the date, Anse Hatfield subsequently claimed that Cassidy approached him and delivered a warning that a slave named Mose had offered him $25 to kill Hatfield.[37] Mose, who was apparently born in 1820, had become the property of Jacob Cline's youngest sons, Jacob J. and Perry A., when the old man died in 1858.[38] Perry Cline, it should be noted, would afterward prove to be Anse's primary foe during the postwar feud. According to family tradition, Mose was particularly devoted to their older brother Peter and frequently stayed with him after the war broke out.[39] Peter's daughter, Josephine, often told of a Rebel raid on Peter Creek early in the war that nearly cost the lives of Mose and her father. Mose ably assisted his master in driving off the attackers, clubbing several Rebels to the ground with an old rifle. The Confederates fell back across the Tug with their wounded, including Cline's brother-in-law, believed to be Randolph "Black Rannel" McCoy—cousin of the future feud chieftain.[40]

Anse claimed that he advised Col. Henry M. Beckley of the warning and was promptly ordered to kill the slave. Cunningham, again the only roughly contemporary narrator, described Mose as "one of the best negroes that ever lived." He added that Hatfield and another Rebel soldier, named Riley Sansom, did enter Mose's cabin "without provocation and shot him dead on the floor."[41] Cline's daughter also related that "poor Mose" was subsequently killed by Rebels from Virginia.[42] While the date of Mose's death is unknown, he was probably killed during the winter of 1862–1863.

After the war, not Hatfield but Riley Sansom, reportedly a member of Witcher's command, was indicted for the murder of "Negro Mose." Not surprisingly, the Hatfields rallied to the defense of their old comrade. Ellison Hatfield, Anse's brother, described Mose as an "armed enemy of Southern soldiers" who frequently threatened to kill Vincent Witcher and his men. Anse testified that Sansom was a "regular soldier" who killed the slave in obedience to military orders. Another witness testified that he frequently saw Mose with "armed men who pretended to be Federal soldiers." He added that Mose was also seen "waylaying the roads to kill the rebels as they passed."[43] Indeed, Peter Cline, his brother William T. Cline, and other home guards participated in several raids along the Tug in late 1862.[44] While "Negro Mose" was apparently unarmed at the time of his death, it is probable that he did fight alongside his pro-Union masters.

Thus, once again, an act attributed after the war to Hatfield turns out to have been the work of others, and that is quite possibly also the case with Anse's next supposed victim. According to Cunningham, Hatfield concealed himself along the road near the mouth of Grapevine Creek in Logan County. When one John Poss came walking down the road sometime later, Anse shot him down without warning.[45] Not a single contemporary record makes reference to Poss or his death.

The withdrawal of Floyd's command from the border to Saltville, Virginia, in late December 1862 might have brought a brief lull in Hatfield's bloody work. The defense of the saltworks, which supplied most of the South east of the Mississippi, was of extreme importance to the Confederacy. However, as Lieutenant Woods of Floyd's staff observed, duty at Saltville consisted only of "mud, rain and idleness."[46] Low morale and desertions plagued the command throughout early 1863. When the men learned that the Virginia legislature intended to transfer control of the State Line to the Confederate government, they deserted in droves. In a letter dated March 3, 1863, Lieutenant Woods reported that Colonel Beckley's regiment virtually melted away overnight.[47] Two days later, Woods reported mass desertions from the regiment to which Anse Hatfield belonged, adding: "I am not at all astonished at the course of these men. They are principally from the border—a region occupied or at the mercy of the enemy—their wifes and families in the majority of cases are helpless and destitute of the absolute necessities of life, and worse than this are subject [to] the insults and depredations of the marauding parties of each side that infest their whole country."[48]

One tradition indicates that Anse might have returned already to the border by the time the State Line fell apart. In 1900 several Logan County residents stated that "about 1863, a party of men such as always infest border territory went to his [Hatfield's] house and in a most brutal manner turned his family out. Nor was this near all the indignities to which they were subjected. On hearing of it, Capt. Hatfield secured leave of absence from the army and promptly settled with the villains."[49] While there is no other evidence that Hatfield's wife and children were abused during the war, his home and family were undoubtedly prime targets for local Unionists. If Cunningham is to be believed, Hatfield was among the Rebel bands that, at one time or another, plundered the homes of more than nineteen Union men on Peter Creek. What Cunningham failed to add was that virtually all of these alleged victims were home guards, including Capt. Bill Francis, his son James M., his son-in-law John Charles, Asa Harmon McCoy, and his brother-in-law, William Trigg Cline.[50]

The partisans of both sides adhered to the ancient law of "an eye for an eye." Undoubtedly, a raid from one side of the Tug was soon followed by retribution from the other. Numerous postwar suits filed in Pike County name members of Francis's or Runyon's Home Guards as alleged participants in the plundering of Southern men in Pike and Logan counties.[51] In 1866 George Hatfield, who lived on Pond Creek in Pike County during the war, charged that in November 1862 an "armed band," including Captain

Francis, Peter Cline, Isaac Smith, Elijah Mounts Sr., and Henry S. Carter, plundered his home. Hatfield claimed that in addition to numerous items, including farm implements and household goods, the Unionists seized "15 head of beef cattle, one yoke of oxen, one mule, 25 head of hogs [and] 15 head of sheep."[52]

Francis was apparently still operating on the Tug in early 1863. According to a report from Floyd's command in the *Richmond Daily Dispatch*, the notorious "Peter's Creek Home Guards, a band of Kentucky Unionists that have made themselves a terror along the Kentucky State line," had been largely dispersed by mid-December. Many Tug Valley Home Guards not killed or captured by Floyd's men, including Captain Runyon himself, joined Col. John Dils's Thirty-ninth Kentucky Mounted Infantry in the winter of 1862–1863. However, Francis, despite the gradual disintegration of his company, apparently retained enough followers to harass local Rebels.[53]

According to tradition, sometime during the war a band of Unionists, including Bill "French" Francis, Harmon McCoy, and the latter's slave, Pete, crossed into Logan County on a raid. When Moses Christian Cline, a Southern sympathizer, attempted to stop them from driving off his stock, he was shot down. Cline lingered near death for some time but eventually recovered from his wound. Cline family tradition claims that shortly after the raid Anse Hatfield visited Cline. Believing the wound was mortal, Anse allegedly swore that he would kill every man connected with the attack, and the Cline family subsequently believed that he did just that. Leading a Rebel detachment into Kentucky, Hatfield took a concealed position near Francis's cabin on the Left Fork of Peter Creek near present-day Phelps. Anse remained in hiding for some time, patiently studying Francis's activities. He soon noticed that the home guard leader stepped outside his cabin every morning to relieve himself after a night's sleep. Early one morning Francis stepped out to urinate, and according to family tradition, "Devil Anse shot him square between his overall galluses."[54]

Despite reporting certain differences in circumstances, Cunningham in the 1890s provided a strikingly similar version of Francis's death: "Bill France [*sic*], a citizen of Pike County Kentucky was at home. A stone fense was just in front of the door[,] a dense thicket of willows extending up to the fense. Ans Hatfield and Randolph McCoy sliped up behind the fense, [and] there diliberations was to each one shoot but on seeing the poor fellow at home and unconscious of his approaching end, McCoy refused to shoot. France steped to his door, his wife began to fasten a neck tie on his neck, when all at once a sharp crack of a rifle fired. France fell dead at the feet of his wife."[55]

While the exact circumstances of Francis's death may never be known, Hatfield family tradition relates that Devil Anse was the slayer of the home guard leader.[56] Another version of the killing, based on information provided by the Hatfield family, was published in the *Logan (W. Va.) Banner* on December 2, 1938. According to this version, Anse was ordered by Capt. John Buchanan of the "Tug River Regiment" to organize a detail and "take, dead or alive, Gen. William Francis, Union officer of Pike." The account continued: "The party sent to 'get' the Union general included Randal [*sic*] McCoy and 'Devil Anse' Hatfield. After several days search and pursuit, General Francis was cornered in his home in Pike County. A fight ensued. What strategy was used to enter General Francis' home is not known but survivors of the party said later that it was 'Devil Anse' who gained entrance and met the trapped general in the room of a house and 'shot it out' with him. Perhaps it was 'Devil Anse'—the facts are dimmed by time—or it might have been another member of the party." The article also states that several years after Anse's death, a party of workmen presented his son, Anderson Jr., or "Cap," with a bullet they found embedded in the old Francis cabin. The relic was discovered while the structure was being torn down, and the workers were convinced that it was the bullet that had killed the home guard chieftain.[57] Francis's death cannot be accurately dated more precisely than sometime in 1863, but it was probably by or before that spring, by which time Hatfield had reenlisted in the Confederate service.[58] Undoubtedly, the slaying of the noted home guard leader greatly enhanced the reputation of the young border fighter.

Throughout the spring of 1863, former State Line officers struggled to bring their men back to the army. By April 22, Col. H. M. Beckley reportedly raised more than fifteen companies in Logan and neighboring counties. Composed of many former members of Floyd's command, Beckley's unit was formally designated the Forty-fifth Battalion Virginia Infantry. Among those to return to the fold were the Hatfield brothers. On May 1, 1863, Anse and Ellison enlisted as privates in Capt. John Buchanan's Company B. Another brother, Elias, better known as "Good Lias," enlisted in the same company on May 7. Ellison was afterward elected to the rank of second lieutenant on May 7, and it is possible that Anse became first lieutenant on the same day.[59]

In many ways, Hatfield's brief connection with the regular Confederate army paralleled his service in the State Line. Beckley's battalion did see service on the border in the early summer and late fall of 1863. The command was frequently pulled back to defend Saltville or protect the vital East Tennessee & Virginia Railroad that ran through southwestern Virginia. However, as before, the border men of the Forty-fifth were soon forced to choose between defending the department and protecting their homes. Although Hatfield later claimed that he resigned his commission, in fact he deserted sometime after August 31, 1863.[60] While the exact date is uncertain, the probable time of his departure was December, when the Forty-fifth withdrew from the border and went into winter quarters in Tazewell County, Virginia.[61] Explanations offered for Hatfield's desertion include disenchantment with the regular army after the death of John B. Floyd on August 26, 1863, or that he went home in disgust when his superiors ordered him to execute two deserters.[62] Neither seems plausible. Given the fact that Hatfield organized an independent company of "home guards" after his return to the Tug, it is much more likely that he deserted in order to defend the border.[63] Many mountaineers apparently felt that the Confederate government expected them to sacrifice not only their lives for the cause, but their homes and families as well. Undoubtedly, Hatfield would have agreed with one Virginia mountaineer who defended his decision to return home with a defiant "Richmond be damned."[64]

At the same time Hatfield formed his company, Capt. William S. "Rebel Bill" Smith was actively engaged in organizing a "Partisan Corps" in the Big Sandy Valley. One of the most noted partisans in western Virginia, the Wayne County native hoped to rally the hundreds of Confederate deserters and absentees in the region with the promise of service on the border. Smith hoped to carve out his own "Confederacy" along the Sandy, as John S. Mosby had done in the Shenandoah Valley.[65] Despite the repeal of the Partisan Ranger Act in early 1864, Rebel Bill continued to petition his superiors to allow his battalion to retain this special status. Smith boasted that he had raised more than 600 men in Wayne, Logan, and Cabell counties in western Virginia as well as the Kentucky counties of Lawrence, Johnson, and Pike. Although his request for partisan ranger status was denied, he was able to retain more than 450 men in his battalion, which camped in Logan County in the late summer of 1864.[66]

Still seeking an independent command, Smith wrote Richmond on August 16, 1864, requesting permission to keep his headquarters in Logan

County. "The section of country in which we operate is isolated from the protection of the Confederate armies, and if we are compelled to vacate the country, it leaves it open to the . . . enemy or to the mercy of deserters from both armies." He warned, "If the authority [to operate independently] is not granted we do not think the men will be willing to enter the Confederate Service as they will not leave their families to the mercies of deserters and whatever organizations may be in the country." Smith also reported that "many men who had joined 'Home Guards' . . . for the purpose of protecting their homes and families have already committed themselves to our cause" by operating with his command against the enemy.[67]

While Hatfield did later refer to the operation of his independent company in Logan and other border counties, he never mentioned any connection with Smith's battalion. However, years later, during the height of the feud, Rebel Bill, in a confidential letter to Kentucky governor Simon Buckner, offered to bring the Hatfields to justice, claiming that they had served in his command during the war.[68] Although Hatfield was not listed among Smith's company commanders in August 1864, other records indicate that he was operating with that officer shortly afterward.

A major Union cavalry raid against Saltville launched from eastern Kentucky in late September left the Sandy Valley stripped of troops. On or about October 12, 1864, Smith's partisans dashed down the Tug and struck Peach Orchard, a small Union outpost in Lawrence County, Kentucky.[69] Located upriver from the main Union base at Louisa, the once-thriving coal mine community was the site of well-stocked stores operated by prominent Pike County Unionists, including John Dils, late colonel of the Thirty-ninth Kentucky.[70] Other Pike County merchants included Morgan, Lewis, and Thomas J. Sowards, the latter two having served under Dils as company commanders.[71] The Rebel raiders seized more than $3,500 worth of goods, primarily clothing, boots, and hats, from the warehouse and store boat of Sowards and Company before putting the property to the torch. In addition to fingering many Pike and Logan county Confederates among the raiders, the Sowards named Anderson, Elias, and "Allison" Hatfield. They claimed other members of the Hatfield and McCoy clans were present, including Johnson McCoy, the brother-in-law for whom Anse named one of his sons.[72]

Still another participant in the raid was Jacob Cline Jr., one of old Jacob's Unionist sons. Young Cline, a former member of Runyon's Home Guards, had deserted from the Thirty-ninth Kentucky on August 10, 1864, and returned to the Tug Valley. Although Cline rejoined the Thirty-ninth in the spring of 1865, he apparently rode with local rebels on at least one raid.[73] It should be noted, however, that Cline was apparently forced to accompany Smith's command on the Peach Orchard raid. Sued by the Sowards in 1866, Cline was defended by Devil Anse himself. Hatfield stated in an 1869 deposition that after Cline returned home from the Union army, he was warned "that if he did not join the rebels . . . they would kill him." In addition to acknowledging his own participation in the raid, Hatfield added that Cline was ordered to accompany the rebels "by men who did kill sometimes."[74]

Given the fate of two of Cline's comrades and kinsmen, Hatfield's remarks about "men who did kill" seem grimly ironic. According to Cunningham's "War History":

> The third year of the war Ashby Hurley and his son only 16 years of age, and Union soldiers came home on a furlow. They soon learned that Ans and his gang was after them. They left home, concealed themselves in a cave. Hatfield found where they was concealed, and upon the promise of old Ans, to treat Hurley and son as prisoners of war, they surrendered. They was taken to a large flat rock [and] tied side by side. Ans went back about 30 paces, fixed a rest, laid his gun on those logs and shot the two soldiers to death[,] the boy begging Hatfield for the privilege to see his mother before he was killed. After they were killed, Hatfield laid them out side by side, on the rock where he killed them.[75]

A resident of Logan County when the conflict began, forty-one-year-old Asbury "As" Hurley was related by marriage to the Mounts and Cline families. He apparently moved to Pike County sometime during the war and settled on the Middle Fork of Elk Creek, which flows into Knox Creek, a tributary of the Tug.[76] On January 8, 1864, he enlisted as a private in Company H of the Thirty-ninth Kentucky Mounted Infantry. His twenty-one-year-old son Fleming had previously joined the same company, in the fall of 1863.[77] Both father and son deserted on August 10, 1864, taking their rifles and equipment. Like young Jacob Cline, the Hurleys were among dozens of members of the Thirty-ninth who deserted in disgust when a black regiment reported for duty at Union headquarters in Louisa. Evidence indicates that the Hurleys spent the next several weeks "lying out" and defying surrender demands from local Rebels.[78] Hurley's old neighbor William Prater claimed he saw the ill-fated Unionists frequently, and his son, John H. Prater, recalled that he often slipped food to the fugitives before they were caught. On Prater's last visit, As Hurley told him that the enemy had "notified him to come in and surrender." However, he refused to do so and allegedly was planning to return to his regiment as soon as he could travel safely. Within days of this secret meeting, however, "some men" arrived at the Prater home and announced that they had killed both of the Hurleys—their luck ran out on or about November 4, 1864, when they were "killed by the rebels" on Lower Elk Creek of Knox.[79]

The killers told the Praters where the bodies were left, but warned that "no one should bury them." Afterward John Prater, who was with the party that found the stripped bodies, recalled that the elder Hurley had been shot twice, his son three times. Despite the Rebel warning, both victims were buried in the woods where they were found.[80] As Hurley's grandson named Devil Anse as the leader of the group that killed his grandfather. According to Harrison Hurley: "Az Hurely and his oldest son discovered a cow missing during the time of the Civil War. They got their rifles and followed the trail of the cow to a clearing where 'Devil Anse' Hatfield and a group of Confederate soldiers were busy butchering the cow. Az and his son, Fleming began firing on the group, killing one of the Confederate soldiers and sending the others fleeing. In the following weeks, 'Devil Anse' Hatfield and his men ambushed Az and Fleming, killing both of them. 'Devil Anse' came and told my grandmaw where they could find their bodies."[81] There is strong reason to believe that Hatfield led the Rebels involved. To Hatfield's men, the Hurleys were "bushwhackers," despite the fact that they, like their Rebel foes, had also deserted the regular service to defend their home. Nevertheless, in fairness to Devil Anse, the Unionists had not only refused to surrender but had apparently killed one of his men. Even if the Hurleys were the victims of summary execution, it is doubtful whether Hatfield's actions would have been questioned by his superiors.

Cunningham alleged that the Hurley killings did not satisfy Hatfield's bloodlust. According to his "War History": "John Sanson [was] one of Ans' pals. Hatfield believed he was a friend to the Hurley family. . . . Ans went deliberately into his house and shot him down. Sanson called for water. Ans gave it to him, raised him up and combed his hair, then Wall Hatfield, shot his brains out before his wife and children. . . . Sanson lived at the mouth of pounding Mill Branch, in Kentucky."[82]

As in the case of the supposed murder of John Poss, Cunningham is the only known source for this alleged incident. A John Sanson and wife were living in Logan County in 1860, and he was apparently the same man who rode with Rebel Bill Smith in 1862–1863.[83] However, with the exception of the fact that Valentine "Wall" Hatfield was riding with his brother in the fall of 1864, there is, as so often, nothing else to corroborate Cunningham regarding the accuracy of this incident.

The arrival of Lt. Col. Vincent Witcher's command on the border in late October resulted in a sharp increase in Rebel activity in the Sandy Valley. On November 5, 1864, Witcher and Rebel Bill Smith attacked Peach Orchard, threatened the Union garrison at Louisa, and captured two armed steamers at nearby Buffalo Shoals.[84] On or about November 9, Smith captured and burned a third vessel on Big Sandy. One Union newspaper lamented: "The Rebel guerrilla, Col. Bill Smith, is now the supreme commander in Wayne and Cabell Counties."[85] Hatfield participated in the raid. John E. Castle, who resided near Rockcastle Creek, afterward charged that Anse and his older brother Wall Hatfield took his horse and saddle. While the horses of many civilians were undoubtedly seized during these operations, it is significant that Castle was captain of a Union militia company that included at least two Pike County refugees, William Trigg Cline and Pleasant McCoy.[86]

At the same time, Smith made a determined effort to disrupt the presidential election proceedings during the raid. On November 8, 1864, a large party of Rebels rode into Lawrence County and took over the polls at the Rockcastle precinct. "Major E. R. Counto," at the head of eighty to a hundred guerrillas, reportedly forced the election officials to permit some of his men to vote: "The clerk took down the names of thirty, all of whom voted for Mr. Lincoln, as they said they thought they could whip him, but did not know about whipping McClellan. The judges did not certify to this compulsory poll-book and the votes of Counto's men were not counted."[87] Shortly after the war, the Lawrence Circuit Court indicted twenty-eight men, most of them residents of Logan County, western Virginia, for "fraudulent voting." While the details of the crime have not survived, the charge undoubtedly stemmed from this wartime incident. The first name listed on the indictment is Anderson Hatfield.[88]

The election incident shows that not all of Hatfield's wartime "deviltry" was of a bloody nature. It also confirms that Anse rode with Maj. Ezekiel K. Counts during the war. Referred to as "E. R. Counto" in a newspaper account and as "E. K. Couns" in the voting fraud indictment, he was more familiarly known as "Devil Zeke" on the border.[89] A former captain in Floyd's State Line, he left the regular service in 1864 and organized a small battalion along the headwaters of the Big Sandy. According to the recollections of one of his men, Counts apparently consolidated his command with Bill Smith's in the fall of 1864. In addition to the Lawrence County raid, Anse and his uncle Jim Vance also rode with Counts on forays in Pike County.[90]

Ironically, although the Confederacy was on the verge of collapse in the winter of 1864–1865, parts of the Big Sandy Valley were still vulnerable to small-scale Rebel raids. The Tug River region in particular remained the domain of Smith and Counts's partisans. Deserters from the regular army continued to return home and join these irregular organizations along the Virginia border, and on December 19, 1864, Lt. Ellison Hatfield, whose 1882 murder sparked the famous postwar vendetta, deserted his post in the Shenandoah Valley, taking four men with him. Family tradition to the contrary, neither Ellison nor any member of the Forty-fifth ever fought at Gettysburg. However, he did fight bravely in the Shenandoah Valley throughout the summer and fall of 1864. His decision to desert was undoubtedly motivated by the miserable conditions within his command at that time. By January 1865 there was only one blanket in the entire battalion, while the seven officers and seventeen men present for active duty were nearly naked.[91]

The last winter of the war also saw the return of Asa Harmon McCoy to the Tug Valley. Several weeks after his release from captivity, he traveled to Ashland, Kentucky, and enlisted as a private in Company E of the Forty-fifth Kentucky Mounted Infantry on October 20, 1863. Based in eastern Kentucky, the Forty-fifth participated in numerous operations against the bands of guerrillas and Rebel cavalry that threatened the region. Although McCoy undoubtedly saw action on several occasions, his next "war wound" resulted from a common accident. On or about May 5, 1864, he was thrown from a buggy and suffered a broken right leg. Treated at the General Hospital in Lexington, Kentucky, he returned to duty on July 1, 1864.[92] According to some accounts, his leg injury might have contributed indirectly to his death a few months later.[93] Since the Forty-fifth was a twelve-month regiment organized for the defense of Kentucky, on December 24, 1864, McCoy was honorably discharged at Catlettsburg, located at the mouth of the Big Sandy.[94]

Sometime afterward he began the perilous journey up the valley to his home on Peter Creek. McCoy family tradition states that shortly after his return, he was threatened by Jim Vance of Hatfield's band. Almost immediately afterward he was fired on from ambush while drawing water from his well. At this point McCoy determined to find shelter in the nearby hills and "lay out" until the danger passed.[95] The details of his subsequent discovery and death at Rebel hands are common knowledge to students of the Hatfield-McCoy feud. Although they all differ in some respects, Cunningham's version generally agrees with other accounts:

Asa H. McCoy, a brother of Randolph, was a union soldier [who] came home on furlough. Ans found out he was coming. For fear of trouble McCoy and his wife took some bed quilts [and] went out in the woods to a rockhouse. This was in the evening and the rain fell in torrents and shortly after dark, the snow began to fall, and about 10 o'clock at night, Ans Hatfield, James Vance, Sr. and others entered McCoy's house.

The snow fell all night, the murder[er]s kept a picket at the door and just before daylight Mary McCoy now Mary Daniels, sliped [by] the guard [as] he dozed, into a sleep, and notified her father, that a gang was waiting for him. McCoy left his place of concealment, went to Peter Creek swam across to a circuitous route of several miles, and came [with]in about one mile of home and stoped under a rock house. The men took the girls' trail at daylight, found where McCoy had slept took his trail and came on him under the rock and shot his brains out.

Mrs. Asa McCoy went down to Tug River to see if she could learn any thing of her husband. She met Old Ans Hatfield [and] asked him concerning her husband. She took Ans Hatfields back trail and came to her husband lying in the snow dead. There was no men in the country, to aid her, she fixed a slide out of pales and the woman hauled Mr. McCoy in [and] buried him.[96]

In other versions, the slayers discovered McCoy's hiding place by following the track of other family members who had been secretly bringing him food—McCoy's wife, according to one account, or a slave named Pete in another. According to Harmon's nephew "Squirrel Hunting" Sam McCoy, the Rebel party included Ans Hatfield, Jim Vance, and several other Logan County men. Harmon supposedly spotted his pursuers and began to run for his life. However, the deep snow caused him to "give out" and he turned to face his enemies. According to Truda McCoy's version, his flight was also hampered by his bad leg and "lung trouble," probably the lingering effects of his old chest wound.[97]

According to Sam McCoy, the Rebels called out that he would not be harmed, and Harmon had just sat down on a nearby log when Jim Vance walked up and shot him to death.[98] Many years later, Harmon's son Larkin told his daughter-in-law that based on the appearance of the body, his father, like the Hurleys, had been stripped and bound before being killed. He added that his mother searched for three days before the body was discovered. Because the neighbors were too terrified to help, he recalled, his mother had trouble getting his father buried.[99]

The killing of Harmon McCoy, which apparently took place in Caney Branch Hollow on January 7, 1865, was the last known war incident linked to Devil Anse. Some accounts claim that he was bedridden with fever at the time of the killing, but virtually all McCoy traditions place him among the Rebels involved. While they were convinced that Jim Vance actually pulled the trigger, the McCoys regarded Devil Anse with equal bitterness during the years immediately after the war.[100]

Recent studies suggest that McCoy's death was not avenged because he was regarded, even by his own family, as an "outcast and traitor" in the predominantly pro-Confederate Tug Valley.[101] However, as previously noted, he was actually one of a sizeable group of Unionists who lived on Peter Creek. Furthermore, while his brother Randolph was an active Rebel, other kinsmen fought for the Union. Indeed, his cousins John and Asa Peter McCoy, whose sisters, like Harmon, married into the pro-Union Cline family, traded shots with Ellison Hatfield and other Rebels in 1863.[102] While many members of the extended McCoy clan did support the Confederacy, it should be noted that several of Anse Hatfield's Kentucky kinsmen, including "Deacon Anse," fought for the Union.[103]

If one accepts local tradition, McCoy's death was an act of revenge. Like Capt. Bill Francis, McCoy could well have been killed to avenge the shooting of Hatfield's friend Moses Christian Cline, or in response to some other act of brutality committed while McCoy rode with the home guards early in the war.[104] Furthermore, because of the rules of civilized warfare, McCoy had been paroled from a Confederate prison once before only to return and bear arms again. Be that as it may, his family might have grudgingly accepted the results of the unwritten law of vengeance that characterized border warfare. As Truda McCoy, the family historian, suggests, Harmon's death was regarded not as a personal killing, but as an act of war that did not violate family honor.[105]

Although sporadic fighting marked the closing days of the war in the Big Sandy Valley, little is known of Hatfield's activities during this period. One tradition maintains that he was in the camp of Capt. Melvin B. Lawson of Logan County at the time Gen. Robert E. Lee surrendered on April 9, 1865.[106] This is entirely plausible, for Lawson, whose company formed part of Rebel Bill Smith's battalion, operated in the same area of the Tug Valley. Indeed, his command, which included several members of the McCoy clan, was held responsible for the deaths of several Pike County Unionists.[107] In the aftermath of Appomattox, Anse, his father, Ephraim, and his brother Ellison, like hundreds of other Confederates, rode to Charleston, West Virginia, and surrendered. For Devil Anse, the war officially ended when he and his kinsmen were paroled on May 4, 1865.[108] Nevertheless, the final surrender did not bring peace overnight.

Conditions remained unsettled along the Kentucky–West Virginia border for years after Appomattox. On March 23, 1866, a Wayne County, West Virginia, Unionist appealed to the governor for troops, claiming that timber crews composed of ex-Rebels from Pike County, Kentucky, and neighboring Logan County, West Virginia, were terrorizing Cassville, which was located on the Big Sandy River near the mouth of the Tug. These die-hard Rebels not only cheered for "Jeff Davis" and cursed the Federal government, but assaulted Union veterans and attacked the local sheriff as well.[109] Reports of threats and violence against Union men became so frequent that Federal troops were sent to Logan and Wayne counties in the summer of 1867 and remained in the region until the spring of 1869.[110]

There is no evidence that Hatfield himself was involved in serious acts of postwar violence. Indeed, by the 1870s the former guerrilla chieftain had become a prosperous farmer and law-abiding citizen of Logan (now Mingo) County, West Virginia, who generally settled his disputes peacefully in court. However, he and his kinsmen apparently never ceased to regard neighboring Pike County as hostile territory, and treated Kentucky law with utter contempt. Beginning in 1866, a series of indictments were handed down in Kentucky against Anse, his ex-Confederate brothers, and their uncle Jim Vance for assault, disturbing the peace, and carrying concealed weapons.[111] Indeed, as late as 1880, when his son Johnson was seized by local authorities on a concealed weapons charge, Anse dashed across the state line at the head of an armed band and forced the Kentuckians to release him at gunpoint.[112]

The outbreak of the notorious feud with the McCoys in 1882 underscored Hatfield's ruthless contempt for Kentucky law. When his brother Ellison was mortally wounded in an Election Day brawl by three of Randolph McCoy's sons, who were immediately arrested, Anse led another armed band across the Tug. The three prisoners were forcibly taken from Kentucky officers, conveyed across the river to West Virginia, and summarily executed. Their bound, bullet-riddled bodies mirrored the deaths of Asa McCoy, the Hurleys, and perhaps other local Unionists taken prisoner by Devil Anse during the war.[113]

Although sparked by family honor and blood vengeance, the feud soon witnessed an alliance between Anse's former Confederate comrade Randolph McCoy and many of Hatfield's wartime foes. One could argue that the true leaders of the McCoy faction were Pikeville attorney Perry A. Cline, who was bound by ties of kinship to some of Hatfield's' wartime victims, and Frank Phillips, whose Unionist father died in a Confederate military prison.[114] Both had strong connections to the former Union community along Peter Creek. Not surprisingly, in letters to the governors of both Kentucky and West Virginia, Cline portrayed the Hatfield faction as die-hard bushwhackers who "have been in arms and violating the laws since the Ware."[115]

While wartime animosity was not the sole factor in the feud, many aspects of it reflected the old hatreds—and fighting ways—spawned by the brutal guerrilla warfare that had ravaged the same vicinity more than twenty years before. Ironically, those closest to Hatfield who had survived that earlier conflict on the border, his brothers Ellison and Valentine, as well as his uncle Jim Vance, lost their lives during the feud. Although the fighting had effectively ceased by 1888, Hatfield did not hold out hope for peace until the death of Perry Cline in 1891. In a subsequent letter to the *Wayne County (W. Va.) News*, "Cap. Hatfield" declared an end to the fighting in language that clearly revealed that he regarded the feud as a continuation of the border warfare he had experienced during the Civil War: "The war spirit in me has abated, and I sincerely rejoice at the prospects of peace. I have devoted my life to arms. We have undergone a fearful loss of noble lives and valuable property in this struggle; all being like Adam not the first transgressors. Now I propose to rest in the spirit of peace."[116]

By the time he died peacefully at his home of old age in 1921, Devil Anse Hatfield had come to symbolize the violence that plagued the Southern mountains in the post–Civil War era. Indeed, the legendary Hatfield-McCoy feud had already become part of American history and folklore. However, Hatfield's Confederate service also symbolized the forgotten war on the Kentucky-Virginia border. While he deserted the regular army, he was among hundreds of men who continued to fight in defense of their homes in an isolated border region largely abandoned by both sides.

The war on Virginia's western border shattered notions of civilized warfare. Far removed from the protection of either army, the people of the Tug Valley fought each other with a desperate fury. Enemies who could not be driven off were hunted down and killed without mercy. Anse Hatfield, like many other partisans on both sides, became a law unto himself. He undoubtedly committed brutal acts of violence; however, such deeds matched the overall pattern of border warfare. To the people of Logan County, he emerged from the war as a man who risked his life in their defense. However, to his Union foes across the border in Kentucky, particularly those along Peter Creek, he was truly the devil in human form.

Without question, the war, the feud, and Hatfield's singular, ruthless personality were inextricably bound. Captain Hatfield's postwar conduct continued to reflect the dual image he won during the conflict—the law-abiding Confederate hero on *his* side of the Tug, and the bold, merciless bushwhacker on the other. Ironically, the legendary feud he waged would come to symbolize the postwar stereotype of the lawless, savage Southern mountaineer. In reality, the feud was deeply rooted in the brutal nature of the Civil War itself on Virginia's western border. As the 1882 execution of the three McCoys revealed, the "devil" spawned by four years of bloody strife was still at large.

Notes

1. James M. McPherson, *Battle Cry of Freedom: The Civil War Era* (New York: Oxford University Press, 1988), 670; and Thomas Lawrence Connelly,

Autumn of Glory: The Army of Tennessee, 1862–1865 (Baton Rouge: Louisiana State University Press, 1971), 148–50, 158–59.

2. Jeffery C. Weaver, *45th Battalion Virginia Infantry, Smith and Count's Battalions of Partisan Rangers* (Lynchburg, Va.: H. E. Howard, 1994), 38–39, 103–5.

3. James A. Garfield, *The Wild Life of the Army: Civil War Letters of James A. Garfield,* ed. Frederick D. Williams (East Lansing: Michigan State University Press, 1964), 64–66.

4. Quoted in Jeffrey C. Weaver, *The Civil War in Buchanan and Wise Counties: Bushwhackers' Paradise* (Lynchburg, Va.: H. E. Howard, 1994), 18.

5. Truda Williams McCoy, *The McCoys: Their Story as Told to the Author by Eye Witnesses and Descendants,* ed. Leonard Roberts (Pikeville, Ky.: Preservation Council Press of the Preservation Council of Pike County, 1976), 5.

6. In a 1966 interview, Willis Hatfield, then Devil Anse's only living son, related that his father and Randolph McCoy served together in the Confederate army. "Devil Anse Helped Trigger Long Feud," unidentified newspaper article in State Library Reference Files, Department for Libraries and Archives, Frankfort, Kentucky. See also Altina Waller, *Feud: Hatfields, McCoys, and Social Change in Appalachia, 1860–1900* (Chapel Hill: University of North Carolina Press, 1988), 17.

7. Waller, *Feud,* 194.

8. Ludwell Johnson, ed., "The Horrible Butcheries of West Virginia: Dan Cunningham on the Hatfield-McCoy Feud," *West Virginia History* 46 (1985–1986): 25–43. Daniel Webster Cunningham's unpublished "The Horrible Butcheries of West Virginia" was written in the 1890s. Intended to chronicle Hatfield's role in the legendary feud, it also includes a brief supplement entitled "Ans Hatfield War History." Cunningham, one of many detectives who sought to "bring the Hatfields to justice," penned a lurid account of the clan leader's guerrilla activities on the border. In addition to Hatfield's supposed involvement in eight killings, Cunningham claimed that his subject shot down two unsuspecting Pike County, Kentucky, Unionists and left them for dead, and further charged that Hatfield's band plundered more than nineteen Union families within a five-mile radius on the Kentucky side of the Tug. But Cunningham was Hatfield's bitter enemy, the son and brother of Union veterans as well as an ardent Republican, and he had little good to say about ex-Confederates and Democrats in general. More important, both Anse Hatfield and his uncle, James Vance, rode with the notorious "Devil Zeke" Counts during the war. The postwar killing of Cunningham's brother by the "Counts gang" led him to tar the Hatfields with the same brush. He condemned the Hatfields as wartime guerrillas

and postwar renegades in a second manuscript, "The Murders of Jackson and Roane County." Cunningham's "war history" was based on hearsay evidence undoubtedly provided by Hatfield's old enemies in Pike County, Kentucky. Nevertheless, this unique source cannot be dismissed lightly. A careful review of this narrative reveals that Hatfield's alleged victims were active Union partisans in the Tug Valley. Furthermore, if one ignores Cunningham's pro-Union bias, the incidents he describes constitute an excellent case study of the pattern of warfare along Virginia's entire western border. This source, when compared with family traditions and local public records, sheds new light on Hatfield's wartime exploits. The picture of Devil Anse that emerges increases our knowledge of the feud and its participants.

9. G. Elliott Hatfield, *The Hatfields* (Stanville, Ky.: Big Sandy Valley Historical Society, 1974), 6, 192.

10. A map of Jacob Cline Sr.'s property found in *Jake Cline vs. Green Taylor* reveals that he owned the land where Delorme is presently located. While there is no evidence that Hatfield was a tenant of the Clines, his first home was located on their lands. Pike County Circuit Court Case No. 3442, Public Records Division, Kentucky Department for Libraries and Archives, Frankfort (hereafter cited as KDLA).

11. In a letter dated November 30, 1993, Debra Basham of the West Virginia Division of Culture and History advised the writer that no record of Hatfield's service in the 129th Regiment of Militia could be located. However, Hatfield claimed to have served in this unit in a postwar interview. See Virgil Carrington Jones, *The Hatfields and the McCoys* (Chapel Hill: University of North Carolina Press, 1948), 169.

12. Scott C. Cole, *34th Battalion Virginia Calvary* (Lynchburg, Va.: H. E. Howard, 1993), 12, 18.

13. Medical Record of Asa H. McCoy, in Series 397: Union Soldiers from Kentucky—"Personal Papers," KDLA.

14. Ibid.

15. Hatfield, *The Hatfields,* 14.

16. Vance testified in *Hatfield vs. Mullens* that he took Richard Hatfield's horse in Pike County, Kentucky, in February 1862. Pike County Circuit Court Case No. 2175, KDLA.

17. *Lynchburg Virginian,* July 31, 1862.

18. *Louisville Daily Journal,* August 14, 1862.

19. *Louisville Daily Journal,* September 9, 1862.

20. Randall Osborne and Jeffrey C. Weaver, *The Virginia State Rangers and State Line* (Lynchburg, Va.: H. E. Howard, 1994), 27–28.

21. Ibid., 200–201.

22. Ibid., 77–78, 201.

23. Ibid., 81.

24. Ibid.

25. Unlike Harmon McCoy, who, according to his service record, was nearly six feet three, Devil Anse, if his records are correct, was only five feet six, not the legendary "six feet of Devil." However, his deadly skill with a rifle undoubtedly evened the odds in personal combat. Compiled Service Records of Forty-fifth Kentucky Mounted Infantry, KDLA; Compiled Service Records of Forty-fifth Virginia Infantry Battalion, West Virginia State Archives, Charleston (hereafter cited as WVSA); Waller, *Feud*, 35.

26. Geraldine F. Davenport to author, January 26, 1994; Pike County Tax Assessment Book (1861) and Pike County Civil Cases 2377 and 2373, KDLA.

27. Records of 167th Militia, Wayne County; Wm. Ratcliff et al. to Gov. F. H. Pierpont, September 21, 1862, Governors Papers, WVSA.

28. Johnson, "Horrible Butcheries," 42.

29. Ibid.

30. 1860 U.S. Census for Pike County, Kentucky, Pike County Order Book K: 397, KDLA; Clyde Runyon, *Marriage Bonds of Pike County, Kentucky, 1822–1865* (Belfry, Ky.: Privately printed, 1984), 195.

31. Johnson, "Horrible Butcheries," 42.

32. Ibid., 40.

33. Governor Thomas E. Bramlette Papers, box 34, file 747, KDLA.

34. 1860 U.S. Census for Logan County, Virginia, KDLA; Records of 167th Militia, Wayne County, WVSA; Virginia M. Bare, "Peter Cline, Sr.: Pioneer Settler," in *Pike County, 1822–1976: Historical Papers Number Two* (Pikeville, Ky.: Pikeville Historical Society, 1976), 60–61.

35. Osborne and Weaver, *Virginia State Rangers*, 85–89.

36. Wm. H. and John McCoy of Pike County were captured the same day. McCoy, "Personal Papers," KDLA.

37. Compiled Service Records of Enoch Cassidy, Thirty-ninth Kentucky Mounted Infantry, KDLA; and Waller, *Feud*, 89.

38. Pike County Will Book A: 63; 1860 Slave Schedules for Logan County, Virginia, KDLA.

39. Eugene Cline, grandson of Peter Cline, interview with author, December 19, 1993.

40. Ibid.

41. Johnson, "Horrible Butcheries," 40.

42. Cline, interview.

43. *State vs. Riley Sansom,* Logan County, West Virginia, Circuit Clerk's Office. Although the date of the incident is given in the indictment as April 1, 1870, this is an error as the testimony clearly indicates that the killing was a wartime event.

44. Pike County Circuit Court Cases 2155, 2177, 2355, 2386, and 2774, KDLA.

45. Johnson, "Horrible Butcheries," 40.

46. Lt. Micajah Woods to "My Dear Father," February 17, 1863, Micajah Woods Papers, Alderman Library, University of Virginia, Charlottesville (hereafter cited as Woods Papers).

47. Osborne and Weaver, *Virginia State Rangers,* 114.

48. Lt. Micajah Woods to "My Dear Father," March 5, 1863, Woods Papers.

49. F. S. Harris, "Noted Character of West Virginia," *Confederate Veteran Magazine* 8 (October 1900): 441–42.

50. Johnson, "Horrible Butcheries," 42; Records of 167th Militia, Wayne County, WVSA.

51. Pike County Circuit Court Cases 2155, 2177, 2355, 2386, and 2774, KDLA.

52. Ibid., cases 2177 and 2183.

53. Ibid. See also *Richmond Daily Dispatch,* December 17, 1862.

54. Harry Dale Cline to author, December 1993; Geraldine Francis Davenport, Genealogical Notes on Cline Family.

55. Johnson, "Horrible Butcheries," 41.

56. Dr. Coleman Hatfield, telephone interview with author, May 18, 1994.

57. *Logan (W.Va.) Banner,* December 2, 1938. Photocopy courtesy of Dana Dorsey, Logan.

58. Pike County Circuit Court Case 2481, KDLA. Given the fact that Randolph McCoy's name does not appear on the rolls of the Forty-fifth Virginia Infantry Battalion, the killing probably occurred during the period between Hatfield's State Line service and his reenlistment in the spring of 1863.

59. Weaver, *45th Battalion,* 27–28, 102–3.

60. Hatfield provided a brief autobiographical sketch to the *Wheeling (W.Va.) Intelligencer* that appeared on November 22, 1889, and is quoted in Jones, *Hatfields and McCoys,* 169–72. However, Hatfield's military file reveals that he "deserted on [illegible] 20, 1863." He may have reenlisted in Co. D of the Forty-fifth on January 1, 1864, and served as a private until he was reported AWOL on February 1, 1864. However, his cousin Anderson Hatfield of Pike

County, Kentucky, was AWOL from the Union army at the same time and could have been forced into the Rebel army. Compiled Service Records of Forty-fifth Virginia Infantry Battalion, WVSA; and Compiled Service Records of Thirty-ninth Kentucky Mounted Infantry, KDLA.

61. Weaver, *45th Virginia*, 42–44.

62. Otis K. Rice, *The Hatfields and the McCoys* (Lexington: University Press of Kentucky, 1978), 10–11.

63. Jones, *Hatfields and McCoys*, 169–72; Rice, *Hatfields and McCoys,* 10–11; and Waller, *Feud,* 31–32.

64. Osborne and Weaver, *Virginia State Rangers,* 115.

65. Weaver, *45th Virginia*, 137–38.

66. Capt. William S. Smith to Gen. Samuel Cooper, August 16, 1864, Letters Received, Confederate Adjutant and Inspector General, Record Group 109, National Archives and Records Administration, Washington, D.C. (hereafter cited as NA).

67. Ibid.

68. William S. Smith to Gov. Buckner, October 12, 1889, Simon B. Buckner Papers, KDLA.

69. Pike County Circuit Court Case 2074, KDLA.

70. Dils afterward reported that Rebels were "swarming" in the area. Vol. 109, Letters Received, Department of Kentucky, Record Group 109, NA.

71. Compiled Service Records of Thirty-ninth Kentucky Mounted Infantry, KDLA.

72. Pike County Circuit Court Case 2074; Lawrence County Circuit Court Civil Case 3183; *Commonwealth vs. Melvin Lawson et al.,* box 13, Lawrence County Circuit Court Criminal Indictments, KDLA.

73. Bare, "Peter Cline"; Records of 167th Militia, Wayne County, WVSA; Compiled Service Records of Thirty-ninth Kentucky Mounted Infantry, KDLA.

74. Pike County Circuit Case 2180, KDLA.

75. Johnson, "Horrible Butcheries," 40.

76. 1860 U.S. Census for Logan County, Virginia, KDLA; Bare, "Peter Cline"; Troy E. Taylor, letter to author, March 29, 1994.

77. Compiled Service Records of Thirty-ninth Kentucky Mounted Infantry, KDLA.

78. Ibid.; Col. Thomas McKinster to D. W. Lindsey, September 22, 1864, Records of Sixty-eighth Kentucky Enrolled Militia, Military Records and Research Library, Department for Military Affairs, Frankfort, Ky. (hereafter cited as MRRL).

79. Pension Files 309.474 and 523.232, NA.

80. Ibid.

81. Taylor, letter to author.

82. Johnson, "Horrible Butcheries," 40.

83. 1860 U.S. Census for Logan County, Virginia; Compiled Service Records of Second Battalion Kentucky Mounted Rifles, KDLA.

84. Cole, *34th Battalion,* 95–97.

85. *Louisville Democrat,* November 18, 1864; *Charleston Journal,* November 9, 1864.

86. *Commonwealth vs. Anderson and Wall Hatfield,* box 12, Lawrence County Circuit Court Criminal Indictments, KDLA; Records of Sixty-eighth Kentucky Enrolled Militia, MRRL.

87. *Louisville Daily Journal,* November 22, 1864.

88. Lawrence County Circuit Court Order Book 6:449, KDLA.

89. Ibid.; Johnson, "Horrible Butcheries," 42; *Louisville Daily Journal,* November 22, 1864.

90. Weaver, *45th Battalion,* 138–39; Pike County Circuit Order Book E:531, KDLA.

91. Weaver, *45th Battalion,* 72, 74, 102, 104.

92. Compiled Service Records of Forty-fifth Kentucky Mounted Infantry, KDLA.

93. McCoy, *The McCoys,* 6.

94. Compiled Service Records of Forty-fifth Kentucky Mounted Infantry, KDLA.

95. McCoy, *The McCoys,* 6–7.

96. Johnson, "Horrible Butcheries," 41–42.

97. McCoy, *The McCoys,* 6–11; Hobert McCoy and Orville McCoy, *Squirrel Huntin' Sam McCoy: His Memoir and Family Tree* (Pikeville, Ky.: Pikeville College Press, 1979), 59–60.

98. McCoy and McCoy, *Squirrel Huntin' Sam,* 59–60.

99. Charlotte Sanders, "Ollie Jane McCoy Smith's Energy Belies Her 80 Years," *Williamson (Ky.) Daily News,* August 2, 1982, clipping in reference files, Phelps Branch, Pike County Public Library, Pikeville, Kentucky.

100. Ibid.; McCoy, *The McCoys,* 11; McCoy and McCoy, *Squirrel Huntin' Sam,* 60; Hatfield, *The Hatfields,* 14.

101. Waller, *Feud,* 17.

102. Pike County Circuit Case 2589, KDLA.

103. James, Joseph, John, Jeremiah, and Thompson Hatfield were allegedly among the Union home guards who plundered Warren Alderson in 1862. Pike

County Circuit Case 2774. See also Compiled Service Records of Thirty-ninth Kentucky Mounted Infantry and 1890 U.S. Veterans Census, Pike County, KDLA.

104. Cline to author; Davenport, Genealogical Notes.

105. McCoy, *The McCoys,* 11.

106. Willis David Staton, *Hatfields and McCoys: True Romance and Tragedies* (Huntington, W.Va.: Algina, 1993), 17.

107. Lawson was identified by Smith as one of his company commanders. Smith to Cooper, August 16, 1864, Letters Received, Confederate Adjutant and Inspector General, Record Group 109, NA.

108. Compiled Service Records of Forty-fifth Virginia Infantry Battalion, WVSA.

109. *Charleston (W.Va.) Journal,* May 5, 1866.

110. Maj. Joseph Collins to Gov. A. J. Boreman, May 6, 1867, Gen. George H. Thomas to Gov. A. J. Boreman, September 17, 1868, Governors Papers, WVSA; *Charleston (W.Va.) Journal,* March 3, 1869.

111. Pike County Circuit Court Order Book F:210, 358–59; Order Book G:189, 263, KDLA. See also, Hatfield, *The Hatfields,* 35; and Rice, *Hatfields and McCoys,* 19.

112. Rice, *Hatfields and McCoys,* 22; Waller, *Feud,* 7; McCoy, *The McCoys,* 46–48.

113. Waller, *Feud,* 74–75.

114. Ibid., esp. 158–81; Bare, "Peter Cline."

115. P. A. Cline et al. to Gov. J. Proctor Knott, Undated Petition, Governors Papers, KDLA.

116. The 1891 letter has been attributed by feud scholars to Hatfield's son Anderson Jr., who was nicknamed "Cap." However, a recently discovered letter from Anse to Governor Buckner, in which he refers to the death of his brother Valentine in the Kentucky State Penitentiary, was signed "Cap. Hatfield," no doubt in reference to Anse's former rank in the Confederate service. Hatfield to Simon B. Buckner, January 21, 1889 [1890], Governors Papers, KDLA. See also *Louisville Courier-Journal,* March 23, 1891.

"Thy will, not ours"

The Wartime Ordeal of Virginia's Churches
David Rolfs

As she looked back in her postwar reminiscences on a year of unprecedented Confederate military disasters during the winter of 1863–1864, Richmond resident Sallie Putnam wondered how anyone could fail to appreciate the enormous wartime sacrifices of the Southern people:

> We sometimes hear of those who did not "feel the war." Situated as we were, we could not exactly understand what the idea imported. If not in fortune at least, in the more delicate and refined sensibilities of our nature, in the loss and absence of dear friends, in the constant anxiety for the probable fate of our country, surely every Southern person must have "felt the war." . . . We had only to step out on our streets to meet here a soldier with one leg, there with one arm . . . or on a passage through a certain quarter of our city where government work was given out to the indigent, we would see hundreds of poor women in waiting for the coarse sewing from which they earned the pittance that saved them from hunger. . . . We took these things to heart, and pondered and meditated, and eagerly looked forward to the end which should decide whether the greater strength lay in moral courage—the force of human will and virtuous endeavor—or in the mere majority of numbers. We lifted our hearts to God, and prayed in the depths of our spirit, and asked His all-powerful help in our weakness; but we rarely said: "Thy will, not ours, oh Lord, be done!" Perhaps therein lay our fault.[1]

At the time Putnam and other Virginians conveniently made Richmond's

German and Jewish shopkeepers the "unfeeling" scapegoats for the terrible extortion and hoarding that plagued the women and children of the Confederacy, but her larger, if unspoken, question remained something of an enigma for the postwar Virginia church. Surely an omniscient and unconditionally loving God also must have "felt" the terrible wartime suffering and heard the earnest spiritual entreaties of the more righteous South, so why had he not come to its aid? Had Putnam's God failed the Confederacy, or had an almost-chosen Southern people either sabotaged their spiritual mission or somehow misconstrued God's purposes in the war?

By the eve of the Civil War, Virginia's antebellum churches had come to occupy an increasingly prominent role in Southern society. While critics had once charged that Jefferson's postrevolutionary proposal to disestablish Virginia's colonial Episcopal Church would undermine true religion in the Commonwealth, to their chagrin his Virginia Act for Establishing Religious Freedom actually helped set the stage for a dramatic nineteenth-century expansion in the number, diversity, and popular influence of Virginia's churches. By the 1850s, Virginia's religious community was expanding at the rate of more than 70 churches a year, and in 1860 at least nineteen religious denominations in Virginia operated a combined total of 3,105 churches. Of that total, 1,403 of the churches were Methodist, 787 Baptist, 290 Presbyterian, and 188 Episcopal. Virginia's rapidly growing evangelical churches had historically been relegated to a subordinate public role in Virginia society by the planter establishment. Presbyterian minister James Henry Thornwell later spiritually justified this Southern church-state relationship with his "spirituality of the church" doctrine, which maintained that ministers should confine themselves to saving individual souls and let politicians deal with the wider problems of Southern society.

As both sections of the country prepared for war in the spring of 1861, the Virginia clergy cast aside any reservations they had had concerning political preaching and publicly sanctioned the creation of the new Confederate government. Rev. Bishop Meade, for one, welcomed the change, explaining that while in the past he had scrupulously avoided making "the least reference to anything partaking of a political character," given "the present circumstances of our country the cause of religion is so deeply involved that I feel not only justified but constrained to offer a few remarks."[2] The stream of ecclesiastical political pronouncements that sprang up quickly turned into a flood, and the Confederate government, anxious to develop a closer relationship with the South's vast network of evangelical churches, either overlooked or in some cases actively promoted such political preaching.

Antebellum Southerners had long maintained that their people practiced a more sincere and orthodox Christian faith than New Englanders, and they now looked for ways to demonstrate this alleged moral advantage by forging the world's first Christian republic. To prove the spiritual superiority of their new cause and government, Southern politicians like Jefferson Davis draped the Confederacy in religious symbolism and asked Southern churches to support their holy experiment. Sincerely convinced they were erecting a "Second City on a Hill," the Richmond government explicitly invoked "the favor and guidance of Almighty God" in the Confederate Constitution and made the phrase *Deo Vindice* (With God as Our Defender) its national motto. To reinforce the idea that the South was upholding America's original political and religious charters far better than the North ever had, Jefferson Davis also appropriated New England's tradition of the Puritan jeremiad, and whenever his government subsequently faced potential wartime crises, he called for official days of fasting, humiliation, and prayer to remind his people of the Confederacy's distinctive Christian identity and mission.

Of course, this spiritual sanctification of the Confederacy could not have been effected without the active support of the Confederacy's churches. In their early wartime sermons, Southern ministers informed their congregations that by seceding from the North the Southern people, just like ancient Israel, had finally separated themselves from an increasingly wicked society and assumed the mantle of a chosen people. By voluntarily embracing this special status, however, the Confederacy was entering into a corporate covenant with God that carried with it both blessings for peoples that proved faithful and curses for nations that stubbornly clung to their sins. Since the consequences of a minority of people failing to uphold God's laws could theoretically subject the entire community to God's terrible wrath, clergymen were always to remain vigilant for any communal sins that might provoke such judgment. Whenever such evil was discerned in the religious community, the Pentateuch instructed that it should be immediately confronted so the people could repent of their sin and restore their proper relationship with God. Since Puritan churches had historically played this prophetic role in New England society, when the Confederacy embraced the Northern jeremiad, it was in effect inviting its churches to take on a new prophetic role in Southern society and publicly address the corporate sins of the Confederacy.[3]

As the South rushed to complete its final military preparations in the momentous spring of 1861, its churchmen eagerly embraced their new wartime mission, as either Old Testament warrior-priests in the line of King David or prophets of the new Confederate Israel. In many cases Southern clerics seemed more interested in the war than their ministries back home. When Jefferson Davis asked his former West Point roommate, Episcopal bishop Leonidas Polk, to accept a commission as major general in the Confederate States Army, Polk immediately suspended his episcopal duties so he could buckle his "sword over the gown" and serve the South as a warrior-priest. In Richmond, Sallie Putnam noted that Virginia clergymen like William N. Pendleton and Dabney Harrison were also shedding their clerical vestments and donning "the armor of the soldier . . . not with a wish to lead in a rebellion . . . but from a stern sense of divine direction and the whisperings of patriotism to which conscience and an innate feeling of duty prompted and would not be stilled."[4]

Ministers from other denominations across the South seemed to share Polk's sentiment that the war should take precedence over their local ministries. Catherine Hopley, an English subject living in Virginia during the war, was shocked when the local Baptist minister she invited to dinner suddenly exclaimed: "I cannot rest here, I believe I must enlist too. I feel that my country calls me, and that I might be as useful on the battlefield as in my church. Has not Bishop Polk set me an example? And there is S. who has volunteered, and M. intends to do the same."[5] Perhaps Hopely's dinner guest and his colleagues were among the dozens of Baptist ministers across Georgia, North Carolina, and Virginia who organized local companies and marched off to war, leaving their congregations to fend for themselves. The Methodist camp was also decimated by the war fever. Bishop George Foster Pierce noted that so many Methodist ministers had enlisted in the Confederate army that the work of the December 1861 Atlanta Conference was impaired. Increasingly concerned with the excessive "war spirit among our preachers," Bishop Pierce announced that in the future, Methodist preachers should go to war as chaplains, not soldiers.[6] Virginian Presbyterian Robert Lewis Dabney also believed that ministers like himself should not compromise their moral power "to act as peace-makers and mediators" and instead urged Virginia's Christians to "arise and conquer in this war by the power of prayer." After taking a leave of absence from his seminary to serve as a chaplain in Beauregard's army, however, Dabney's earlier convictions and noncombatant status did not prevent him from serving as a battlefield courier in the First Battle of Manassas, or from later serving as "Stonewall" Jackson's chief of staff.[7]

While other clergy continued to labor faithfully in their pulpits back home, many now also took up Davis's call to preach the new Confederate jeremiad and ensure that their congregations both understood its terms and lived up to its vigorous requirements. As both sides prepared for the first major battle of the war, Jefferson Davis designated June 13, 1861, as the Confederacy's First National Day of Humiliation, Fasting, and Prayer, and from this date forward, the clergy began to introduce similar themes of corporate reconciliation to their congregations and use them to create a new sense of both national identity and communal sin in Southern society. In his first national fast day sermon, the Virginia reverend O. S. Barten helped illustrate the meaning of the jeremiad by contrasting the old U.S. Constitution with the new Confederate Constitution, happily observing that the latter specifically acknowledged "Almighty God" and invoked his blessings. According to Barten, this was because the Confederacy, unlike the old Union government, was striving to become the world's greatest Christian republic and would thus work much more closely with churches to ensure that it fulfilled its divine mission.[8] Barten then used an analogy his congregation was intimately acquainted with to help describe this process of corporate sanctification—the quest for individual salvation. Barten explained that unlike human beings, nations lacked eternal souls that could be rewarded and punished in the afterlife, so God had to judge them in this world with either communal blessings or curses. Thus, the entire nation had to faithfully observe his Commandments if it wished to avoid divine "retributions and punishments."[9] Other Virginia Fast Day sermons the next year followed similar lines. On November 15, 1861, Rev. Thomas V. Moore reminded his fellow Presbyterians that "war is a part of the agency by which God disciplines nations," and that during such judgments it behooved believers to turn to their God, acknowledge their sins, and repent, so that he would once again favor their cause.[10]

Despite several serious military setbacks throughout the first two years of the war, Virginian Christians remained firmly convinced of the spiritual superiority of their cause and most faithfully observed the government's fast days, as well as the official days of thanksgiving that followed important Southern victories. Catherine Hopley noted that some churches had formal sermons, while others just gathered together for informal thanksgiving and worship, but regardless of the format: "There was no parade of piety, no boasting of religious zeal; but a spirit of thankfulness, adoration, and submission, breathed through all the prayers. The exhortations were for resolution and self-denial. They thanked their Almighty Protector for the favors he had yet displayed toward his people; while they prayed for strength to be rightly guided in the great and trying duties before them."[11] The services on days of thanksgiving followed a similar liturgical formula, but since they usually occurred a few days or weeks after a major battle, the local churches were often filled with wounded soldiers that were still convalescing at local homes.[12]

Given Virginia's precarious position as the Confederate state closest to its enemy's heartland—with only about a hundred miles separating the rival capitals—Virginia experienced the full wrath of the Union armies in the first two years of the war. The most serious early military reverses included the loss of western Virginia, which had never really been in the Rebel camp anyway, the Northern occupation of Alexandria and the lower Shenandoah Valley, and the costly Peninsula and Antietam campaigns. Under Lee's brilliant leadership, the Army of Northern Virginia had successfully deflected the most serious Yankee blows in 1862, and with the exception of a few extreme northern and southeastern counties, most of the state remained securely in Confederate hands. Of course, this proved little comfort to the unlucky citizens living in the newly occupied Union areas. The sudden arrival of war changed everything for Judith McGuire, a resident of Alexandria, Virginia: "Our friends and neighbors have left us. Everything is broken up. The Theological Seminary is closed; the High School dismissed. Scarcely any one is left of the many families which surrounded us . . . our children are all gone—the girls to Clarke, where they may be safer . . . and the boys, the dear, dear boys, to the camp to be drilled and prepared to meet any emergency. Can it be our country is to be carried on to the horrors of civil war?"[13]

By the end of 1862, most northern Virginian communities had experienced the bitter fruits of war firsthand, and while they still expressed complete confidence in the righteousness and ultimate triumph of their cause, they were tired of the endless violence. Although Lee's military genius had spared much of the state from the horrors of Northern occupation, it did little to alleviate the suffering on the civilian home front. With fathers and sons off serving in the army, Virginia's families struggled to make ends meet, especially with rising inflation and wide-scale speculation plaguing the Confederate economy. Between August 1862 and March 1863, the prices of most foodstuffs increased almost threefold. A barrel of flour that had cost $7.50 in 1861 now cost as much as $30, but the government offered no commensurate increase in soldiers' salaries to match the tornadic increase in prices.[14] Women and children lived in constant uncertainty and fear, always wondering where their next meal would come from and whether their husbands, sons, or fiancées had survived the latest battle or winter camp epidemic. The unexpected length of the war and increasing number of casualties only heightened such concerns. The death of the family patriarch or his sons often meant economic ruin for the grief-stricken survivors or, at best, years of profound economic hardship.

Even when loved ones in the army were spared, Virginia's families were increasingly victimized by the war as each new Northern incursion into the Old Dominion created further economic disruptions, harsh military occupations, and a growing sea of refugees who—stripped of their homes and treasure—were now left completely dependent on the charity of their relatives and neighbors. With their communities suddenly besieged by a host of new wartime evils, Virginia's Christians naturally turned to their churches for material and spiritual assistance, and their clergy worked conscientiously to address their congregations' changing wartime expectations.

A common problem confronting northern Virginia communities throughout the war was the flood of wounded that invariably engulfed their towns after each major campaign. In a harbinger of greater evils to come, following First Manassas a number of Warrenton homes became impromptu hospitals, including Susan Caldwell's. On July 31 alone some seventy injured or sick soldiers came into town. "Our town is filled with sick soldiers," she wrote her husband with the army. "Some die each day." A captain from Georgia died of typhoid in Susan's home two days before his wife came to minister to him. She "went into spasms," Susan wrote to her husband in late September. "Yesterday she went to the Graveyard and stretched herself on her husband's grave."[15]

Since the healing of the sick had been such a vital component of Christ's ministry on earth, Virginians naturally expected their churches to help alleviate the physical and emotional suffering of these stricken soldiers and comfort their families. To their credit, the churches rose to the challenge. In 1862 the Episcopal Diocese of Virginia began to hire full-time missionaries to serve the emotional needs of wounded soldiers convalescing in Richmond and Petersburg. In other parts of the South, churches helped local women organize ladies' hospital aid associations. In addition to collecting contributions and medical supplies, at least one of these—Rev. Robert Woodward Barnwell's South Carolina Aid Association—began recruiting nurses for service in Virginia.[16] Later, hospital chaplains also organized on-site reading and writing classes for severely disabled veterans so the former farmers could secure teaching jobs after the war and continue to provide for their families.[17]

As their husbands and sons enthusiastically marched off to war in 1861, few Virginian families imagined the fighting would be so terrible, that it would last so long, or that so many of their men would never return. Over the course of the dreadful wartime judgment, Virginians expected their churches to pray daily for their absent menfolk, help provide for their physical and spiritual needs, and, should their families' worst nightmares be realized, ensure that they received a proper Christian burial. After celebrating the Confederate victory at First Manassas, Bishop Pierce told his son Lovick, an adjutant serving with the Fifteenth Georgia in Virginia, that the entire community was constantly thinking of the regiment: "We all think of you, talk about you, and pray for you."[18] To help meet the physical needs of the departed soldiers, churches began to serve as meeting places for voluntary aid societies that cooked nonperishable foodstuffs and knitted clothing for the troops or raised money to help provide for soldiers' families during their absence. In some cases, churches themselves provided money, food, and clothing to the families of departed soldiers, wartime refugees, and widows.[19] When a locally organized unit finally did see major action, the consequences could be devastating, with the community sometimes losing—literally overnight—most of its finest sons. In the aftermath of such tragedies, Virginians expected their churches to serve as centers of mourning. The clergy would deliver moving eulogies in praise of the fallen Confederate heroes, and celebrate their lives and wartime sacrifices as worthy of imitation. Even after the fallen soldier had received a proper Christian wake, funeral, and burial, the church remained a house of mourning for his grieving family and friends. When Union soldier Elisha Hunt Rhodes visited an Episcopal church in Winchester, Virginia, he was surprised to find so many women dressed in black.[20]

Northern invasions and occupations of their local communities presented Virginia's churches with a host of difficulties. From the outset, such military incursions always proved disruptive. When a Yankee column approached Warrenton, Virginia, in the spring of 1862, a runner burst into a church service and warned the minister to dismiss his flock because the enemy had arrived. Parishioners rushed out onto the street, where some of the curious women later lingered, apparently anxious to see what their Yankee tormentors actually looked like.[21] Once established, Northern soldiers often began plundering fencing, farm animals, and other supplies from the town, and the churches found themselves at the mercy of the conquering army. At best, they could expect unwanted Northern guests at their next services, and at worst, their churches might be vandalized or commandeered for use as a Northern headquarters or field hospital.[22] Women's daily routines and regular church attendance were disrupted by the presence of intimidating Yankee sentries and fears that their homes might be looted in their absence.[23] As Lucy Caldwell's family soon discovered, the Yankee raids on Virginian communities often proved most vexing of all. In a late April 1863 raid, enemy troops detained some civilians, confiscated provisions from farmers, and imposed a 7:00 P.M. curfew and a "lights-out" at nine. Then, after departing, they suddenly returned and arbitrarily arrested anyone found out on the street.[24] In the face of Yankee usurpations deliberately designed to demoralize Southern resistance, Confederate women brazenly defied their would-be conquerors and expected their churches to lead and spiritually sustain the community's resistance to the Union occupation. Camouflaged in heavy brown veils to mask their faces from the enemy, some women continued attending church as an act of resistance. Most refused to tolerate any deviation from their clergy's assigned roles as leaders of the Confederate resistance. When one Falmouth, Virginia, pastor made the mistake of praying for Lincoln and the country, the ladies stormed out of the service and boycotted the church until their pastor saw the light.[25]

When confronted with early defeats, the churches simply took their lead from Richmond and dutifully preached their jeremiad sermons on Davis's appointed fast days. Grateful for its unprecedented influence and new prophetic role in the Confederate society, the church committed most of its resources to the Southern cause, absolutely convinced that God would not let it fail. To help ensure it did not, Southern clergy like Bishop Pierce used the same successful prewar revivalist tactics that had won souls for Christ to enlist replacement soldiers for the Confederacy. Even the church bells that had once summoned the faithful to sanctuaries supported the cause, as they were melted to forge Southern cannon. If defeats produced doubts, then, as Winchester resident Cornelia McDonald said, "We have only, as Bishop Meade said in his dying message to his people, 'to stand firm and think of our dead.'"[26]

In the first week of May 1863 Lee won his most decisive victory yet over the Army of the Potomac, but the success was marred by the death of one of his most able lieutenants—Stonewall Jackson. Jackson's death created something of a theological dilemma for the Confederacy. At the height of his military career, the churches had attributed his remarkable feats on the battlefield to his deep religious faith, proclaiming that Jackson was heaven-sent to lead the Southern armies to victory. What then, was the South to think now, when its divinely appointed military savior had not only been struck down on the battlefield but also killed by his own men? His wounds need not have proven fatal, but they had; and as if to emphasize the spiritual significance of his death, God had taken him home on a Sunday. Judith McGuire articulated the most common answer presented in Southern pulpits over the next month: "Stonewall Jackson is numbered with the dead! Humanly speaking we cannot do without him; but the same God who raised him up, took him from us. . . . Perhaps we have trusted too much to an arm of flesh; for he was the nation's idol."[27] Since Jackson's life had come to represent a microcosm of the Confederate jeremiad, Southern ministers had to develop some meaningful spiritual rationalization for his death. Otherwise they would be forced to admit that either God had abandoned their holy experiment or they had completely misinterpreted his wartime purposes.

Jackson's death appeared all the more ominous when it was followed in quick succession by two decisive Confederate defeats at Gettysburg and Vicksburg. With growing speculation at home and mounting military disasters in the East and West, thoughtful Virginia Christians instinctively sensed that there had to be some spiritual problem plaguing their cause. The fiery wartime judgment had undoubtedly altered many Virginians' prewar faith, religious practices, and feelings about God. Had any of these changes somehow allowed sin to creep into the Southern camp?

If so, Virginia's churches would be hard pressed to meet the challenge.

By 1863, most of the major denominations were suffering from a shortage of ministers—with many off fighting at the front and others soon to depart for temporary missions in the army.[28] Even when qualified ministers were available, there was no guarantee a suitable public meeting place could be found. This was because by 1863, the Northern armies had adopted harsher war measures, including the confiscation of Southern churches for use as Northern hospitals, headquarters, and stables. In some limited cases, this had even resulted in some churches being deliberately vandalized or damaged.

These factors, coupled with the difficulties and dangers women faced in traveling to church in a war zone without their husbands' protection, prevented many women from attending regular weekly religious services. Hard pressed by wartime shortages, skyrocketing consumer prices, and the continued absence of their men, Southern women increasingly turned to their faith for the emotional strength and comfort they needed to endure their wartime suffering. Since many found it increasingly difficult to regularly attend their traditional public church services, they simply continued saying their family prayers at home and began participating in more local prayer meetings. Armed with appropriate denominational prayer books and hymnals, a few women even organized and conducted their own religious services at home with their neighbors.[29] Although these private religious practices could be a source of great spiritual comfort and edification, they effectively removed Virginian women and their children from the teaching, encouragement, and moral accountability of their pastors and churches. More important, by removing themselves from formal religious society, these women lost the spiritual support systems that had been helping them to overcome their spiritual doubts and to resign themselves to the will of God. Combined with a worsening war situation, this spiritual isolation sometimes caused women to experience spiritual crises, as nagging doubts about the justice of God or their leaders grew into open bitterness or rebellion.

For many women, the stumbling block proved to be the senseless death of a loved one. Try as she might, Lucy Breckinridge could not stop thinking about Johnny, the seventeen-year-old brother she lost at the Battle of Seven Pines: "I miss him more than I ever did and find it harder to be reconciled to the death of one who might have been so useful."[30] Disconsolate over the death of her cousin, Lucy Buck tried to find comfort in the fact that he had died in the service of a noble cause and was probably in heaven now but found that "that was not enough, nor was the reading of the Ninetieth Psalm . . . or the singing of hymns."[31] Mary Gay refused to resign herself to her brother's death. "I did not believe that my brother should die," she said, "and I could not say to that Holy being, 'Thy will be done.'"[32] As some women began to question the providential unfolding of God's will for them and their families, they found it increasingly difficult to love him and submit to his seemingly capricious judgments.

Most Virginian women, however, were still directing their venom at Yankees. Phoebe Yates Pember, a young Jewish matron at the Chimborazo Hospital, was shocked to discover her Christian friends were replacing their gospel of love with a harsher, more vindictive Old Testament faith based on vengeance. After listening to her pious Christian friends brag about their Yankee bone collections one evening, she proposed that they "all join the Jewish Church, let forgiveness and peace and good will alone and put their trust in the sword of the Lord and Gideon."[33]

In 1863 the Southern clergy were still fulfilling their responsibility to preach the Confederate jeremiad, but with what results? Frustrated with the South's inexplicable military failures, some Virginia clergy, like Robert Dabney, had dramatically shifted their prewar positions concerning Christians' wartime roles. Having once urged Christians to conquer in this war by "the power of prayer," by late 1863 Dabney had embraced an Old Testament vision of retributive justice and vengeance that countenanced the use of guerrilla warfare against the North.[34] In light of recent events, other Southern clerics had also lost their former sense of certainty concerning the war's outcome. The previous year Bishop Pierce had confided to his son that he feared the Southern people's spiritual shortcomings would fatally undermine their cause: "I am troubled because the calamities which ought to humble us seem only to harden. Wickedness increases I fear. . . . We are a guilty people and whether there are righteous enough to save us, I doubt. But I will hope to the end." In an 1863 address to the Georgia General Assembly Pierce elaborated upon the reasons for his growing pessimism: "Pitiless extortion, is making havoc in the land. We are devouring each other. Avarice, with full barns, puts the bounties of Providence under bolts and bars, waiting with eager longings for higher prices. The widow's wail and childhood's cry fall upon his ears unheeded. . . . Speculation in salt and bread and meat runs riot in defiance of the thunders of the pulpit, executive interference, and the horrors of threatened famine."[35]

In a March 27, 1863, sermon, Rev. William Norwood also named speculators as the principal cause of God's continued judgments since they increased the price of food "beyond the means of the greater part of their neighbors" and apparently loved "their wealth more than their country, or even the lives of their sons." Raising the ominous specter of the jeremiad, Norwood then asked: "And may we not expect still heavier chastisements unless this demoralizing, this degrading, this idolatrous spirit of gain is repressed and we humble ourselves before God for this sin?"[36]

Although they, too, castigated the speculators, the Annual Council of the Episcopal Diocese of Virginia and 1863 Meetings of the Baptist General Association hinted at another potential scapegoat for the recent disasters besetting the Confederacy—Southern women. Without identifying women in particular, after discussing the abysmal state of Virginia's Sunday schools, an Episcopal education committee concluded that the heart of the problem was parents' failure to enroll their children in the church school and ensure their regular attendance. In similar fashion, the Address of the Baptist General Association ended with a mild rebuke to members who were not assembling regularly to hear the gospel preached. Since women had generally outnumbered men two to one in the antebellum churches, and most of the men were off serving in the army, by default these remarks were primarily directed at Virginia's women.[37]

Perhaps disenchanted with the jeremiad's constant search for spiritual scapegoats, and after hinting that women's moral failures were a sin provoking God's disenchantment with the Confederacy, the Episcopal council quickly moved on to other points of business. Observing that shortly before his death, Gen. Stonewall Jackson had asked the churches to send clergy to minister to his men, the conference decided to temporarily detach some priests from their local parishes and send them on short-term mission trips to the army. In what appeared to be the beginning of a gradual shift in policy, the Episcopal council also asked that its ministers stop preaching sermons "on the times and the war and the objects of our country's hopes" and focus instead on "the glad tidings of salvation, just the eternal message of grace and love to perishing sinners."[38] In other words, the churches should shift the emphasis of their preaching from the Confederate jeremiad back to the pursuit of individual salvation. Although the churches would never completely abandon the jeremiad, and it would be energetically preached in some quarters until 1865, they had taken an important step back from a New

England doctrine they sensed was failing, and reemphasized the importance of the South's traditional "spirituality of the church" doctrine. The churches' decision to strip clergy from their already hard-pressed home ministries and reassign them as missionaries to the army, despite their knowledge of growing communal sin at home, seemed to confirm the shift in focus.

At the end of 1863, Southern churches remained firmly committed to final victory, but they had apparently lost some of their earlier enthusiasm for erecting a Confederate City on a Hill. The new Confederate church-state alliance had successfully appropriated New England's principal religious motif, and its churches had done their best to preach it, but by the third year of the war this foreign implant did not seem to be bearing any fruit for the South. Indeed, the jeremiad had shackled Southern churches with a seemingly irreconcilable spiritual dilemma. It proclaimed that the South was the true Christian Republic, and that only national righteousness could secure final victory. But it also kept reminding the flawed Southern home front of its carnal and communal sins and lack of revival. Indeed, the practical implications of its theology seemed to indicate that, if anything, the South was spiritually regressing because it was identifying or embracing new sins, something the churches themselves readily acknowledged. The South had never completely repented of its earlier sins of national pride, Sabbath-breaking, drunkenness, and cursing, but now in the public mind these had been superceded by the seemingly worse evils of greed, idolatry, merciless speculation, selfishness and increasing bitterness, factionalism, and rebellion against God and government. So even as the church enthusiastically proclaimed Southern national righteousness, the need for Christian perfectionism, and the inevitability of Southern victory, it seemed to be in complete denial. Where was that elusive national righteousness, that spirit of revival on the home front, and why had military events turned so decisively against the Confederacy? Uncomfortable with the direction their Confederate experiment had taken, many Virginia clergy finally shifted the focus of their ministries from the necessity of securing the South's corporate salvation to something they were more historically comfortable with, and successful at pursuing—the path to individual salvation.

The shift came on the eve of Ulysses S. Grant's relentless Wilderness Campaign in late 1864 and 1865. Since at heart the war was spiritual in nature, the message was that faith was the key to final Southern victory. The Southern churches' decision to shift their spiritual emphasis from communal sanctification to individual salvation would reap handsome eternal rewards, as major revivals began to blaze through the Army of Northern Virginia. Having failed to redeem the home front, the churches would continue to redirect their pastoral ministries to help feed the burgeoning revivals at the front. At home popular interest in the military revivals soared as many hoped the spiritual enthusiasm in the army would somehow spill over to their communities and help spiritually renew the home front as well. In the final hours of the Confederacy, the Southern churches thought they saw a ray of hope in the gathering storm clouds. Although the North had recently won a series of heady victories, it was now foolishly placing its faith in the size and strength of its armies instead of trusting God alone for the final victory, and this would be its downfall. As long as the Southern people remained faithful and performed their duty, surely God would not abandon their cause.

Subsequent military events in the spring of 1865 soon dispelled such spiritual illusions, and the final defeat of the Confederacy provoked a profound spiritual crisis as the churches tried to ascertain what had gone wrong with the Confederate experiment. Demoralized by their society's catastrophic defeat and chagrined by their faulty spiritual prognostications, Virginia clerics were forced to reassess their wartime ministries. Had a backslidden Southern home front ultimately robbed the Confederacy of final victory or, as Lincoln so eloquently observed in his Second Inaugural Address, had both sides simply assumed too much concerning the morality of their prewar causes and misconstrued God's ultimate purposes in the war? Still convinced of the righteousness of their Lost Cause, the Southern churches could only conclude that, like the examples of Job and Christ, the life and death of the Confederacy was intended to accomplish some higher, presently unknown, purpose. Although temporarily embittered with his ways, few Virginians abandoned their belief in God, and after the war, their severely tested but proven faith would help a chastened people and church process the meaning of Virginia's catastrophic defeat and endure its consequences. Once again Southerners could take comfort in a literal, commonsense exegesis of the Scriptures that assured them God had never intended the churches' final victory to occur in this world, and when the Christian soldiers of the Confederacy returned, they would help their churches pursue revival at home with the same spirit it had been pursued in the army.

Notes

1. Sallie A. Brock Putnam, *In Richmond during the Confederacy: By a Lady of Richmond* (New York: R. M. McBride, 1961), 272–74. Original title page reads *Richmond during the War: Four Years of Personal Observation; By a Richmond Lady* (New York: G. W. Carlton, 1867).

2. Bishop Meade, *Address on the Day of Fasting and Prayer June 13 1861 Delivered at Christ Church, Millwood, Virginia* (Richmond: Richmond Enquirer Book and Job Press, 1861), 15.

3. Drew Gilpin Faust, *The Creation of Confederate Nationalism: Ideology and Identity in the Civil War South* (Baton Rouge: Louisiana State University Press, 1988), 26–29.

4. Putnam, *In Richmond during the Confederacy*, 49.

5. Catherine C. Hopley, *Life in the South; From the Commencement of the War. By a Blockaded British Subject. Being a Social History of Those Who Took Part in the Battles, from a Personal Acquaintance with Them in Their Own Homes. From the Spring of 1860 to August 1862* (1863; repr., New York: Augustus M. Kelley, 1971), 1:329–30.

6. George G. Smith, *The Life and Times of George Foster Pierce, D.D., LL.D., Bishop of the Methodist Church, South, with His Sketch of Lovick Pierce, D.D., His Father* (Sparta, Ga.: Hancock, 1888), 447; Christopher H. Owen, *The Sacred Flame of Love: Methodism and Society in Nineteenth-Century Georgia* (Athens: University of Georgia Press, 1998), 103–5.

7. Thomas C. Johnson, *The Life and Letters of Robert Lewis Dabney* (Richmond: Presbyterian Committee of Publication, 1903), 221, 237, 241, 262–72.

8. Harry S. Stout and Christopher Grasso, "Civil War, Religion, and Communications: The Case of Richmond," in Randal Miller, Harry S. Stout, and Charles Reagan Wilson, eds., *Religion and the American Civil War* (New York: Oxford University Press, 1998), 322.

9. O. S. Barten, *A Sermon Preached in St. James' Church, Warrenton, Virginia . . .* (Richmond: N.p., 1861), 7–9.

10. Thomas Verner Moore, *God Our Refuge and Strength in This War: A Discourse before the Congregations of the First and Second Presbyterian Churches on the Day of Humiliation, Fasting and Prayer, Appointed by President Davis, Friday Nov. 15, 1861* (Richmond: N.p., 1861), 7, 13–18.

11. Hopley, *Life in the South*, 1:353–56.

12. Ibid., 2:17–19.

13. Matthew Page Andrews, ed., *The Women of the South in War Times* (Baltimore: Norman, Remington, 1920), 72–73.

14. William Blair, *Virginia's Private War: Feeding Body and Soul in the Confederacy, 1861–1865* (New York: Oxford University Press, 1998), 69.

15. John G. Selby, *Virginians at War* (Wilmington, Del.: Scholarly Resources, 2002), 45.

16. Fort Ward Museum and Historic Site, *Unhappiness Abroad: Civil War Refugees*, n.d., http://oha.alexandriava.gov/fortward/special-sections/refugees/ (August 20, 2006); Jean V. Berlin, ed., *Ada W. Bacot Diary: A Confederate Nurse* (Columbia: University of South Carolina Press, 1994), 5.

17. Kurt O. Berends, "'Wholesome Reading Purifies and Elevates the Man': The Religious Military Press in the Confederacy," in Miller, Stout, and Wilson, *Religion and the American Civil War*, 147.

18. Smith, *Life and Times*, 442, 443.

19. Margaret E. Wagner, Gary W. Gallagher, and Paul Finkelman, eds., *The Library of Congress Civil War Desk Reference* (New York: Simon and Schuster, 2002), 688.

20. Robert Hunt Rhodes, ed. *All for the Union: A History of the 2nd Rhode Island Volunteer Infantry in the War of the Great Rebellion as Told by the Diary and Letters of Elisha Hunt Rhodes, Who Enlisted as a Private in '61 and Rose to the Command of His Regiment* (Lincoln, R.I.: A. Mowbray, 1985), 188–93; Berlin, *Confederate Nurse*, 123.

21. Selby, *Virginians at War*, 51.

22. Steven E. Woodworth, *While God Is Marching On: The Religious World of Civil War Soldiers* (Lawrence: University Press of Kansas, 2001), 200, 205, 247–48.

23. Cornelia Peake McDonald, *A Woman's Civil War: A Diary, with Reminiscences of the War from March 1862*, ed. Minrose C. Gwin (Madison: University of Wisconsin Press, 1992), 107, 114.

24. Selby, *Virginians at War*, 98–99.

25. Ibid., 51; McDonald, *Woman's Civil War*, 106; Woodworth, *While God Is Marching On*, 141.

26. Smith, *Life and Times*, 451; Wagner, Gallagher, and Finkelman, *Civil War Desk Reference*, 687; Woodworth, *While God Is Marching On*, 124–25; McDonald, *Woman's Civil War*, 117.

27. Andrews, *Women of the South*, 180.

28. To cite just one such example, the parish from which W. N. Pendleton resigned, Grace Church in Lexington, had still not found a replacement minister more than a year later. Documenting the American South, *Journal of the Sixty-eighth Annual Council of the Protestant Episcopal Church in Virginia. Held in St. Paul's Church, Richmond on the 20th, 21st and 22nd*

May, 1863, http://docsouth.unc.edu/imls/episc68th/menu.html (September 15, 2006), 18.

29. Drew Gilpin Faust, Thavolia Glymph, and George C. Rable, "A Woman's War: Southern Women in the Civil War," in Edward D. C. Campbell Jr. and Kym S. Rice, eds., *A Woman's War: Southern Women, Civil War, and the Confederate Legacy* (Richmond and Charlottesville: Museum of the Confederacy and the University Press of Virginia, 1996), 13.

30. Lucy Breckinridge, *Lucy Breckinridge of Grove Hill: The Journal of a Virginia Girl, 1862–1864,* ed. Mary D. Robertson (Columbia: University of South Carolina Press, 1994), 126.

31. Selby, *Virginians at War,* 133.

32. Quoted in Drew Gilpin Faust, "Without Pilot or Compass," in Miller, Stout, and Wilson, *Religion and the American Civil War,* 257.

33. Phoebe Yates Pember, *A Southern Woman's Story: Life in Confederate Richmond,* ed. Bell Irvin Wiley (Jackson, Tenn.: McCowat-Mercer, 1959), 123.

34. Johnson, *Life and Letters,* 260–90. The guerrilla warfare scheme was actually developed by another Richmond cleric, M. D. Hoge, but Dabney's biographer claims Dabney was an early supporter of the policy.

35. Smith, *Life and Times,* 454, 475–76.

36. Rev. William Norwood, *God and Our Country* (Richmond: Smith, Bailey, 1863), 13–15.

37. Documenting the American South, *Address of the Baptist General Association [of] Virginia: June 4, 1863,* n.d., http://docsouth.unc.edu/imls/baptist/baptist.html (September 15, 2006), 6–8; Documenting the American South, *Journal of the Sixty-eighth Annual Council of the Protestant Episcopal Church in Virginia,* 16–39.

38. Documenting the American South, *Journal of the Sixty-eighth Annual Council of the Protestant Episcopal Church in Virginia,* 39.

The Virginian Wartime Scrapbook

Preserving Memories on Paper
William C. Davis

The history of scrapbook keeping is clouded and uncertain, riddled with the mythology and misconception that surrounds most popular pastimes. For instance, it is often asserted that the ancient Romans and Greeks like Cicero and Aristotle used notebooks to collect information.[1] The problem with that is that the codex, the "book" as we know it as a bound bundle of paper with discrete leaves or pages, did not appear until the first century A.D., long after both Cicero and Aristotle, and even then it did not become a commonplace or preferred form of book structure for another three centuries after that.

By the second millennium the codex had become ubiquitous in the West. Virtually all books from A.D. 400 onward were handwritten manuscript copies of the Bible and other religious, philosophical, and literary tomes. At some time over the centuries there also appeared for the first time the substantial bound volume of blank pages for miscellaneous use. The advent of printing only accelerated the output of books of both kinds, and both would have been used on an ersatz basis for pressing or preserving mementoes: flowers and leaves, love poems, locks of hair, even legal documents. Thanks to its weight and bulk, the Bible became an early and perennial favorite for such storage of odd bits. By the sixteenth century most middle-class families had a copy, if no other books, and its sacred and special place among family possessions made it the natural repository for other, more ephemeral items that were treasured by an owner.

Perhaps the earliest reference to what later centuries knew and called scrapbooks came in 1598, when the spread of culture and literacy led to a huge explosion in the number and availability of printed and souvenir items that people wanted to save. The result was the "commonplace book," in which scholars and laypeople collected poems, witticisms, quotations, kitchen and medicinal recipes, and copied them into blank books for preservation. There was no theme necessary; it was all just material of interest to the idiosyncratic compiler. At the same time Western culture saw the beginning of the great collections of art, and a corresponding interest among the middle classes in compiling for themselves lithographs, prints, broadsides, illustrations from playbooks, and more. In 1550 in Florence the Italian Giorgio Vasari published *The Lives of the Most Excellent Painters, Sculptors and Architects,* in which he advised literati to put their prints and drawings in large albums for preservation. In London alone at that time the square around St. Paul's Cathedral teemed with print sellers hawking one-penny ballads, satires, sonnets, and more, many of which found their way in between the leaves of commonplace books.

By the late sixteenth century such a book was sometimes called a *silva rerum,* which literally meant "a forest of things." When boys of the middle classes began going to school in Tudor times, teachers required them to keep commonplace books, and in them write down and learn by rote quotations, idioms, mathematical equations, and the other things deemed necessary for a decent elementary education.[2] After another century the pastime had become itself a commonplace. In 1706 the English philosopher John Locke published his *A New Method of a Common-Place-Book.* He owed it to the world to share his method, he said, "in an age so full of useful inventions." He gave instructions even on how to prepare a useful index, as well as how to organize religious proverbs, useful quotations on any subject, and whatever else "I would put . . . in my Common-Place-Book."[3] Then in 1769 the Reverend James Granger published his two-volume *Biographical History of England from Egbert the Great to the Revolution* in London. It achieved instant popularity, and Granger repeatedly updated it in later editions. Then, after his death, his editor Mark Noble published more editions in which he expanded the original work by using plagiarized illustrations taken from other works, an approach that became known as "grangerizing." In the subtitle to the later versions this process was lauded as a means of collecting portraits that would familiarize Britons with their famed ancestors and better help to catalog the history of the island people. Blank pages at the back of the Granger volumes were soon being used by owners for collecting and preserving prints of their own, yet another variant on the commonplace book.

In America the commonplace book arrived with the first settlers or soon thereafter, and by the time Granger was achieving popularity it had become widespread in Virginia and elsewhere. "I was in the habit of abridging and commonplacing what I read," Thomas Jefferson recalled of his schooldays, "and of sometimes mixing my own reflections on the subject."[4] All of his life Jefferson would be a habitual hoarder of newspaper clippings and other memorabilia, keeping them in an extensive number of blank books or albums. By the time Jefferson was president in 1801, the album had evolved into something essentially recognizable today. Often they were used to collect signatures as well as to store ephemera, in the process becoming a sort of general repository for an individual's memory. More affluent customers had their names embossed on the covers of their albums, and sometimes even had locks built into the binding to keep them private. At the same time the women's popular "friendship album" appeared, used to save quotes, calling cards, locks of hair, poems, and more.

And then emerged the name by which such albums were destined to be known in posterity. It has been claimed that the word *scrapbook* came about because people developed a penchant for taking colorful pieces of paper from printing waste and using the "scraps" to decorate their albums, or alternately because paper photographs not mounted on card stock were called "scraps," and thus the albums in which people pasted them became scrapbooks.[5] The former explanation is unlikely, because the general population did not have access to printing scraps, which were recycled as a rule into new paper or used to stiffen bindings. The latter explanation is a nonsense. Photographs on paper did not appear until the 1840s in England and were not widespread until the 1850s. However, the word *scrapbook* used in its modern sense came into use at least as early as 1820, when the Scots newspaper publisher John M'Diarmid brought out his first volume of *The Scrap Book: A Collection of Amusing and Striking Pieces, in Prose and in Verse* in Edinburgh. It went through several subsequent editions, firmly associating the name scrapbook with a collection of literary miscellanea, and with the concept of blank book pages being filled with newspaper clippings, pictures, and other things of interest or curiosity.

Then in 1826 John Poole published *Manuscript Gleanings and Literary Scrapbook,* which illustrated ways to create albums at home using personal writings, poems, newspaper articles, and even decorative things like bits of wallpaper and fabric. Just a decade later the first purpose-made scrapbook was printed and put on the market, with decorative covers, a title page proclaiming its intended use, and even frame lines on the pages to set off the contents to be added by the owner.[6] Within another fifteen years the developments in photography did add paper photographs to the range of available scrapbook fillers, and while most photos of the period went instead into special *carte-de-visite* albums, many did find their way into scrapbooks as well.

Meanwhile, three other important phenomena occurred that put the scrapbook within reach and aspiration of the common man, and certainly the majority of Virginians. The explosion in the newspaper press in America during the first half of the nineteenth century meant that the South went from having fewer than a hundred presses in operation in 1800 to more than five hundred by 1850. In the following decade the number of presses doubled, and in 1860, at the outbreak of the secession crisis, Virginia alone had 130 functioning journals.[7] Thus the raw material for thousands of scrapbooks was coming off those presses every day, five of them in Richmond alone. Meanwhile, the invention and spread of the telegraph meant that up-to-the-minute news could be transmitted to those waiting presses, providing a reading public with the most interesting—and therefore memorable—information. And the spread of virtually universal free public education for white males and many females in the South guaranteed that there was a population out there capable of reading the news, and wanting to preserve it. Supply and demand came together just at the time that the major experience of the century was about to erupt, and thus Virginians all across the Commonwealth were ready with scissors and scrapbooks to create their own volumes of war memories.

There is simply no means of determining how many Virginians kept war scrapbooks. It must have been in the thousands, yet probably the majority of them disappeared during or soon after the war. Paper is by its very nature ephemeral. Dampness or inadequate storage could ruin a scrapbook quickly. Yankee raiders could and did pillage and vandalize homes occasionally, destroying books simply because they could. The fire that gutted Richmond in April 1865 no doubt took many scrapbooks with it, and then in the years after the war many owners simply disposed of their scrapbooks either from disinterest or because they housed now unhappy memories. Still, scores survive. The Virginia Historical Society holds at least twenty of them. The Virginia Military Institute and Virginia Tech have several, and the Museum of the Confederacy has the most of all, with at least twenty-two scrapbooks that are in whole or part wartime compilations.

Most scrapbook keepers were women, like Richmond girl Lizzie Ellis Munford with her modest compilation of verses and mementoes.[8] Ellen Tompkins was just sixteen when she began compiling her commonplace book of clippings from Richmond papers.[9] At least one woman, Nannie E. Kent of Lynchburg, used her scrapbook not only for the usual clippings of verse and the like, but also as a copybook to preserve military orders issued by a local Confederate officer.[10] Other, male collectors were educators like Philip Barbour Ambler, an instructor at the Hollins Institute, a women's college in the Roanoke Valley. Addison Brown Roler, a student at the University of Virginia before he enlisted in July 1861, kept a scrapbook of articles on secession, the Union blockade, and foreign viewpoints on the war.[11]

Some Virginian scrapbooks are nothing short of Homeric in ambition. Virginia E. Price began keeping newspaper clippings, including battle reports, in 1861, and continued to do so through late 1864, compiling six scrapbook volumes that also included obituaries of Confederate luminaries and local Richmond soldiers, poetry and songs, official proclamations, and even a homemade silk miniature of the Confederate battle flag. Cassius F. Lee Jr. of Alexandria, cousin of Gen. Robert E. Lee, was even more ambitious. He began collecting at least as early as December 18, 1859, just days after the execution of John Brown for his raid on Harpers Ferry. He continued clipping articles and saving ephemera until September 17, 1863, and in the process put together a minimum of eighteen volumes of scrapbooks, chiefly of military and political content, some material drawn from Union as well as Virginian newspapers. So voluminous was his collecting that some volumes are filled just by clippings from a single month, and two volumes are devoted to February 1862. In Richmond, Petersburg, Staunton, Winchester, Alexandria—anywhere newspapers were available—Confederate citizens and a few soldiers were cutting out clippings and putting them in scrapbooks or holding them for a later opportunity, along with stamps, letters, even currency, especially when Confederate paper money ceased to have much value except as melancholy souvenirs. One man called his book "Confederate Scraps," while Edward T. George of King George County actually titled his compilation "Miscellaneous Clippings: A Scrapbook of Collections Made during the War of the Confederacy."

Very few soldiers in the field had the opportunity to keep scrapbooks, though many did clip newspapers articles and carry them with them, along with letters from home and a few other keepsakes. But space in the knapsack was limited, and the wear of constant packing and unpacking, soakings from river crossings, bleaching by the sun, and the like generally reduced paper items to tatters and shreds. Still, a few soldiers located out of the way in stationary defenses were able to keep the nucleus of scrapbooks occasionally. Holmes Conrad, who after the war was responsible for obtaining in a U.S. Supreme Court decision a substantial reparation from West Virginia to pay its share of the public debt of Virginia, intermittently kept a scrapbook during the time he was in the First Virginia Cavalry.[12]

Clippings and ephemera dealing with the loss of Gen. Thomas J. "Stonewall" Jackson seem to be the most common items to all of these scrapbooks, reflecting just how deeply his wounding and death affected Virginians. Certainly, they make up a large component in what might be taken as a typical example of a Virginian wartime scrapbook, the one kept in Richmond by Orrin L. Cottrell. The son of a city harness maker, he was only fifteen when the war began, thus too young yet to enlist. In 1864, aged eighteen, he took a job with the Confederate States Armory in Richmond, which made him exempt from the draft, but in that same year, like thousands of other government clerks and officeholders, he joined the local defense forces, becoming a private in Company B of the First Battalion Virginia Infantry Local Defense. During the balance of the war he occasionally left the city on armory business, and in the weeks immediately preceding the fall of the city on April 2, 1865, Cottrell was sent to Amelia Springs, very possibly in connection with the buildup of supplies there for Lee's army in anticipation of a retreat westward. After the war he went into the hardware business, and in the 1890s was a member of the executive committee of the Virginia Historical Society.[13]

The interest in history represented in Cottrell's latter-day involvement with the historical society is no doubt a reflection of an earlier passion that impelled him to become a collector of oddments and clippings, the raw material for his commonplace or scrapbook. Indeed, based on the arrangement of items in Cottrell's scrapbook, with newspaper clippings from the war years scattered and interspersed with items from many years afterward, it is evident that he kept his memorabilia unsorted and in raw form for years, both during the war and afterward, and then, perhaps in the 1870s, began to assemble it into the blank pages of an old ledger.

Some of the items reflected his wartime occupation. He kept passes issued by the armory and the Richmond provost marshal's office allowing him to enter and leave the city on business. He kept the passes allowing him travel on the Danville Railroad for his trips to Amelia Springs. Most of the wartime mementoes, however, were simply artifacts of living as a Confederate and a Richmonder. Like hundreds of scrapbook keepers, he filled many of his pages with Confederate Treasury notes left on hand at the collapse. He pasted nearly a hundred of them of all denominations, including banknotes from several of the Confederate state banks, and even scrip printed by localities. None of it was worth a cent after 1865, and much of it represented a nostalgic curiosity. Curiously, Cottrell also gathered a few early examples of postwar reproductions of Confederate money. He also had a Confederate cotton loan certificate from the February 20, 1863, issue of bonds, with all of the coupons still attached, showing that he had not had an opportunity to collect any of the interest that was due him on the note. His father's stock certificate for shares in the Bank of Richmond were somehow also destined to be worthless artifacts of the war, as were even receipts for deposits in the Virginia Savings Banks.

Then there were some things that would seem otherwise unusual had Cottrell not been living in Richmond. Somehow he came into possession of two receipts for provisions from the Chimborazo Hospital, one dated March 24, 1865, and the other one for the payment by the government of $1,070 on April 1. It may have been the last government funds actually paid out by that hospital before the collapse. It could have been the last payment of any kind by the government in Richmond. Whatever the case, Cottrell and the armory had no official reason for interaction with the hospital, and the payment was not to Cottrell himself. Most likely, these two receipts represent some of the tens of thousands of scraps of government paperwork that were scattered all over the city during the evacuation, much of it burned by fleeing Confederates, and the rest abandoned to the spreading fires and the wind.

There are items that one would expect to find in the scrapbook of many citizens of the Confederate capital, especially since the Richmond press dominated Confederate journalism overall. Newspapers would always contribute the great bulk of scrapbook contents. The text of Jefferson Davis's February 1862 inaugural speech appeared in a special edition of the *Examiner,* and Cottrell cut it out for safekeeping, including the ominous little news item at the end, used to fill out the column, announcing the evacuation of Nashville.

Naturally, some articles on war events especially interesting to Richmonders were included, especially coverage of the 1864 Kilpatrick-Dahlgren raid on the city that almost penetrated its environs, along with panicked rumors of plans to burn the capital, free Union prisoners in Libby Prison, and kill or kidnap Davis and his leaders. Stories of daring exploits were also wont to be clipped and saved, like the accounts of the cruise of the Confederate commerce raider *Tallahassee,* written by William Shepardson for the *Dispatch* in 1864. A few leaflets or broadsides of popular patriotic poetry were also collected, like "Farewell to the Star Spangled Banner," and broadsides and leaflets soliciting contributions for the care and comfort of sick soldiers. And Davis's February 10, 1864, exhortation to the soldiers of the Confederates thanking them for their massive reenlistments were certainly a worthy memento. Not surprisingly, Cottrell, like many other scrapbook keepers, selected articles on slavery, justifying its history and defending its beneficial nature. If the Yankees were going to try to link this war with slavery, then Confederates needed to be informed as to the true nature of the institution.

Equally typical, though, were the number of poems taken from the press, especially those dealing with death and dying, and the loss of loved ones, especially soldiers. In a culture obsessed with ritualized death and grieving, Richmond Confederates surrounded themselves with mementoes reminding them of life's transient nature. There were the leaflets hastily printed only hours after a death, announcing the event and inviting mourners to funeral ceremonies a day or two hence. There were obituaries from the newspapers and printed eulogies. So concerned were Richmond Confederates with death that scrapbooks also often included articles likes the ones in Cottrell's detailing rumored stories of bodies being mixed up and returned to the wrong widows and families.

Amid all this more conventional content, however, Cottrell showed an eye for comedy, satire, and the incongruous in wartime. Humor was formulaic, strained, and heavy-handed in those times, but it was what they laughed at. Cottrell was taken by a parody of the Lord's Prayer that began: "Our father who art in Washington, Abraham Lincoln be thy name . . ." When the *Dispatch* printed an acrostic in 1861 that took the first letters of Jefferson Davis's name to spell out a message welcoming the new president to Richmond, Cottrell thought it worthy of preserving. At the other end of the war, within a week of the fall of Richmond, Cottrell clipped another grim witticism from a Richmond paper, now censored by the Union. It read as an obituary: "Died on April 3d, 1865, Southern Confederacy, son of Jefferson Davis, aged three years and ten months. Died of strangulation. No funeral."

Occasionally Cottrell selected something that was purely outlandish, delicious for its wit as well as for its viciously mean underpinnings. Interestingly, one of the most avid scrapbook keepers in Virginia was himself a newspaperman, George W. Bagby, a popular freelance journalist who wrote essays and editorials for the Richmond papers but also for those elsewhere in the Confederacy. He specialized in biting and often venomous sarcasm, and so entertaining were his fulminations that they appeared not only in his own five volumes of scrapbooks compiled during the war but also in countless others all over the South.[14] Probably nothing else from his pen carried quite the venom as his essay "A Modest Proposal for the Relief of Richmond," which appeared in the *Examiner* on October 14, 1863, and which Cottrell duly clipped for his scrapbook. Bagby's satire identified several classes of individuals as the source of all the evils besetting the city and the Confederacy: prostitutes, Jews, unscrupulous restaurateurs, and Negroes. They were overcrowding the capital, so they should all be forced—six at a time—to live in empty barrels. The blacks did not have to be fed, for they could subsist on eating dirt. Gamblers and prostitutes would eat each other, the Jews would eat the restaurant keepers, and those who remained could subsist by eating the fattened Jews. The blacks, tired of eating dirt, would then eat the poor. Thus, he said, "the dangerous classes will be destroyed at a blow, and nobody left but Government and negroes." No one would eat the blacks, of course. It would be a social outrage given their inferiority, and also they were property and therefore worth something, as the gamblers, whores, Jews, and restaurants keepers were not. And for those poor not eaten, they could subsist on Confederate money, which was worthless for any other purpose he could imagine. Mixed with bacon rind and rolled in bran, the paper would be quite edible. "If Confederate notes will pass in no other way," he concluded, "they certainly will in this."

Cottrell, like many another scrapbook keeper, may not actually have thought of putting the items he collected into an organized commonplace book until after the war. Indeed, during the conflict he may have been too busy. But shortly after the war, even as he continued to clip articles and gather leaflets and other memorabilia, he found an unused ledger book and started the work, pasting in his wartime passes and documents first. Along with the Confederate money there was space for a few Confederate stamps, as there would be in the years ahead for some United States stamps as well, with no particular purpose evident, but that is in the nature of scrapbooks of the time.

Most of the wartime scrapbooks simply went into closets and bureau drawers after the war, though many Virginians continued to add to them in after years, mostly with clippings dealing with wartime reminiscences, veterans' events, or monument dedications. Cottrell's scrapbook, for instance, is more than half filled with postwar clippings and materials. He added obituary and funeral notices of friends and fellow Richmond citizens and a few things dealing with postwar life, but mostly he included articles dealing with the Confederate experience. Indeed, perhaps more Virginia scrapbooks covering the conflict were started after the war than during it. The state's presses, especially in Richmond, turned out innumerable articles on battles and campaigns, reminiscences by officers and men, and even more on the deaths of great chieftains like Jackson and J. E. B. "Jeb" Stuart. The surrender at Appomattox became a special subject for endless print, and for Richmonders especially the evacuation and fall of the Confederate capital attracted a lot of work with the scissors. At the same time, Cottrell included quite a bit of coverage on Union loyalists in Richmond during the war—called "ferrets" afterward—and the presumed outrages of the Reconstruction regime, and even some interesting tidbits on the rise of Civil War tourism as visitors came to the Old Dominion seeking war relics.

Anything on a Confederate anniversary celebration, a veterans' gathering, or a monument dedication was fair game for his pages. Cottrell, at least, even made space in his pages for a March 1865 obituary of John M. Daniel, editor of the *Richmond Examiner,* a man whose work had produced a great deal of the fodder that fed Virginian scrapbooks. Not surprisingly, Cottrell pasted in a copy of a December 1865 letter that appeared in the press written by Gen. Jubal A. Early from exile in Havana. Not only did Early defend his unsuccessful late-war career, but he also begged Southerners and the nations of the world "not to commit the further injustice of receiving the history of this struggle from the mouths and pens of our enemies." He would spend the rest of his life creating and promoting his own version of the war story, and Cottrell and almost all other scrapbook keepers were willing accomplices when they pasted down articles by Early and others revealing the beginnings and development of the Lost Cause myth that was to prevail in the state and the South for most of the next century. Gettysburg especially predominated in interest, as writers sought to explain away the defeat, arguing that it should have been the victory that won Southern independence, while generals expostulated at length trying to explain away their defeats or shift blame to others. In preserving history, Confederate veterans—and Confederate scrapbook keepers—were also shaping it in the image they preferred.

At least one wartime commonplace book was actually published, Lizzie Daniel Cary's *Confederate Scrap-Book,* which came off the presses of the J. L. Hill Printing Company in Richmond in 1893. The publisher declared that it was "copied from a Scrap-book kept by a young girl during and immediately after the war, with additions from war copies of the 'Southern Literary Messenger' and '[Southern] Illustrated News' loaned by friends, and other selections as accredited." Not surprisingly, she brought it out of safekeeping to help raise money for a Confederate memorial fund.

Few of the scrapbook keepers had fought in the war. Most of them watched it from the sidelines, forced to experience the conflict vicariously, their battlefields a sheet of newsprint, their weapons penknife and scissors, their casualties the news of the loss of friends and family that they found in their newspapers. Yet, ironically, they performed a great service for Confederate posterity, if not for the wartime effort itself, and not just in raising funds for memorials. Not only did they preserve the story of the war as Confederate Virginians wanted it to be remembered with their postwar clippings. They also saved much of the actual history of the war itself. Hundreds of journals ceased publishing during the war, and many of them saw virtually all extant copies of their issues disappear in the years following. There are Confederate—and Virginian—newspapers from the 1860s from which not a single issue survives. But in the articles laboriously clipped and pasted into scrapbooks by these earnest civilians, invaluable material otherwise lost can still be found—battle reports, official communications, casualty lists, letters from commanders, even serialized contemporary accounts of campaigns, not to mention all that appeared to reveal the hardships endured by civilians on the home front. The result is that the Virginian scrapbook is like history itself—flawed, incomplete, highly biased, and yet indispensable in understanding the experience of the population of the Old Dominion in its most trying time.

Notes

The author would like to thank John Coski, Robert K. Krick, and Robert E. L. Krick for their advice and assistance with this essay.

1. http://www.pagesoftheheart.net/artman/publish/article_727.shtml.

2. Craig R. Thompson, *Schools in Tudor England* (Washington, D.C.: Folger Shakespeare Library, 1958), 16.

3. http://oll.libertyfund.org/Texts/Locke0154/Works/HTMLs/0128-02_Pt07_CPBook.html#hd_lf128.2.head.056.

4. Noble E. Cunningham, *In Pursuit of Reason: The Life of Thomas Jefferson* (Baton Rouge: Louisiana State University Press, 1987), 9.

5. http://lmm.confederationcentre.com/english/learning/learning-4.html.

6. http://www.littlebit.com/ideas_scrap/history_scrap.htm.

7. Joseph C. G. Kennedy, *Preliminary Report on the Eighth Census, 1860* (Washington, D.C.: Government Printing Office, 1862), 103, 211.

8. Munford-Ellis Family Papers, Duke University, Durham, North Carolina.

9. Tompkins Family Papers, Virginia Historical Society, Richmond.

10. Nannie E. Kent Scrapbook, Virginia Historical Society.

11. Addison Brown Roler Scrapbook, 1861, Virginia Historical Society.

12. The scrapbooks referenced here are all at the Museum of the Confederacy in Richmond, Virginia. The author is indebted to John Coski for his assistance in surveying the museum's scrapbook holdings.

13. 1850, 1860, 1880 U.S. Census, Hanover County, Virginia; Orrin L. Cottrell Scrapbook, in possession of the author.

14. Bagby's scrapbooks are in the Bagby Family Papers at the Virginia Historical Society in Richmond.

"Lincoln acted the clown"

Virginia's Newspapers and the Gettysburg Address
Jared Peatman

By the fall of 1863, Richmond, Virginia, was the heart and soul of the Confederacy. Richmond housed the Confederate government, was the home to the South's most famous and successful army, and was economically the most important city in the eleven seceded states. During the war Richmond's population swelled from 37,000 in 1860 to more than 100,000 at the peak of the war. Due to these factors, the newspapers of the city dominated those of the Confederacy, particularly when it came to reporting Northern events. However, in the fall of 1863 the Richmond press failed its readers by inaccurately reporting the dedication of the Soldiers' National Cemetery in Gettysburg, Pennsylvania, and Lincoln's Gettysburg Address. While early reports of the event confused Lincoln's role at Gettysburg, later editorials omitted the words that Lincoln spoke. An analysis of what the editors said, how they covered Lincoln's other major speeches, and the individual biographies of the editors and papers indicates that the Richmond press dismissed the Gettysburg Address because of Lincoln's statements on equality and freedom. Examining the spread of reporting about the dedication ceremonies throughout the state and eventually the rest of the South shows the reliance of the Confederate press on the Richmond papers. As a result, the editors of the five major Richmond newspapers had an enormous impact on the way the Gettysburg Address was reported in Virginia and throughout the Confederacy.

When the Battle of Gettysburg concluded on July 3, 1863, thousands of corpses lay on the formerly peaceful farms. Pennsylvania governor Andrew Curtin visited a week later and appointed local lawyer David Wills to arrange for the interment of the Keystone State's fallen sons. Before the summer ended the cemetery had become national in scope, and Governor Curtin asked Wills to turn his attention to "the proper consecration of the grounds."[1]

On Wills's behalf, Boston mayor F. W. Lincoln visited Edward Everett, a nationally renowned orator and statesman, on September 23 and privately inquired whether he would be willing to prepare and deliver an oration at the dedication of the cemetery. Everett indicated his acceptance, and that same day David Wills sent a formal invitation. In response to Wills's letter Everett replied that he would be happy to speak at the ceremonies but could not possibly be prepared before November 19. Wills agreed to the date.[2]

Wills sent Lincoln a formal letter on November 2 asking him to attend the ceremonies, noting, "[I]t is the desire that, after the Oration, You as Chief Executive of the Nation formally set apart these grounds to their Sacred use by a few appropriate remarks."[3] Historians have traditionally cited this last-minute letter as the first time that Lincoln was approached about participating in the dedication ceremonies, but that may not be the case.

On August 28 Curtin visited President Lincoln in Washington, D.C., to discuss draft quotas for Pennsylvania. However, if the same method was employed to ask Lincoln to participate in the ceremonies as was used with Everett in September, it is likely that Curtin extended an invitation to Lincoln at this late-summer meeting. Between August 28 and November 2 there were no recorded meetings between Lincoln and anyone else in a position to ask him to speak at Gettysburg, increasing the likelihood that he and Curtin had discussed the dedication ceremonies and Lincoln's potential role in them on August 28. Lincoln never responded in writing to Wills's letter of November 2, likely because he had already committed himself to attending the ceremonies. Furthermore, on October 13, nearly three weeks before the formal invitation, the *Philadelphia Inquirer* reported that David Wills had told its Baltimore correspondent that Lincoln was "expected to perform the consecrational service" at the dedication ceremonies.[4]

For more than a century historians have argued that Lincoln was asked to speak at the ceremonies as an afterthought, that his presence was not exactly welcomed by those in charge of planning the ceremony, and that he had no time to prepare an address until the day before the dedication.[5] If Lincoln had been asked to participate in the ceremonies as early as August 28, then clearly he was not an afterthought, and in fact was likely the first person asked to participate in the ceremonies. And if this is so, there can be no question about the planners' desire to have Lincoln at the ceremonies given the early date they approached him. Lastly, Lincoln certainly had time to prepare his thoughts before giving the address, making the stories of his cobbling the speech together at the last minute highly unlikely. Rarely during the war did Lincoln leave Washington, D.C., indicating that he viewed this as an important event and one to be taken seriously.[6]

President Lincoln arrived in Gettysburg at dinnertime on November 18, 1863. Before long, a crowd gathered outside the house where he was staying and began calling for a speech. Lincoln came to a second-floor window and spoke to those below:

> I appear before you, fellow-citizens, merely to thank you for this compliment. The inference is a very fair one that you would hear me for a little while at least, were I to commence to make a speech. I do not appear before you for the purpose of doing so, and for several very substantial reasons. The most substantial of these is that I have no speech to make. [Laughter.] In my position it is somewhat important that I should not say any foolish things.
>
> A VOICE—If you can help it.
>
> MR. LINCOLN—It very often happens that the only way to help it is to say nothing at all. [Laughter.] Believing this is my present condition this evening, I must beg of you to excuse me from addressing you further.

Lincoln then "retired amidst loud cheers," not knowing that these remarks would be reported and perceived to be *the* Gettysburg Address by some. After dinner, Lincoln retired to his room and refined the remarks he had planned for the next day.[7]

At 10:00 on the morning of November 19, Lincoln took his place in the parade that would travel a half mile from the center of Gettysburg to the cemetery. A little more than an hour later, the procession arrived at the cemetery, and Lincoln took his seat on the speakers' platform. The program of events called for music, a prayer, more music, Edward Everett's two-hour oration, more music, and then "Dedicatory Remarks, by the President of the United States."[8] Holding the text of his remarks in his hands, Lincoln began to speak:

Four score and seven years ago our fathers brought forth upon this continent a new Nation, conceived in Liberty, and dedicated to the proposition that all men are created equal. [Applause.] Now we are engaged in a great civil war, testing whether that Nation, or any Nation so conceived and so dedicated, can long endure. We are met on a great battle-field of that war. We are met to dedicate a portion of it as the final resting-place of those who here gave their lives that that nation might live. It is altogether fitting and proper that we should do this. But in a larger sense we cannot dedicate, we cannot consecrate, we cannot hallow this ground. The brave men living and dead who struggled here have consecrated it, far above our power to add or detract. [Applause.] The world will little note nor long remember what we say here, but it can never forget what they did here. [Applause.] It is for us, the living, rather to be dedicated here to the unfinished work that they have thus far so nobly carried on. [Applause.] It is rather for us to be here dedicated to the great task remaining before us, that from these honored dead we take increased devotion to that cause for which they here gave the last full measure of devotion; that we here highly resolve that the dead shall not have died in vain; that the nation shall, under God, have a new birth of freedom; and that Governments of the people, by the people, and for the people shall not perish from this earth. [Long-continued applause.][9]

After more music, a benediction brought the ceremonies to a close three hours after they had begun.[10]

Joseph Gilbert of the Associated Press was the most prominent reporter at the dedication ceremonies. As Lincoln spoke, Gilbert recorded the address in shorthand, or at least as much of it as he could. Upon the completion of the ceremonies Gilbert looked at Lincoln's original manuscript and corrected his version against that document. As it was Gilbert's report that would eventually find its way to the Richmond papers via the *New York Herald,* it is his transcription of the Gettysburg Address that is reprinted above.[11] Many of the major Northern newspapers had already received an advance copy of Edward Everett's printed oration, which Gilbert embellished with a full account of the ceremonies delivered to the subscribers of the Associated Press by telegraph that night. The following day the *New York Herald* was one of the several papers that used Gilbert's account.[12] The *Herald* had the largest circulation of any paper in North America, with a daily subscription rate of 75,000, about half again that of the *Times* of London and more than four times that of the *Richmond Dispatch,* Richmond's most popular paper.[13]

On November 20, 1863, the *Herald* covered the dedication ceremonies on pages 3–5 before breaking and finishing the coverage on page 10. A large map on the third page is entitled "The American Necropolis," with the ensuing column entitled "The National Necropolis." The term *necropolis* means a large, elaborate cemetery. That column includes the following subheads:

THE NATIONAL NECROPOLIS.
Our Heroic Dead at Gettysburg.
Consecration of a National Cemetery for the Union Soldiers who Fell There.
Arrival of the President and Cabinet.
Speeches by Mr. Lincoln, Mr. Seward and Gov. Seymour.
SOLEMN AND IMPRESSIVE CEREMONY.
Imposing Civil and Military Procession.
THE CROWDS OF THE BATTLE FIELD.
ORATION BY EDWARD EVERETT.
History of the Three Days' Fighting at Gettysburg.
Upon Whom the Responsibility of the War Rests.
The Question of the Restoration of Concord Between the North and the South,
&c., &c., &c.,

On the fourth page the *Herald* reported the brief words Lincoln spoke on November 18 under the headline, "SERENADE TO THE PRESIDENT—HIS SPEECH." Following this brief report is an account of the procession to the ceremony and then six columns containing the text of "MR. EVERETT'S ORATION." With the conclusion of Everett's speech, the paper announced that coverage of the events continued on page 10. It was not until that tenth page that the November 19 remarks of President Lincoln were reprinted, accurately and with breaks for applause.

Over the next few days an edition of the November 20 *New York Herald* made its way south, most likely passed through the lines during a prisoner exchange, and arrived in Richmond by the night of November 23. The content of the Richmond newspapers over the next few days make it clear that all the pertinent pages made it to Richmond intact, including the tenth page containing the text of the Gettysburg Address.[14]

On November 24, 1863, the *Richmond Dispatch, Richmond Examiner, Richmond Sentinel,* and *Richmond Whig* all carried the exact same account of the ceremonies at Gettysburg:

> Several columns of the *Herald* are occupied with a description of the "National Necropolis," or cemetery at Gettysburg. Lincoln, [Secretary of State William H.] Seward, several foreign ministers, and other dignitaries were present. Lincoln was serenaded the night preceding the day on which the ceremony took place. He declined to make a speech on the ground that "in his position it was somewhat important that he should not say foolish things." A voice—"If you can help it." Lincoln—"It very often happens that the only way to help it is to say nothing at all." [Laughter.]
>
> Seward was also serenaded and responded in an anti-slavery speech. He thanked God for the hope that when slavery is abolished the country will be again united.
>
> The notorious [John H.] Forney was also serenaded. In his speech he declared that he was in favor of Lincoln's election in 1860, but did not want it to appear so, that he might the better accomplish the breaking up of the Democracy.
>
> Everett's oration is published at length in the *Herald,* occupying six columns of small type. He predicted the reconstruction of the Union.[15]

The coverage of that event was part of a much longer column of general news from the North. It is difficult to know exactly where this account originated, but the author was likely John Graeme Jr., the Richmond agent of the Confederate Press Association.

In 1860 the major Southern newspapers belonged to the Associated Press, but the inauguration of war ended that affiliation. In the early spring of 1863, several major Southern daily newspapers formed the Press Association of the Confederate States of America (also known as the Confederate Press Association). By May 1863 forty-four of the Confederacy's papers belonged, including all the Richmond newspapers except the *Sentinel.* Because of the importance of Richmond, the Confederate Press Association hired John Graeme Jr. to be their Richmond agent to facilitate the gathering of news in the Confederacy's most important city. The article in the Richmond papers on November 24 was clearly a product of the Confederate Press Association, making it likely that it was Graeme who wrote the piece.[16]

Graeme's account was fewer than two hundred words in length and spent all but two sentences discussing the events that occurred on the night of November 18. The only mention of the November 19 ceremonies was a statement that Everett "predicted the reconstruction of the Union." Nearly all of the information discussed in this account came directly from the subheads at the top of the *New York Herald*'s coverage on page 3.

It is difficult to escape the impression that Graeme did little more than skim the report in the *New York Herald,* relied mainly on the subheads, and either did not read or ignored the page that discussed Abraham Lincoln's part in the ceremonies.[17] Perhaps the sentence that Everett's oration consumed "six columns of small type" in the *New York Herald* explains why Graeme passed over the small column on Lincoln. The editor of the *Richmond Dispatch* commented that the news from the North, including Graeme's account, was "not of much interest."[18]

The *Richmond Examiner* of November 25, 1863, offered some of the most extensive reporting of the events accompanying the dedication ceremonies. Noting an abundance of coverage in the "Yankee papers," the *Examiner* promised "to give only the portion of their accounts likely to interest our readers."[19] The *Examiner*'s article on the ceremonies was a reflection of its editor, John Moncure Daniel. Daniel was born in Stafford County, Virginia, on October 24, 1825. After stints reading the law in Fredericksburg and serving as a librarian in Richmond, Daniel found his true calling as a journalist, first for the *Southern Planter* and then for the *Richmond Examiner.* He was a polarizing figure, and as a result of his staunchly Democratic editorials, Daniel fought several duels before and during the war.[20]

In 1853 Daniel became minister to the court of Victor Emmanuel in Turin, Italy. While in Turin, Daniel was sued for libel by a New Yorker on the basis of an editorial he had written before leaving Richmond. Daniel lost the case and was forced to pay several thousand dollars in damages. The outcome of the trial unfavorably disposed Daniel to the North and its citizens, a prejudice that frequently appeared in his writings. The Virginian returned home at the beginning of the Civil War and cast his lot with his native state.

He joined the Confederate army and was eventually assigned to Maj. Gen. A. P. Hill's staff, where he served until wounded during the Seven Days' battles in June 1862. His injury made it impossible for Daniel to continue to serve in the field, and he returned to the editor's desk at the *Richmond Examiner,* a paper he owned. Daniel was an unorthodox editor in that he wrote few of the editorials that appeared in the *Examiner.* He preferred to let others compose the pieces and then edited them so heavily that at times they were unrecognizable to their authors. Nothing made it into the *Examiner* that Daniel did not approve. Daniel was a known racist and supporter of slavery, leaving little doubt that he would have found repugnant Lincoln's assertion in the Gettysburg Address that "all men are created equal," and disdained the call for a "new birth of freedom."[21]

Daniel's biases manifested themselves in his editorial on the Gettysburg Address. The first part of the editorial was a straightforward recounting, in remarkable detail, of the parade on the morning of November 19. The *Examiner* notes that Dr. Thomas Stockton's prayer, the oration by Edward Everett, and the address of Lincoln had already been reported. In fact nowhere in prior editions of any Richmond newspapers did these accounts appear. In contrast to the lack of coverage of these three central speeches is the full reprinting of a dirge that was sung at the conclusion of Lincoln's remarks and a verbatim recounting of the benediction that concluded the ceremonies. Following a description of the cemetery was "LINCOLN'S RECEPTION AT GETTYSBURG—HE MAKES A SPEECH." Yet rather than the Gettysburg Address, the subject of this section was Lincoln's few remarks of November 18. While complimenting the crowd that serenaded Lincoln for its respect and orderliness, Daniel chided Lincoln for behaving in a "humorous manner" despite the obvious "solemnity and reverence" that such a place and occasion deserved. Three days later, the *Examiner* condemned the ceremonies as "the substitution of glittering foil and worthless paste for real brilliants and pure gold." In Daniel's opinion, Lincoln was fool's gold. The paper added, "The Yankees have an invincible conviction that they are the successors of the Romans in empire, and of the Athenians in genius." Edward Everett "'took down his THUCYDIDES,' and fancied himself a PERICLES . . . the play was strictly classic." Classic, at least, until Lincoln took the stage: "A vein of comedy was permitted to mingle with the deep pathos of the piece. This singular novelty, and the deviation from classic propriety, was heightened by assigning this part to the chief personage. Kings are usually made to speak in the magniloquent language supposed to be suited to their elevated position. On the present occasion Lincoln acted the clown." However, the following line asserts that Lincoln "declined to speak for fear he should perpetrate a folly," revealing that the speech in question was that of November 18. The following sentences confirm that point by mentioning the disappointment of the crowd that Lincoln would not speak. The editorial also pointed out the comments of the heckler who joked that Lincoln "could only avoid talking nonsense by holding his tongue." What at first appeared to be an evaluation of the Gettysburg Address quickly revealed itself instead as a reference to Lincoln's November 18 remarks. Rather than giving a magnificent address, Lincoln was portrayed to have muttered only insignificant words inappropriate for the occasion.[22]

On November 25, the *Richmond Dispatch* published an account of "THE GETTYSBURG CEMETERY CELEBRATION—THE SPEECHES." It appears that the *Dispatch* obtained a copy of the *New York Herald* the day after the initial report on the dedication. Derisively calling the ceremonies "entirely Yankee-ish," the paper gave a rundown of the speeches on November 18, including the full text of Lincoln's comments and a summary of the speech by William Seward before reprinting parts of Edward Everett's November 19 oration.[23] The *Richmond Dispatch* was founded on October 19, 1850. Unlike the other Richmond papers, the *Dispatch* was not affiliated with a particular political party, vowing that news would not be subordinated to politics. The *Dispatch* cost only a penny, and quickly attracted the younger crowd in the city and surrounding areas. By 1860 it had a circulation of 18,000, the largest of any paper in the state, and was probably the third largest daily in the South, just behind two of the New Orleans papers.[24]

The *Richmond Dispatch* focused most of its editorial on "Edward Everett, of 'Boasting' [Boston], that secondary and most disgusting edition and representative of the Pilgrim Fathers." In his speech, Everett had contended that he did not believe "there has been a day since the election of President Lincoln when, if an ordinance of secession could have been fairly submitted to the mass of the people, in any single Southern State a majority of ballots would have been given in its favor." This predictably drew fire from the editor of the *Dispatch*, who noted that "the stiff corpses of one thousand two hundred and eight eighty [*sic*] men lying in a semi-circle around him, killed dead" served the "purpose of giving the lie to all such statements." The editor was somewhat disingenuous in his assertion that Virginians were united on the question of secession. Virginia had been one of the last states to secede, and the *Dispatch* itself had not fully supported secession until 1861. Two years into the war, however, those past vacillations were glossed over in the name of Confederate unity. The account ended after discussing Everett's oration, making no mention of Lincoln's speech on November 19.[25]

Edward Everett was despised by many Virginians long before his comments at Gettysburg. In 1860 Everett had been the vice presidential candidate on John Bell's Constitutional-Union ticket, which sought to decrease sectional tensions and avoid war by a strict adherence to the Constitution. Bell and Everett won the electoral votes of two states: Kentucky and Virginia. However, once the war began Everett threw his support behind Lincoln and the war to preserve the Union. The man that many Virginians had voted for as their choice to hold the second-highest office in the nation had turned his back on them. In short, Southern comments about Everett's oration may have had as much to do with his past as with his words at Gettysburg.[26] On November 27, Edward Everett was the subject of the editor's column in the *Richmond Dispatch*. "Everett's oration at Gettysburg is what might have been expected of that unreal, metaphorical, moonlight orator. It matters little to him what the facts [might be]." The editor dedicated the entire column to further chastising Everett's statement questioning Southern support of secession. Much like the *Richmond Examiner,* the *Dispatch* editor censored any mention of Lincoln's role in the dedication ceremonies, and offered no commentary on his speech.[27]

The *Richmond Enquirer* was the oldest of the Richmond newspapers, having been founded on May 9, 1804. A prewar Democratic paper, the *Enquirer* in 1863 was owned and edited by Nathaniel Tyler and William J. Dunnavant.[28] On November 27 the paper reported that Lincoln had played a part in the dedication ceremonies, and it was the first Richmond newspaper to print a direct reaction to Lincoln's speech of November 19. The paper identified Lincoln as the "stage manager and Edward Everett as the 'Orator of the day.'" It further commented that "Mr. Everett produced the expected allusions to Marathon and Waterloo, in the best style of the sophomores of Harvard." Edward Everett had attended Harvard, taught at the university, and served as its president for three years in the 1840s, making the reference personal and pointed. "After the Orator of the day, President Pericles, or rather Abe, made the dedicatory speech; but had to limit his observations within small compass, lest he should tell some funny story over the graves of the Immortals." In stating that Lincoln spoke after Edward Everett, the *Enquirer* demonstrated an understanding of Lincoln's role in the ceremonies on November 19. The *Enquirer* did not respond to the content of Lincoln's speech, instead dismissing it out of hand because of its brevity.[29]

Two of Richmond's daily newspapers, the *Whig* and the *Sentinel,* carried the Confederate Press Association account of the cemetery dedication on November 24 but offered no further reporting on the event. While the other three Richmond papers all printed at least one other substantial article on the dedication ceremonies, none of the papers reprinted the words that Lincoln spoke at the dedication ceremonies. This was a marked contrast to their coverage of Lincoln's two inaugural addresses. In both 1861 and 1865 the *Richmond Dispatch* reprinted Lincoln's inaugurals. In 1861 the paper offered substantial commentary on the event, while the reporting was more descriptive in nature in 1865.[30] In both the inaugurals and the Gettysburg Address, Lincoln advocated a strong national government and indicated his personal opposition to slavery, stances that most Southerners opposed, but only in the Gettysburg Address did Lincoln implicitly declare that whites and African Americans were "equal." Is it mere coincidence that Richmond's papers did not reprint the speech containing this assertion, even though the text was available to them? As is often the case, what the newspapers did not report is as important as what they did.

From Richmond the news of the events at Gettysburg and Lincoln's role spread to the rest of the state and Confederacy. On November 27, 1863, the *Lynchburg Virginian* offered extensive reporting on "THE CEM-ETERY—SPEECH AND WIT OF LINCOLN." The account occupied a full column with details of the procession to the cemetery. After describing the parade, the *Virginian* explained, "The dedication ceremonies were then performed, the oration being delivered by Edward Everett, after which the crowd dispersed." The article then gave a description of the cemetery itself. This account is full of details, making it remarkable that it contains no mention of the part played by President Lincoln. The reference in the headline to the speech by Lincoln was to an entirely different event that had taken place on November 18 in Hanover, Pennsylvania, before Lincoln even arrived in Gettysburg. Throughout this column there is no mention of the sources used to compile the account.[31]

The editors corrected their earlier omission in the December 4, 1863, edition of the *Virginian.* The editorial that day was titled "Old Abe's Last." Taking their account from the *New York World,* the editors quoted the opening sentence of Lincoln's Gettysburg Address. The *Virginian* was the only newspaper in the state to reprint any of Lincoln's actual words on November 19. Despite reporting part of Lincoln's oration, the Lynchburg editor thought no more of Lincoln than his Richmond colleagues: "Really, the ignorance and coarseness of this man would repel and disgust any other people than the Yankees. . . . What a commentary is this on the character of our enemies."[32]

The *Staunton Vindicator* of December 4 provided additional comments on Everett and his "unkind criticism" of the South based wholly on the reporting of the *Richmond Dispatch*. Noting that "many of our contemporaries are much disturbed at the consecration of the field at Gettysburg as a huge Yankee Necropolis and give vent to unkind criticism of the part taken by Edward Everett," the *Vindicator* editor offered a sarcastic invitation for Everett to come dedicate the final resting places of Union soldiers who had fallen in Virginia. There were a good many, the editor noted, and there would be more if the North continued the war. The entire column in the *Staunton Vindicator* centered on the role of Edward Everett in the dedication ceremonies. Not once did Abraham Lincoln's name appear.[33] The other Staunton paper, the *Staunton Spectator,* offered no comment on the dedication ceremonies or Lincoln's address.

The piece authored by John Graeme Jr. of the Confederate Press Association appeared in papers across the South over the following ten days. On November 24, the *Atlanta Daily Constitutionalist, Atlanta Southern Confederacy, Augusta (Ga.) Daily Chronicle & Sentinel, Macon Telegraph, Memphis Appeal, Mobile Daily Advertiser and Register,* and *Savannah Daily Morning News* carried an abbreviated version of Graeme's account that stated: "Several columns of the Herald are occupied with an account of the dedication of the national Necropolis at Gettysburg. Lincoln was serenaded the night previous, but declined to make any speech, saying that in his position it was important that he should not say any foolish things. [A voice—'If you can help it.' Lincoln—'It often happens the best way is to say nothing.']"

The formatting of these accounts varied slightly, but the wording was the same. The November 24 *Daily Journal,* published in Wilmington, North Carolina, carried substantially the same account with a few changes in wording. That same day the *Daily South Carolinian* carried an even more abbreviated version. "Several columns in the *Herald* is [sic] occupied with an account of the dedication of the National Necropolis at Gettysburg."

The *Charleston Mercury, Atlanta Daily Intelligencer,* and Atlanta's *Daily Constitutionalist* all carried Graeme's full account, the *Mercury* and *Daily Constitutionalist* on November 27 and the *Daily Intelligencer* on November 29. The November 27 edition of the *Augusta (Ga.) Daily Chronicle & Sentinel* carried an account so abbreviated it did not even mention the small detail that Lincoln had been present at the dedication.

A few days after these telegraphic accounts appeared, Southern newspapers began to receive copies of the Richmond papers. They were quick to plagiarize their Virginia brethren. This was nothing new during the Civil War era; George Smalley's account of the battle of Antietam originally appeared in the *New York Tribune* but was reportedly reprinted by 1,400 newspapers. According to one authority, in order to put together the paper for each day's edition, the editor "would first select two important newspapers from each of the larger cities represented among his newspaper exchanges and clip a dozen or so small articles . . . then he would clip articles for solid matter, leaving just enough space for the lead editorial."[34]

On November 30, the *Memphis Appeal* reprinted the *Richmond Enquirer*'s account of three days earlier. On December 2, the *Atlanta Daily Intelligencer* carried that same account. The *Macon Telegraph* reprinted the account from the November 25, 1863, *Richmond Dispatch*. The *Mobile Daily Advertiser and Register* reprinted another account from the *Richmond Dispatch*. None of these papers wrote their own editorials about the events surrounding the dedication of the Soldiers' National Cemetery and Lincoln's Gettysburg Address. Instead, they simply reprinted articles from the Richmond newspapers. It is a telling indication of the influence the Richmond editors had over the Southern press, and shows that when it comes to Southern reporting on the Gettysburg Address, one need look no farther than the city of Richmond.

In many ways this is not surprising. Following the battle of Chancellorsville in May 1863, two papers, the *Savannah Republican* and the *Wilmington Daily Journal,* both complained that the Richmond papers had not printed the casualty lists of out-of-state regiments or discussed their roles in the battle. Rather, they focused on Virginia regiments. It is clear that these two papers thought the Richmond press should be national in scope, much like today's *New York Times* or *Washington Post*.[35]

While all the Richmond papers mentioned the events in Pennsylvania, it seems as though few people paid any attention to those stories. Jefferson Davis offered no preserved comments on the address. The same can be said for John B. Jones, the famous Confederate War Department diarist who wrote about nearly everything newsworthy during the war. Josiah Gorgas, head of Confederate ordnance, was also silent on the Gettysburg Address, as were the famous women diarists Mary Chesnut and Judith McGuire.[36] Yet Southern readers were used to news stories about Abraham Lincoln. Virginia newspapers mentioned Lincoln in nearly every issue, eventually desensitizing their readers to stories about the Union president. One such example is a December 8, 1863, article from the *Richmond Dispatch,* which notes, "Yankee papers say that 'Lincoln has got the varioloid,'" and wondered, "what the varioloid has done that Lincoln should 'get it,' we cannot imagine, but it is just like Lincoln to seize some harmless object, and just like the Yankee papers to make a grand fuss over it."[37] With daily articles like this, it is little wonder that most readers found Southern reporting of the dedication ceremonies to be nothing out of the ordinary.

As a result of the censorship by the Richmond editors, Virginians and Southerners in 1863 had no idea what Lincoln said at the dedication of the cemetery in Gettysburg. The November 20, 1863, edition of the *New York Herald* that arrived in Richmond by November 23 carried four full pages of coverage on the dedication of the Soldiers' National Cemetery in Gettysburg, including the full text of Lincoln's speech. While the Richmond papers reprinted some of the dirges and excerpts of the other speeches at the dedication ceremonies, they never provided their readers any hint of what Lincoln said in his Gettysburg Address. Lincoln's affirmation "that all men are created equal" and his call for "a new birth of freedom" linked his words at Gettysburg to the Emancipation Proclamation. As a result, the Richmond editors lampooned Lincoln's appearance and words without ever telling their readers what those words were. The domination of the Richmond press ensured that it was their version of the ceremonies that would be disseminated throughout the Confederacy, condemning Lincoln's most famous speech to obscurity in the wartime Confederacy.

Notes

1. *Revised Report of the Select Committee Relative to the Soldiers' National Cemetery Together with the House of Representatives and the Commonwealth of Pennsylvania* (Harrisburg, Penn.: Singerly and Myers, 1865), 161–67.

2. Ibid., 184; *Edward Everett at Gettysburg* (Boston: N.p., 1863), 1.

3. David Wills to Lincoln, November 2, 1863, Robert Todd Lincoln Papers, Library of Congress, Washington, D.C.

4. The only other person who may have been in a position to speak with Lincoln about participating in the dedication ceremonies was Massachusetts governor John Andrew. Andrew visited Lincoln at the White House on September 14, 1863. It is not known what they discussed. Lincoln Sesquicentennial Commission, *Lincoln Day by Day: A Chronology, 1809–1865,* ed. Earl Schenck Miers (Washington, D.C.: Lincoln Sesquicentennial Commission, 1960), 3:204, 207; *Philadelphia Inquirer,* October 13, 1863.

5. See, for example, William E. Barton, *Lincoln at Gettysburg: What He Intended to Say; What He Said; What He Was Reported to Have Said; What He Wished He Had Said* (New York: P. Smith, 1930), 48; and Ward Hill Lamon, *Recollections of Abraham Lincoln, 1847–1865,* ed. Dorothy Lamon Teillard (Washington, D.C.: The editor, 1911), 172–73.

6. *Revised Report,* 161–65.

7. *New York Herald,* November 20, 1863; Barton, *Lincoln at Gettysburg,* 59–61, 191.

8. *Revised Report,* 177–78.

9. Abraham Lincoln, *The Collected Works of Abraham Lincoln,* ed. Roy P. Basler, Marion Dolores Pratt, and Lloyd A. Dunlap (New Brunswick, N.J.: Rutgers University Press, 1953–1955), 7:19–21.

10. Louis Austin Warren, *Lincoln's Gettysburg Declaration: "A New Birth of Freedom"* (Fort Wayne, Ind.: Lincoln National Life Foundation, 1964), 130–31, 136.

11. Lincoln, *Collected Works,* 7:19–21.

12. Barton, *Lincoln at Gettysburg,* 15.

13. James M. Lee, *History of American Journalism* (Boston: Houghton, Mifflin, 1917), 284.

14. On November 27 the *Richmond Enquirer* reprinted part of a dirge that had been sung at Gettysburg, a dirge whose lyrics first appeared on the tenth page of the *New York Herald* of November 20 right next to the text of the Gettysburg Address, indicating that the editor of the *Enquirer,* and likely all of the Richmond editors, had to have seen the speech.

15. This account is from the November 24, 1863, editions of the *Richmond Examiner, Richmond Sentinel,* and *Richmond Whig.* The *Richmond Dispatch* carried the exact same account with one exception; it noted the year as 1864. The only Richmond daily that did not carry the account was the *Richmond Enquirer.*

16. Ford Risely, "The Confederate Press Association: Cooperative News Reporting of the War," *Civil War History* 47 (2001): 224–28; J. Cutler Andrews, *The South Reports the Civil War* (Princeton, N.J.: Princeton University Press, 1970), 44, 56–57.

17. Graeme is not the only person to have missed the part of the *New York Herald* containing Lincoln's Gettysburg Address. In his 1963 work on the Gettysburg Address, *The Enduring Impact of Lincoln's Gettysburg Address* (Philadelphia: Privately printed, 1963), Herman Blum said that the *Herald* "mentioned the address as the 'dedicatory remarks of the President,' without reporting what he said" (10).

18. *Richmond Dispatch,* November 24, 1863.

19. *Richmond Examiner,* November 25, 1863.

20. Lyon Gardiner Tyler, "John Moncure Daniel," in *Encyclopedia of Virginia Biography* (New York: Genealogical Publishing, 1915), 3:153.

21. Ibid.; Andrews, *South Reports,* 29–30; Peter Bridges, *Pen of Fire: John Moncure Daniel* (Kent, Ohio: Kent State University Press, 2002), 32, 100.

22. *Richmond Examiner,* November 25, 1863.

23. *Richmond Dispatch,* November 25, 1863.

24. Marvin Evans, "The Richmond Press on the Eve of the Civil War," *The John P. Branch Historical Papers of Randolph-Macon College* 1 (January 1951): 25–26.

25. Ibid.

26. Mark R. Cheathem, "Constitutional Union Party (1860)," in David S. Heidler and Jeanne T. Heidler, eds., *Encyclopedia of the American Civil War: A Political, Social, and Military History* (Santa Barbara, Calif.: ABC-CLIO, 2000), 1:490–91.

27. *Richmond Dispatch,* November 27, 1863.

28. Evans, "Richmond Press," 17–18.

29. *Richmond Enquirer,* November 27, 1863.

30. *Richmond Dispatch,* March 5, 1861; *Richmond Dispatch,* March 8, 1865.

31. *Lynchburg Virginian,* November 27, 1863.

32. *Lynchburg Virginian,* December 4, 1863.

33. *Staunton Vindicator,* December 4, 1863.

34. Brayton Harris, *Blue and Gray in Black and White: Newspapers in the Civil War* (Washington, D.C.: Brassey's, 1999), 182; Andrews, *South Reports,* 25.

35. Andrews, *South Reports,* 299–300.

36. A search of the following has revealed no comment on the address: Jefferson Davis, *The Papers of Jefferson Davis,* vol. 10, ed. Lynda Lasswell Crist,

Kenneth H. Williams, and Peggy L. Dillard (Baton Rouge: Louisiana State University Press, 1999); John B. Jones, *A Rebel War Clerk's Diary at the Confederate States Capital* (Philadelphia: Lippincott, 1866); Josiah Gorgas, *The Civil War Diary of General Josiah Gorgas,* ed. Frank E. Vandiver (Tuscaloosa: University of Alabama Press, 1947); Mary Boykin Miller Chesnut, *Mary Chesnut's Civil War,* ed. C. Vann Woodward (New Haven, Conn.: Yale University Press, 1981); Judith W. McGuire, *Diary of a Southern Refugee during the War* (New York: E. J. Hale and Son, 1867).

   37. *Richmond Dispatch,* December 8, 1863.

Diary of a Southern Refugee during the War, September 1862–May 1863

Judith Brockenbrough McGuire

Edited by James I. Robertson Jr.

In the ten-month period of this segment of Mrs. Judith McGuire's diary, she endured the aftershocks of four major battles: Second Manassas (August), Antietam (September), Fredericksburg (December), and Chancellorsville (May). Each came like a new, destructive wave, testing faith as well as hope.

Mrs. McGuire and her minister husband were expatriates staying with friends in Lynchburg in late summer 1862. From there, they visited acquaintances in Charlottesville and family in Hanover County before finding a temporary home in Ashland. The village was twelve miles north of Richmond and astride the Richmond, Fredericksburg & Potomac Railroad. For almost a year, the McGuires shared an eight-room home with three other families. Despite the overcrowded conditions and innumerable problems, Mrs. McGuire thought the Ashland sojourn to be the most pleasant period of her wartime displacement.

Her husband secured a clerical position with the Confederate government in Richmond. One or two days a week, Mrs. McGuire was a volunteer nurse at the soldier hospital superintended by the now-famous Sally Tompkins. The McGuires commuted to the capital by rail. Mrs. McGuire supplemented the family's meager income by making and selling soap.

While she continually expressed hope that the South would win the awful civil war, Mrs. McGuire's emotions centered around the young men wrenched from earth by war's killing hand. She took personal interest in a number of soldier-patients, including a favorite nephew who almost died from a battle wound. News of a battle to the north always sent Mrs. McGuire and other women to the Ashland railroad station. There they provided aid to wounded men en route to Richmond hospitals. Like all Southerners, Mrs. McGuire was grief-stricken at the May 1863 death of Gen. "Stonewall" Jackson. Her pen picture of the single-car train carrying the general's remains to the capital is unique.

Here, as in previous installments, the diarist sometimes deviated from her own thoughts to describe the plight of other Southern women undergoing ordeals worse than her own. Nevertheless, three themes are consistent throughout this extraordinary journal.

Mrs. McGuire was always proudly aware of her native roots. She noted in April 1863: "It is grievous to think how much of Virginia is down-trodden and lying in ruins. The old State has bared her breast to the destroyer, and borne the brunt of battle for the good of the Confederacy." In contrast, the middle-aged minister's wife saw few redeeming qualities in Union soldiers. Commenting on superior Union numbers in the field, Mrs. McGuire stated: "[T]hey come like the frogs, the flies, the locusts, and the rest of the vermin which infested the land of Egypt, to destroy our peace." The third theme apparent in her diary is a religious faith that no ill fortune could blunt. Her diary is a mixture of incisive observations on society, ruminations on past glories, and descriptions of present hardships. Yet underneath it all is an unwavering dedication to the will of God. At one low point, Mrs. McGuire wrote: "God will give us the fruits of the earth abundantly, as in days past, and if we are reduced, which I do not anticipate, to bread and water, we will bear it cheerfully, thank God, and take courage."

Diary of a Southern Refugee

Lynchburg, September 2—The papers to-day give glorious news of a victory to our arms on the plains of Manassas, on the 28th, 29th, and 30th. I will give General Lee's telegram:

Army of Northern Virginia
Groveton, *August* 30—10 P.M.
Via Rapidan.

To President Davis:—This army achieved to-day, on the plains of Manassas, a signal victory over the combined forces of McClellan and Pope. On the 28th and 29th, each wing, under Generals [James] Longstreet and Jackson, repulsed with valour attacks made on them separately. We mourn the loss of our gallant dead in every conflict, yet our gratitude to Almighty God for his mercies rises higher each day. To Him and to the valour of our troops a nation's gratitude is due.

R. E. Lee[1]

Nothing more to-day—my heart is full. The papers give no news of the dead and wounded. The dreaded black-list yet to come. In the mean time we must let no evil forebodings mar our joy and thankfulness.

3d—Wild stories on the street this morning, of the capture of prisoners, killing of generals, etc. Burnside and staff captured, they say. The last too good to be true.[2]

4th—Our victory at Manassas complete; the fight lasted four days. General Kearney was killed in a cavalry fight at Chantilly.[3] Beautiful Chantilly has become a glorious battle-field. The splendid trees and other lovely surroundings all gone; but it is classic ground for this time. In those fights I had eight nephews! Are they all safe? I have heard from two, who fought gallantly, and are unscathed. It is said that our army is to go to Maryland.

5th—Our son J[ohn] arrived last night with quite a party, his health greatly suffering from over-work in Richmond during these exciting times. One of the party told me an anecdote of General J. E. B. Stuart, which pleased me greatly. Mrs. S[tuart] was in the cars, and near her sat a youth, in all the pride of his first Confederate uniform, who had attended General S[tuart] during his late raid as one of his guides through his native county of Hanover. At one of the water stations he was interesting the passengers by an animated account of their hair-breadth escapes by flood and field, and concluded by saying, "In all the tight places we got into, I never heard the General swear an oath, and I never saw him drink a drop." Mrs. S[tuart] was an amused auditor of the excited narrative, and after the cars were in motion she leaned forward, introduced herself to the boy, and asked him if he knew the reason why General S[tuart] never swears nor drinks; adding, "It is because he is a Christian and loves God, and nothing will induce him to do what he thinks wrong, and I want you and all his soldiers to follow his example."

September 12—No news from the army, except a letter in the morning's paper speaking of General Lee's being pleased with his reception in Maryland, and that our troops are foraging in Pennsylvania.[4] I hope so; I like the idea of our army subsisting on the enemy; they certainly have subsisted on us enough to be willing that we should return the compliment. Took leave of our nephew, B. H. M.,[5] this morning; he has been there on sick-leave, and has gone in pursuit of his regiment, which is now across the Potomac. Poor child! It was hard to see him go off alone, with his child-like countenance and slender figure; but he is already a veteran in the service, and has a most unflinching, undaunted spirit.

Took a ride this evening with Mrs. D[aniel] through the beautiful environs of this city. After getting beyond the hospitals, there was nothing to remind us of war; all was peaceful loveliness; we talked of days long passed, and almost forgot that our land was the scene of bitter strife. Sometimes I almost fancy that we are taking one of our usual summer trips, with power to return when it terminates; and then I am aroused, as from a sweet dream, to find myself a homeless wanderer, surrounded by horrors of which my wildest fancy had never conceived a possibility in this Christian land and enlightened day.

Sunday—Just returned from church. Mr. K.[6] gave us a delightful sermon on our dependence on God as a people. "When Moses held up his hand, then Israel prevailed; and when he let down his hand, then Amalek prevailed."[7] Oh, that our hands may always be "held up" for our cause and armies! Next Thursday (18th) is the day appointed by our President as a day of thanksgiving for our success. His proclamation is so beautiful that I will copy it:

> To the people of the Confederate States:
> Once more upon the plains of Manassas have our armies been blessed by the Lord of Hosts with a triumph over our enemies. It is my privilege to invite you once more to His footstool, not now in the garb of fasting and sorrow, but with joy and gladness, to render

thanks for the great mercies received at His hands. A few months since our enemies poured forth their invading legions upon our soil. They laid waste our fields, polluted our altars, and violated the sanctity of our homes. Around our capital, they gathered their forces, and with boastful threats claimed it as already their prize. The brave troops which rallied to its defence have extinguished their vain hopes, and under the guidance of the same Almighty hand, have scattered our enemies and driven them back in dismay. Uniting those defeated forces and the various armies which had been ravaging our coasts with the army of invasion in Northern Virginia, our enemies have renewed their attempt to subjugate us at the very place where their first effort was defeated, and the vengeance of retributive justice has overtaken their entire host in a second and complete overthrow. To this signal success accorded our armies in the East has been graciously added another, equally brilliant, in the West. On the very day on which our forces were led to victory on the plains of Manassas, in Virginia, the same Almighty arm assisted us to overcome our enemies at Richmond, in Kentucky.[8] Thus, at one and the same time, have two great hostile armies been stricken down, and the wicked designs of our enemies set to naught. In such circumstances it is meet and right that, as a people, we should bow down in adoring thankfulness to that gracious God who has been our bulwark and defence, and to offer unto Him the tribute of thanksgiving and praise. In His hand is the issue of all events, and to Him should we in a special manner ascribe the honour of this great deliverance. Now, therefore, I, Jefferson Davis, President of the Confederate States, do issue this, my proclamation setting apart Thursday, the 18th day of September, as a day of thanksgiving and prayer to Almighty God, for the great mercies vouchsafed to our people, and more especially for the triumph of our arms at Richmond and Manassas, in Virginia, and at Richmond, in Kentucky; and I do hereby invite the people of the Confederate States to meet on that day, at their respective places of public worship, and to unite in rendering thanks and praise to God for these great mercies, and to implore Him to conduct our country safely through the perils which surround us, to the final attainment of the blessings of peace and security.

Given under my hand and the seal of the Confederate States, at Richmond, this fourth day of September, A.D. 1862.

> Jeff. Davis, Pres. of the C. S.
> J. P. Benjamin, Sec. of State.[9]

Tuesday, September 16th—The papers to-day give no account of our army in Maryland. General Loring has been successful in the Kanawha Valley, in driving the enemy, taking prisoners, and 5,000 stand of arms, etc.[10] Our success in the West still continues. Kentucky is represented to be in a flame of excitement.[11] General Kirby Smith asks for 20,000 stand of arms to be sent to arm Kentuckians, who are rushing to his standard. Cincinnati preparing for defence, etc.

Yesterday I was surprised and delighted to see my nephew, W. B. C.[12] After passing through the bloody fight at Manassas, he found he could not march into Maryland, in consequence of the soreness of his wound received last spring at Kernstown. He gives a graphic account of our army's trial, tribulations, and successes at Manassas. Our dear ones all passed safely through the fights.

Winchester once more disenthralled. My dear S[ally] B[land] S[mith] about to return to her home there—but in what state will she find it? When Jackson drove Banks down the Valley, Dr. S[mith], in passing through Winchester, stepped into the open door of his house; found it had been Banks's headquarters; the floors covered with papers torn up in haste; the remnants of the General's breakfast on the dining-room table, and other unmistakable signs of a recent and *very* hurried departure.

September 18th—Thanksgiving-day for our victories! We went to church this morning and heard Mr. K[inckle]'s admirable sermon from 1st Sam., chap. vii, v. 12: "Then Samuel took a stone, and set it between Mizpeh and Shen, and called the name of it Ebenezer, saying Hitherto hath the Lord helped me." Oh! I trust that this day has been observed throughout the Confederacy. If all our duties were as easily performed, we should be very good Christians; but, alas! Our hearts are often heavy, and do not cheerfully respond to the calls of duty. In prosperity, praise and thanksgiving seems to rise spontaneously to our lips, but to humble ourselves, and feel our entire dependence, is a much more difficult duty.

Saturday, September 20th—An official account in the morning's paper of the surrender of Harper's Ferry to our men on Sunday last.[13] Colonel Miles, the Federal commander, surrendered, unconditionally, to General Jackson, 11,000 prisoners, 50 pieces of artillery, 12,000 stand of arms, ammunition, quartermaster and commissary stores in large quantities. McClellan attempted to come to the rescue of Harper's Ferry. A courier was captured, sent by him to Miles, imploring him to hold out until he could bring him reinforcements. General Lee ordered General D. H. Hill to keep McClellan in check, and, for this purpose, placed him on the road to Boonesborough. It is said that McClellan had a force of 80,000 men, and that General Hill, on Saturday and Sunday, kept him in check all day—General Longstreet getting up at night. Next day they attacked him, repulsed and drove him five miles.[14] The details of the battle have not yet appeared. We have further rumours of fighting, but nothing definite. It is impossible for me to say how miserable we are about our dear boys.

The body of Brigadier-General Garland[15] was brought to this, his native city [Lynchburg], and his home, yesterday for interment. He was killed in the battle near Boonesborough. This event was a great shock to the community, where he was loved, admired, and respected. His funeral yesterday evening was attended by an immense concourse of mourning friends. It made my heart ache, as a soldier's funeral always does. I did not know him, but I know that he was "the only child of his mother, and she is a widow;" and I know, moreover, that the country cannot spare her chivalric sons.

Monday Night, September 22d—Probably the most desperate battle of the war was fought last Wednesday near Sharpsburg, Maryland. Great loss on both sides.[16] The Yankees claim a great victory, while our men do the same. We were left in possession of the field on Wednesday night, and buried our dead on Thursday. Want of food and other stores compelled our generals to remove our forces to the Virginia side of the [Potomac] river, which they did on Thursday night, without molestation. This is all I can gather from the confused and contradictory accounts of the newspapers.

24th—Still no official account of the Sharpsburg fight, and no list of casualties. The Yankee loss in generals very great—they must have fought desperately. [Jesse] Reno, [Joseph K. F.] Mansfield, and Miles were killed; others badly wounded. The Yankee papers say that their loss of "field officers is unaccountable"; and add, that but for the wounding of General [Joseph] Hooker, they would have driven us *into the Potomac.*

25th—The tables were turned on Saturday, as we succeeded in driving a good many of them into the Potomac. Ten thousand Yankees crossed at Shepherdstown, but unfortunately for them, they found the glorious Stonewall there.[17] A fight ensued at Boteler's Mill, in which General Jackson totally routed General Pleasanton and his command. The account of the Yankee slaughter is fearful. As they were recrossing the river our cannon was suddenly turned upon them. They were fording. The river is represented as being blocked up with the dead and dying, crimsoned with blood. Horrible to think of! But why will they have it so? At any time they might stop fighting, and return to their own homes. We do not want their blood, but only to be separated from them as a people, eternally and everlastingly. Mr. [McGuire], Mrs. D[aniel], and myself, went to church this evening, and after an address from Mr. K[inckle] we took a delightful ride.

A letter from B. H. M.,[18] the first she has been able to write for six months, except by "underground railroad," with every danger of having them read, and perhaps published by the enemy. How, in the still beautiful but much injured Valley, they do rejoice in their freedom! Their captivity—for surrounded as they were by implacable enemies, it is captivity of the most trying kind—has been very oppressive to them. Their cattle, grain, and every thing else, have been taken from them. The gentlemen are actually keeping their horses in their cellars to protect them. Now they are rejoicing in having their own Southern soldiers around them; they are busily engaged nursing the wounded; hospitals are established in Winchester, Berryville, and other places.

Letters from my nephews, W[illiam] B. N[ewton] and W[illoughby] N[ewton]. The first describes the fights at Boonesborough, Sharpsburg, and Shepherdstown. He says the first of these was the severest hand-to-hand cavalry fight of the war. All were terrific. W[illiam] speaks of his feelings the day of the surrender of Harper's Ferry. As they were about to charge the enemy's intrenchments, he felt as if he were marching into the jaws of death, with scarcely a hope of escape. The position was very strong, and the charge would be up a tremendous hill over felled timber, which lay thickly upon it—the enemy's guns, supported by infantry in intrenchments, playing upon them all the while. What was their relief, therefore, to descry the *white flag* waving from the battlements! He thinks that, in the hands of resolute men, the position would have been impregnable. Thank God, the Yankees thought differently, and surrendered, thus saving many valuable lives, and giving us a grand success. May they ever be thus minded!

30th—The *Richmond Examiner* of yesterday contains Lincoln's Proclamation, declaring all the negroes free from the 1st of January next![19] The Abolition papers are in ecstasies; as if they did not know that it can only be carried out *within their* lines, and there they have been practically free from the moment we were invaded. The *New York Tribune* is greatly incensed at the capture of Harper's Ferry; acknowledges that the battle of Sharpsburg was a disaster to them—Sumner's corps alone having lost 5,000 men in killed and wounded.[20] It says it was the "fiercest, bloodiest, and most indecisive battle of the war." Oh, that their losses could convince them of the wickedness of this contest! But their appetite seems to grow on what it feeds upon. Blood, blood, is still their cry. My heart sickens at the thought of what our dear soldiers have yet to pass through. Arise, O God, in thy strength, and save us from our relentless foes, for thy great name's sake!

Mr. [McGuire] has improved so much in health that we return in a few days to Richmond, that he may again enter upon the duties of his office. Ashland is our destiny for next year; the difficulty of obtaining a house or board in Richmond has induced us to join a party of refugee friends in taking a cottage there. Our children are already there, and write that a comfortable room is awaiting us. Last night we received a message from Mr. and Mrs. S., of Alexandria, that they were in the place, having run the *blockade,* from their oppressed home, during the battles around Richmond, when many of the soldiers had been withdrawn, and of course the surveillance of the old town had become less severe. Mrs. D[inkins], of Alexandria, and myself went directly after breakfast to see them. They had much to tell of the reign of terror through which they had gone, and nothing very satisfactory of our homes. Mrs. D[inkins]'s house was occupied as a barracks, and ours as a hospital. Miss —— had accompanied our friend Mrs. [Corse] there one day during the last winter; it was used as a hospital, except the front rooms, which were occupied by General N.[21] (a renegade Virginian) as headquarters. Can it be that any native of Virginia can be untrue to her now? Let General Scott, General Newton, and Captain Fairfax[22] answer! General N[ewton] married a Northern wife, which must account for his defection. The ladies drove up to our poor old home, the road winding among stumps of trees, which had been our beautiful oak grove; but one tree was left to show where it had been; they inquired for Mrs. N[ewton]. She was out, and they determined to walk over the house, that they might see the state of our furniture, etc. They went up-stairs, but, on opening the door of our daughter's room, they found a lady standing at a bed, cutting out work. Mrs. —— closed the door and turned to my chamber; this she found occupied by a family, children running about the room, etc.; these she afterwards found were the families of the surgeons. With no very *amiable* feelings she closed that door and went to another room, which, to her relief, was unoccupied; the old familiar furniture stood in its place, and hanging over the mantel was my husband's portrait. We left it put away with other pictures. The wardrobe, which we left packed with valuables, stood open and empty; just by it was a large travelling-trunk filled with clothing, which, she supposed, was about to be transferred to the wardrobe. She turned away, and on going down-stairs, met Mrs. N[ewton], who politely invited her into her (!) parlour. The piano, sofas, etc., were arranged precisely as she had been accustomed to see them arranged, she supposed by our servants, some of whom were still there. This furniture we had left carefully together, and covered, in another room. The weather was cold, and the floor was covered with matting, but no carpet. Mrs. N[ewton] apologized, saying that she had lately arrived, and did not know that there was a carpet in the house until, the day before, she was "exploring" the third story, and found in a locked room some very nice ones, which the soldiers were now shaking, and "she should make herself comfortable." She had just before been expressing holy horror at the soldiers in Alexandria having injured and appropriated the property of others. Mrs. —— looked at her wonderingly! Does she consider these carpets her own? Our parlour curtains were upon the passage-table, ready to be put up. She found them, no doubt, while exploring the third story, for there we left them securely wrapped up to protect them from moths. Ah! there are some species of moths (bipeds) from which bars and bolts could not protect them. This we did not anticipate. We thought that Federal officers were gentlemen!

October 1—Letters from Winchester, giving cheering accounts of our army. It is stationed at Bunker's Hill, twelve miles from Winchester, greatly increased since our recent fights, and in fine spirits. We leave Lynchburg to-morrow, and after spending a few days with our friends at the University, proceed to Richmond and Ashland.

3d—University of Virginia—Arrived here yesterday, and met with a glowing reception from the friends of my youth, Professor and Mrs. Maupin.[23] My sister, Mrs. C[olston], and daughters, staying next door, at Professor Minor's.[24] In less than five minutes we were all together—the first time for many anxious months. They are refugees, and can only hear from home when our army finds it convenient to clear "The Valley" of invaders. One of her sons, dear R.,[25] was ordered last winter, by General Jackson, to command a body of soldiers, whom he sent to break the dam in the Potomac, which at that point supplied the Ohio and Chesapeake Canal with water—(it also worked his mother's mill)—and the breaking of which, if effectually done, would prevent the Yankees from using the canal for transportation. This dangerous project was undertaken most cheerfully, and was most thoroughly effected. It was necessarily done in the night, to elude the vigilance of the Yankees on the Maryland shore. In the dead hour of the winter's night did some of the first gentlemen's sons in the South, who happened to belong to that portion of the army, work up to their waists in water, silently, quietly, until the work was finished; nor were they discovered until day dawned, and revealed them retiring; then shot and shell began to fall among them furiously. One of the brave band fell! Notwithstanding their danger, his companions could not leave him, but lifted him tenderly, and carried him to a place of safety, where he might at least have Christian burial by sympathizing friends. The large old mill, which had for many years sent its hundreds and thousands of barrels of flour to the Baltimore and Georgetown markets, still stood, though its wheels were hushed by the daring act of the night before. It had been used of late by the Yankees for their own purposes. The enemy seemed to have forgotten to destroy it, but the Union men could not allow their old friend and neighbour, though the widow of one whom they had once delighted to honour, to have such valuable property left to her; they immediately communicated to the Yankees that it belonged to the mother of the leader of the party who broke the dam. It was, of course, shelled and burned to the ground, except its old stone walls, which defied their fury; but if it helped the *cause*, the loss of the property did not weigh a feather with the family. The son has just been promoted to the lieutenant-colonelcy of the Second Regiment. His mother expressed her gratification, but added, that he had been so successful as captain of the company which he had raised, drilled, and led out from his own county, that she dreaded a change; besides, in that Second Regiment so many field-officers had fallen, that she had almost a superstitious dread of it. My dear R[aleigh], his heart is bound up in the cause, that self-preservation is the last thing that ever occurs to him. Oh! I trust that all evil may be averted from him.

It is sad to see these elegant University buildings, and that beautiful lawn, which I have always seen teeming with life and animation, now almost deserted. Two of the Professors are on the field; the Professor of Medicine and Surgery are surgeons in the neighbouring hospitals, and Dr. B.[26] is Assistant Secretary of War. Others, unfitted by age and other circumstances for the service, are here pursuing their usual avocations with assiduity, but through many difficulties. The students are mere boys, not arrived at military age, or, in a few instances, wounded soldiers unfit for service. The hospitals at Charlottesville are very large, and said to be ad- mirably managed. Every lady at this place, or in town, seems to be actively engaged in making the patients comfortable. The kitchens are presided over by ladies; each lady knows her own day to go to a particular kitchen to see that the food is prepared properly and served to the patients—I mean those who are confined to their beds or wards—the regular "matrons" do every thing else. This rich country supplies milk, butter, fruit, vegetables, fresh meat, etc.; and all kinds of delicacies are prepared by the ladies. Our friends, Dr. and Mrs. M[aupin], have sons in the field.[27] The elder, though not of military age at the time, shouldered his musket at the first tap of the drum; he would not be restrained. When I saw him, with his slight figure and boyish look, in his uniform and soldier's trappings, my heart sank within me, as I remembered that 'twas but as yesterday that this child, with his picture beauty, was the pet of the household. Now he is quite a veteran; has fought on many a field; scorns the idea of danger; prides himself on being a good soldier; never unnecessarily asking for fur- loughs, and always being present at roll-call. The second son, but sixteen, as his father would not allow him to enlist, has gone as an independent in a cavalry company, merely, he said, for the "summer campaign." Ah! in this "summer campaign," scarcely equaled in the annals of history, what horrors might have come! But he has passed through safely, and his father has recalled him to his college duties. Their mother bears the separation from them, as women of the South invariably do, calmly and quietly, with a humble trust in God, and an unwavering confidence in the justice and righteousness of our cause.

W[estwood], Hanover County, October 6th—We left the University on the 4th, and finding J. B. N.[28] on the cars, on "sick leave," I determined to stop with him here to spend a few days with my sisters, while Mr. [McGuire] went on to Richmond and Ashland. I do nothing but listen—for my life during the last three months has been quiet, compared with that of others. J[ohn] gives most interesting accounts of all he has seen, from the time he came up the Peninsula with the army in May, until he was broken down, and had to leave it, in Maryland, after the battle of Sharpsburg. As a surgeon, his personal danger has not been so great as that of others, but he has passed through scenes the most trying and the most glorious. My sisters and M[ary] give graphic descriptions of troubles while in the enemy's lines, but, with the exception of loss of property, our whole family has passed through the summer unscathed. Many friends have fallen, and one noble young relative, E. B.,[29] of Richmond County; and I often ask myself, in deep humility of soul, why we have been thus blessed, for since our dear W[illiam] P[helps] and General [James] McIntosh fell, the one in December, the other in March, we have been singularly blessed. Can this last, when we have so many exposed to danger? O God, spare our sons! Our friend, Dr. T., of this neighbourhood, lost *two* sons at Sharpsburg![30] Poor old gentleman! It is so sad to see his deeply-furrowed, resigned face.

McClellan's troops were very *well-behaved* while in this neighbourhood; they took nothing but what they considered contraband, such as grain, horses, cattle, sheep, etc., and induced the servants to go off. Many have gone—it is only wonderful that more did not go, considering the inducements that were offered. No houses were burned, and not much fencing. The ladies' rooms were not entered except when a house was searched, which always occurred in unoccupied houses; but I do not think that much was stolen from them. Of course, silver, jewelry, watches, etc., were not put in their way. Our man Nat, and some others who went off, have returned—the reason they assign is, that the Yankees made them work too hard! It is so hard to find both families without carriage horses, and with only some mules which happened to be in Richmond when the place was surrounded. A wagon, drawn by mules, was sent to the depot for us. So many of us are now together that we feel more like quiet enjoyment than we have done for months.

8th—Mr. [Willoughby] N[ewton] joined us this morning, and we all gathered here for the day. It seemed so much like old times, that C[atherine] broke a war rule, and gave us pound-cake for supper.

9th—A very pleasant stay at S[ummer] H[ill]. The ladies all busily knitting for our soldiers—oh, that we could make them comfortable for the winter!

10th—Bad news! The papers bring an account of the defeat of our army at Corinth.[31] It was commanded by General Van Dorn—the Federals by Rosecranz. They fought Friday, Saturday, and Sunday. The fight said to have been very bloody—great loss on both sides. The first two days we had the advantage, but on Sunday the Yankees "brought up reinforcements," and our men had to retire to Ripley. The Northern papers do not brag quite so much as usual; they say their loss was very great, particularly in officers; from which, I hope it was not quite so bad with us as our first accounts represent. The bringing up of reinforcements, which the Yankees do in such numbers, is ruinous to us. Ah! if we could only fight them on an equal footing, we could expunge them from the face of the earth; but we have to put forth every energy to get rid of them, while they come like the frogs, the flies, the locusts, and the rest of the vermin which infested the land of Egypt, to destroy our peace.

Richmond, October 15th—Yesterday morning my sister M[ary], J. W.,[32] and myself, drove up from W[estwood] to the depot, seven miles, in a wagon, with four mules. It was a charming morning, and we had a delightful ride; took the accommodation cars at twelve and arrived here at two. We drove to the Exchange [Hotel], and were delighted to find there our dear J[udith] McI[ntosh], and her little Bessie, on her way to W[estwood] to spend the winter. Poor thing, her lot is a sad one! She was excited by seeing us, and was more cheerful than I expected to see her; though she spoke constantly of her husband, and dwelt on her last days with him. She was in Memphis; her little Jemmie was extremely ill; she telegraphed for her husband in Arkansas. He came at once, and determined that it would be better off to take the little boy to the house of his aunt in Louisiana, that J[udith] might be with her sister. They took the boat, and after a few hours arrived at Mr. K[eene]'s house. The child grew gradually worse, and was dying, when a telegram came to General McIntosh from General [Sterling] Price, "Come at

once—a battle is imminent." He did not hesitate; the next steamer bore him
from his dying child and sorrowing wife to the field of battle at Pea Ridge.
He wrote to her, immediately on his arrival at camp, the most beautifully
resigned letter, full of sorrow for her and for his child, but expressing the
most noble Christian sentiments. Oh, how she treasures it! The lovely boy
died the day after his father left him! The mother said, "For a week H[arriet]
and myself did nothing but decorate my little grave, and I took a melancholy pleasure in it; but darker days came, and I could not go even to that
spot." She dreamed, a few nights after little Jemmie's death, of being at Fort
Smith, her home before the war; standing on the balcony of her husband's
quarters, her attention was arrested by a procession—an officer's funeral.
As it passed under the balcony she called to a passer-by: "Whose funeral is
that?" "General McIntosh's, madam." She was at once aroused, and ran to
her sister's room in agony. She did what she could to comfort her, but the
dream haunted her imagination. A few days afterwards she saw a servant
ride into the yard, with a note for Mrs. [Harriet Phelps] K[eene]. Though
no circumstance was more common, she at once exclaimed, "It is about my
husband." She did not know that the battle had taken place; it was the fatal
telegram. The soldiers carried his body to Fort Smith, and buried it there.
To-morrow she returns, with her aunt to W[estwood]. She wishes to get
to her mother's home in Kentucky, but it is impossible for her to run the
blockade with her baby, and there is no other way open to her.

Ashland, October 19—We are now snugly fixed in Ashland. Our mess consists
of Bishop J[ohns] and family, Major J[ohns][33] and wife [Julia], Lieutenant
J[ohn] J[ohns] and wife (our daughter), Mrs. S[tuart] and daughter of
Chantilly, Mr. [McGuire], myself, and our two young daughters—a goodly
number for a cottage with eight small rooms; but we are very comfortable.
All from one neighbourhood, all refugees, and *none able to do better,* we
are determined to take every thing cheerfully. Many remarks are jestingly
made suggestive of unpleasant collisions among so many families in one
house; but we anticipate no evils of that kind; each has her own place, and
her own duties to perform; the young married ladies of the establishment
are by common consent to have the house-keeping troubles; their husbands
are to be masters, with the onerous duties of caterers, treasurers, etc. We old
ladies have promised to give our sage advice and experience, whenever it is
desired. The girls will assist their sisters, with their nimble fingers, in cases

of emergency; and the *clerical* gentlemen are to have their own way, and to do their own work without let or hindrance. All that is *required* of them is, that they shall be household chaplains, and that Mr. [McGuire] shall have service every Sunday at the neglected village church. With these discreet regulations, we confidently expect a most pleasant and harmonious establishment. Our young gentlemen are officers stationed in Richmond. Mr. [McGuire] and themselves go in every morning in the cars, after an early breakfast, and return to dinner at five o'clock. J[ulia] J[ohns] and myself have free tickets to go on the cars to attend to our hospital duties. I go in twice a week for that purpose.

A dispatch just received from General Bragg claiming a signal victory at Perryville; but in consequence of the arrival of large reinforcements to the enemy, he had fallen back to Cumberland Gap.[34] These victories without permanent results do us no good, and so much blood is spilled. There seems to be a revolution going on in the North. Ohio, Indiana, and Pennsylvania have given the Democrats a large majority for Congress![35] So may it be!

November 4—A letter from my dear S[ally Smith] at Winchester. She says she is wearing herself down in the Confederate service; but there are so many soldiers in the hospitals that she is too much interested to give up nursing them even for a day. Our army still at Bunker's Hill. We are expecting daily to hear that it is falling back. When they leave the Valley all the sick that can be moved will be brought down to the Richmond hospitals, which are now comparatively empty.[36]

November 7—The snow falling rapidly—the trees and shrubs in full leaf, and the rose-bushes, in bright bloom, are borne down by the snow. Our poor soldiers! What are they to do to-night, without shelter, and without blankets? Everybody seems to be doing what they can to supply their wants; many persons are having carpets made into soldiers' blankets. My brother J[ohn White Brockenbrough] told me that he had every chamber carpet in the house, except one, converted into coverlets; and this is by no means a singular instance. A number of coverlets, made of the most elegant Brussels carpeting, were sent by Mr. B.,[37] of Halifax County, the other day, to our hospital, with a request to Miss T[ompkins][38] that the blankets should be given from the hospital to the camp, as more easily transported from place to place, and the carpeting retained in the hospital. This was immediately done. The blankets that could be spared from private houses were given last winter. How it gladdens my heart when I see a vessel has run the blockade, and arrived safely at some Southern port, laden with ammunition, arms, and clothing for the army! The Bishop and J[ulia] have just left us, for the council of the Southern Church, to meet at Augusta, Georgia. Oh that their proceedings may be directed by an all-wise Counsellor!

13th—Spent yesterday at the hospital—very few patients. Our army in the Valley falling back; and the two armies said to be very near each other, and much skirmishing. Our dear W. B. N[ewton] had his horse shot under him a few days ago. This is fearful. Our country is greatly afflicted, and our dear ones in great peril; but the Lord reigneth—He, who stilleth the raging of the seas, can surely save us from our enemies and all that hate us—to Him do we look for help.

 A Baltimore paper of the 11th gives an account of McClellan having been superseded by Burnside.[39] We are delighted at this, for we believe McC[lellan] to be the better general of the two. It is said that he was complained of by [Gen. in Chief Henry W.] Halleck for not pushing the army on, and preventing the capture of Harper's Ferry and the 11,000. McC[lellan] knew it could not be done, for he had General Jackson to oppose him! His removal was an unexpected blow to the North, producing great excitement. Oh that the parties there would fight among themselves! The Northern papers are insisting upon another "On to Richmond" [offensive], and hint that McC[lellan] was too slow about every thing. The "Young Napoleon" has fallen from his high estate, and returns to his family at Trenton! The Yankees are surely an absurd race, to say the least of them. At one moment extolling their generals as demi-gods, the next hurling them to the dust—none so poor as to do them reverence. "General McClellan is *believed* to have passed through Washington last night," is the announcement of a late Yankee paper, of the idol of last week.

18th—Another raid upon Fredericksburg; much mischief done![40] They are preparing for a second evacuation of the town! The number of refugees will be greatly increased, and where are they to go? Poor homeless wanderers, leaving business and the means of support to the mercy of a vindictive soldiery!

 Letters from our Valley friends taking leave of us, written some time ago, when the enemy were again closing around them. We are very anxious about them. Their situation is becoming pitiable; every new set of troops help themselves to whatever suits their fancy—stock of all sorts, grain, meat, every thing valuable and portable! Silver, glass, china, has to be buried, and very adroitly, or it is found. Some of the servants are very unfaithful, and let the enemy in to the most private places. There are some honourable exceptions to this last remark. Our relative, Mr. [John E.] P[age], has moved below the mountains for security; but he was in the habit, when at home, of intrusting every thing to his house-servant, including his wine and ardent spirits—and it was kept sacredly—the master knew not where; but on each departure of the enemy every thing would be returned to its accustomed place, in good order.

November 23—Poor Fredericksburg! The enemy on the Stafford side of the river in force; their cannon planted on the hills. Day before yesterday they demanded the surrender of the town, which was declined by General Lee. They then threatened to shell it, at nine o'clock this morning; but it is now night and it has not been done. It is hourly expected, however, and women and children are being hurried off, leaving every thing behind except what they can get off in bundles, boxes, etc. There is no transportation for heavy articles. The Vandals threw a shell at a train of cars filled with women and children. It burst very near them, but they were providentially protected.[41] A battle is daily expected. In the meantime the sufferings of wandering women and children are very great.

November 25—Just from the depot. The cars have gone to Richmond, filled with non-combatants from Fredericksburg—ladies, with their children, many of whom know not where to go. They will get to Richmond after dark, and many propose staying in the cars this cold night, and seeking a resting-place to-morrow. The feeling of desolation among them is dreadful. Oh, how I wish that I had even one room to offer! The bombardment has not commenced, but General Lee requested last night that the women and children who had not gone should go without delay. This seems to portend hot work.

29th—Nothing of importance from the army. The people of Fredericksburg suffering greatly from the sudden move.[42] I know a family, accustomed to every luxury at home, now in a damp basement-room in Richmond. The mother and three young daughters cooking, washing, etc.; the father, a merchant, is sick and cut off from business, friends, and every thing else. Another family, consisting of mother and four daughters, in one room, supported by the work of one of the daughters who has an office in the Note-Signing Department. To keep starvation from the house is all that they can do; their supplies in Fredericksburg can't be brought to them—no transportation. I cannot mention the numbers who are similarly situated; the country is filled with them. Country houses, as usual, show a marvelous degree of elasticity. A small house accommodating any number who may apply; pallets spread on the floor; every sofa and couch *sheeted* for visitors of whom they never heard before.[43] If the city people would do more in that way, there would be less suffering.[44] Every cottage in this village is full; and now families are looking with wistful eyes at the ball-room belonging to the hotel, which, it seems to me, might be partitioned off to accommodate several families. The billiard-rooms are taken, it is said, though not yet occupied. Yet how everybody is to be supported is a difficult question to decide. Luxuries have been given up long ago, by many persons. Coffee is $4 per pound, and good tea from $18 to $20; butter ranges from $1.50 to $2 per pound; lard 50 cents; corn $15 per barrel; and wheat $4.50 per bushel. We can't get a muslin dress for less than $6 or $8 per yard; calico $1.75, etc.[45] This last is no great hardship, for we will all resort to homespun. We are knitting our own stockings, and regret that we did not learn to spin and weave. The North Carolina homespun is exceedingly pretty, and makes a genteel dress; the only difficulty is in the dye; the colours are pretty, but we have not learned the art of *setting* the wood colours; but we are improving in that art too, and when the first dye fades, we can dip them again in the dye.

30th—The Yankee army ravaging Stafford County dreadfully, but they do not cross the river.[46] Burnside, with the "greatest army on the planet,"[47] is quietly waiting and watching our little band on the opposite side. Is he afraid to venture over? His "On to Richmond" seems slow.

December 10—Just returned from a visit of a week to my old friend Mrs. C.[48] Her home in Richmond is the very picture of comfort and hospitality; having wealth, she uses it freely, in these troublous times, for the comfort of others. If all hearts were as *large* as hers, there would be no refugees in garrets and cellars. I was touched by her attention to Mr. [McGuire], whom she had always seen engaged in his duties as a minister of the Gospels. She seemed to think it a kind of sacrilege to see him employed from nine until four o'clock in the duties of his secular office, and "to think of his reverend and hoary head bending over a clerk's desk"; she would say, "Oh, what awful times!" I told her that she must not think of it in that light; that he had been greatly blessed to get the office, which supported us so much better than many other refugees. While talking this way, she would be suiting the action to the word, by rolling up a most delightful chair to the fire, placing a small table before it, ready for some nice refreshment when he returned. It is trying to see him work so hard for our support, in his delicate state of health. The girls and myself are very anxious to get work from Government, signing notes, copying—any thing to assist in supporting ourselves; but we have tried in vain, and I suppose it is right, for there are so many widows and orphans who have a much higher claim to any thing that Government can do for them. We have heard heavy firing to-day. The car passengers report that there is skirmishing near Port Royal.

13th—Our hearts are full of apprehension! A battle is going on at or near Fredericksburg. The Federal army passed over the river on their pontoons night before last. They attempted to throw the bridges over it at three places; from two of these they were driven back with much slaughter; at the third they crossed. Our army was too small to guard all points. The firing is very heavy and incessant. We hear it with terrible distinctness from our portico.[49] God of mercy, be with our people, and drive back the invaders! I ask not for their destruction; but that they may be driven to their own homes, never more to put foot on our soil; that we may enjoy the sweets of peace and security once more. Our dear boys—now as ever—I commit them into Thy hands.

Night—Passengers report heavy skirmishing before they left Fredericksburg this morning, but cannonading tells us of bloody work since.[50] A few wounded men were carried by to-night. We went to the depot to see if there were any particular friends among them, but found none.

14th—Firing in the direction of Fredericksburg renewed this morning, but at irregular intervals. Telegraph wires are cut. No news except from passengers in the trains. The cars are not allowed to go to the town, but stop at a point some miles below. They report that every thing goes on well for us, of which we were sure, from the receding sound of the cannon. Praise the Lord, O my soul, and all that is within me praise His holy name! How can we be thankful enough for such men as General Lee, General Jackson, and our glorious army, rank and file!

Nine o'Clock at Night—A sad, sad train passed down a short time ago, bearing the bodies of Generals Cobb, of Georgia, and Maxcy Gregg, of South Carolina.[51] Two noble spirits have thus passed away from us. Peace to their honoured remains! The gentlemen report many wounded on the train, but not severely. I fear it has been another bloody Sabbath. The host of wounded will pass to-morrow; we must be up early to prepare to administer to their comfort. The sound of cannon this evening was much more distant, and not constant enough for a regular fight. We are victorious again! Will they now go from our shores forever? We dread to hear of the casualties. Who may not be among the wounded to-morrow?

15th—An exciting day. Trains have been constantly passing with the wounded for the Richmond hospitals. Every lady, every child, every servant in the village, has been engaged preparing and carrying food to the wounded as the cars stopped at the depot—coffee, tea, soup, milk, and every thing we could obtain.[52] With eager eyes and beating hearts we watched for those most dear to us. Sometimes they were so slightly injured as to sit at the windows and answer our questions, which they were eager to do. They exult in the victory. I saw several poor fellows shot through the mouth—they only wanted milk; it was soothing and cooling to their lacerated flesh. One, whom I did not see, had both eyes shot out. Nothing but an undying effort to administer to their comfort could have kept us up. The Bishop was with us all day, and the few gentlemen who remained in the village. When our gentlemen came home at five o'clock they joined us, and were enabled to do what we could not—walk through each car, giving comfort as they went. The gratitude of those who were able to express it was so touching! They said that the ladies were at every depot with refreshments. As the cars would move off, those who were able would *shout* their blessings on the ladies of Virginia: "We will fight, we will protect the ladies of Virginia." Ah, poor fellows, what can the ladies of Virginia ever do to compensate them for all they have done and suffered for us? As a train approached late this evening, we saw comparatively few sitting up. It was immediately surmised that it contained the desperately wounded—perhaps many of the dead. With eager eyes we watched, and before it stopped I saw Surgeon J. P. Smith (my connection) spring from the platform, and come towards me; my heart stood still. "What is it, Doctor? Tell me at once." "Your nephews, Major B[rockenbrough] and Captain C[olston], are both on the train, dangerously wounded."[53] "Mortally?" "We hope not. You will not be allowed to enter the car; come to Richmond to-morrow morning; B[rockenbrough] will be there for you to nurse. I shall carry W[illiam] C[olston] on the morning cars to his mother at the University. We will do our best for both." In a moment he was gone. Of course I shall go down in the early cars, and devote my life to B[rockenbrough] until his parents arrive. I am writing now because I can't sleep, and must be occupied. The cars passed on, and we filled our pitchers, bowls and baskets, to be ready for others. We cannot yield to private feelings now; they may surge up and rush through our hearts until they almost burst them, but they must not overwhelm us. We must do our duty to our country, and it can't be done by nursing our own sorrows.

January 8th [1863]—On the 16th of December, the day after the last entry in my diary, I went to Richmond, and found B[owyer] B[rockenbrough] at the house of Mr. P.,[54] on Grace Street, surrounded by luxury, and the recipient of unnumbered kindnesses; but so desperately ill! The surgeons had been up all night in the various hospitals, and, as numerous as they were, they were sadly deficient in numbers that night. The benevolent Dr. Bolton[55] had taken his wife and her sister, who had learned the art of binding up wounds, to his hospital, and all night long they had been engaged most efficiently in their labour of love. Other ladies were engaged in offices of mercy. Women who had been brought up surrounded by the delicacies and refinements of the most polished society, and who would have paled at the sight of blood under other circumstances, were bathing the most frightful gashes, while others were placing the bandages. I found B[owyer] suffering the most intense agony, and Mrs. P[aine] agitated and anxious. No surgeon could be obtained for private houses. I sent for one, who was not an army surgeon, to come at once. He sent me word that he had been up all night, and had just retired. Again I sent to implore him to come; in five minutes he was there.[56] He told me at once that his [Bowyer's] situation was critical in the extreme; the Minie ball had not been extracted; he must die, if not soon relieved. He wanted assistance—another surgeon. To send in pursuit for Dr. Gibson[57] for my brother,[58] then stationed at Camp Winder, and to telegraph for his father, occupied but a few moments; but the surgeons could not come. Hour after hour I sat by him. To *cut* off his bloody clothes, and replace them by fresh ones, and to administer the immense doses of morphine, was all that Mrs. P[aine] and myself could do. At dark Surgeons G[ibson] and B[olton], accompanied by my brother, arrived. They did what they could, but considered the case hopeless. His uncle, General C.,[59] arrived, to our great relief. He joined us in nursing him during the night. The cars were constantly coming in. Shouts of victory and wails for the dead were strangely blended. I was glad that I did not hear during that dreadful night that the body of that bright, beautiful boy, that young Christian hero, Randolph Fairfax,[60] had been brought to town. The father, mother, sisters!—can they bear the blighting stroke? The hope, the pride, almost the idol of the family, thus suddenly cut down! We, too, mourn him dead, as we had loved and admired him living. We had watched his boyhood and youth, the gradual development of that brilliant mind and lofty character. His Christian parents are bowed down, but not crushed; their future on earth is clouded; but by faith they see his abundant entrance into the kingdom of heaven, his glorious future, and are comforted.[61] Another young Christian soldier of the same battery was shot down about the same moment—our young friend David Barton,[62] of Winchester. Three months ago his parents buried their oldest son, who fell nobly defending his native town [Winchester], and now their second has passed into heaven. The Church mourns him as one who was about to devote his life to her sacred cause, but who felt it his duty to defend her against the hosts who are desecrating her hallowed precincts. How many, oh, how many of the young soldiers of the Cross are obliged to take up carnal weapons, to "save from spoil the sacred place!" Poor fellows! Their life's blood oozes out in a great cause. But our church!

> Will she ever lift her head
> From dust, and darkness, and the dead?

Yes, the time is at hand when she, our Southern Church, shall

> Put all her beauteous garments on,
> And let her excellence be known.

Decked in the robes of righteousness,
The world her glory shall confess.

No more shall foes unclean invade
And fill her hallowed halls with dread;
No more shall hell's insulting host
Their victory and thy sorrows boast.[63]

The churches of Fredericksburg suffered dreadfully during the bombardment. Some were torn to pieces. Our dear old St. George's suffered very little; but a shell burst through her revered walls, and her steeple was broken by a passing shot.[64] She stands a monument of Vandalism, though still a Christian chapel, from which the Gospel will, I trust, be poured forth for many years, when we shall no longer be surrounded by those who cry, "Raze it, raze it, even to the foundations thereof."

But to return to my patient. After days and nights of watching, I left him improving, and in the hands of his parents. The physicians still seem doubtful of the result, but I am full of hope. The ball, after much difficulty, was extracted, since which time he has gradually improved; but his sufferings have been indescribable. W. B. C[olston] is also slowly convalescing. One night while sitting up with B[owyer], together with a surgeon and General C[olston], when we had not been able to raise him up for two days, we were startled by his springing from the bed in agony, and running to the fire; the surgeon (his uncle) gently put his arm around him and laid him on the couch. I hastened to the bed to make it comfortable; but it was so large that I could not raise it up; at last I called out, "General, help me to make up this bed; come quickly." In an instant the large feather bed was grasped by him with strength and skill, and turned over and beaten thoroughly, the mattress replaced; then to help me to spread the sheets, smooth the pillows, etc., was the work of a moment. The patient was replaced in bed and soothed to sleep. Not till then did I remember that my companion in making the bed was one who but a short time before had led his brigade in the hottest of the fight, and would, perhaps, do it again and again. I complimented him on his versatility of talent, and a pleasant laugh ensued. During the Christmas holidays, while most anxious about our wounded, a letter from Kentucky reached us, announcing the death of my lovely niece, Mrs. K[eene]. As soon as her home on the Mississippi became surrounded by the enemy, she was obliged to leave it. She then joined her husband,[65] who is on General [John Cabell] Breckinridge's staff, and stationed near Knoxville. As her health was very delicate, she determined as soon as General B[reckinridge] was ordered off, to attempt to get to her mother in Kentucky; her husband placed her in the care of en elderly physician and friend, who accompanied her in a carriage across the mountains, as the public conveyances between those hostile regions are, of course, discontinued. Before she had travelled many days she was compelled to stop at a small house on the roadside, and there, with much kindness from the hostess, and from her travelling companion, but none of the comforts to which she had been accustomed, she suffered intensely for many days, and then attempted to go on. She reached George-town, Kentucky, which was her summer home; her mother was telegraphed for, and reached her just three days before she breathed her last. Dear H[arriet]! another victim of the war; as much so as was her brother, who received his mortal wound at Dranesville, or her brother-in-law, who was shot through the heart at Pea Ridge. Her poor mother deemed it a blessed privilege to be able to be with her in her dying hour; a comfort which she did not experience after her long trip to see her son. I fear she will sink under accumulated misfortunes, cut off as she is from all that makes life bearable under such circumstances. During the campaign of last summer around Richmond, she describes her feelings as being anxious and nervous beyond expression. She heard nothing but threats against us; and braggadocio, until she believed that we must be crushed; the many Southerners around her could not express their feelings except in subdued whispers. The Cincinnati and Covington papers expressed their confidence of success. Each day she would go to Cincinnati to hear the news, and come back depressed; but on the sixth day after the battles commenced, as she took her usual morning walk, she observed that the crowd around the telegraph office was more quiet than usual. As she approached, "curses, not loud, but deep," reached her ear. Hope dawned upon her subdued spirit. "Is there any thing the matter?" she asked, meekly, of the first gentlemanly-looking man she saw. "The matter!" he exclaimed. "Oh! madam, we are defeated. McClellan is retreating down the river towards Harrison's Landing. I don't know *where* that is, but we are shamefully beaten." She did not allow herself to speak, but rapidly wended her way home, her face bathed in tears of thankfulness, and singing the *Gloria in Excelsis*.

Several days ago General Bragg reported a victory at Murfreesboro,

Tennessee.[66] There was certainly a victory on the first day, as 4,000 prisoners were secured, with thirty-one pieces of cannon, and sent to Chattanooga. On the third day the enemy were reinforced, and our army was obliged to fall back. A friend remarked that the Bragg victories never seem to do us much good. The truth is, the Western Yankees fight much better than the Eastern, and outnumber us fearfully. They claim the victory, but acknowledge the loss of 30,000 men. It must have been a most severe conflict. At Vicksburg they have made another attack, and been repulsed;[67] and yet another misfortune for them was the sinking of their brag gun-boat *Monitor*.[68] It went down off Cape Hatteras. In Philadelphia the negroes and Abolitionists celebrated the 1st of January with mad demonstrations of delight, as the day on which Lincoln's proclamation to abolish slavery would take effect. In Norfolk the negroes were deluded by the Abolitionists into great excitement. Speeches were made, encouraging them to take up arms against their masters. Hale[69] has offered a resolution in the Northern Congress to raise two hundred regiments of negroes! The valiant knight, I hope, will be generalissimo of the corps. He is worthy of the position!

16th—Just returned from Richmond. B[owyer]'s situation still precarious, and I am obliged to stay with him a great deal. I see a number of officers and other gentlemen in his room; they seem to be in fine spirits about the country. Our President's Message[70] has been enthusiastically received. It is a noble production, worthy of its great author. I think the European public must contrast it with the Northern "Message" most favourably to us.

Several friends have just arrived from Yankeedom in a vessel fitted out by the Northern Government to receive the exchanged prisoners. About six hundred women and children were allowed to come in it from Washington. They submitted to the most humiliating search, before they left the wharf, from men and women. The former searched their trunks, the latter their persons. Mrs. Hale, of California, and the wife of Senator Harlan, of Iowa,[71] *presided* at the search. Dignified and lady-like! One young friend of mine was bringing five pairs of shoes to her sisters; they were taken as contraband. A friend brought me one pound of tea; this she was allowed to do; but woe betide the bundle of more than one pound! Some trunks were sadly pillaged if they happened to contain more clothes than the Northern Government thought proper for a rebel to possess. No material was allowed to come which was not made into garments. My friend brought me some pocket handkerchiefs and stockings, scattered in various parts of the trunk, so as not to seem to have too many. She brought her son, who is in our service, a suit of clothes made into a cloak which she wore. Many a gray cloth travelling-dress and petticoat which was on that boat is now in camp, decking the person of a Confederate soldier; having undergone a transformation into jackets and pant. The searchers found it a troublesome business; not the least assistance did they get from the searched. The ladies would take their seats, and put out first one foot and than the other to the Yankee woman, who would pull off the shoes and stockings—not a pin would they remove, not a string untie. The fare of the boat was miserable, served in tin plates and cups; but, as it was served gratis, the "*Rebs*" had no right to complain, and they reached Dixie in safety, bringing many a contraband article, not-withstanding the search.

The hated vessel, *Harriet Lane*,[72] which, like the *Pawnee,* seemed to be ubiquitous, has been captured near Galveston by General Magruder. Its commander, Captain Wainwright,[73] and others were killed. Captain W[ainwright] was most intimately connected with our relatives in the "Valley," having married in Clarke County. He wrote to them in the beginning of the war, to give them warning of their danger. He spoke of the power of the North and the impotency of the South. He thought that we would be subjugated in a few months—little did he anticipate his own fate, or that of his devoted fleet.

19th—Colonel Bradley Johnson[74] has been with us for some days. He is nephew to Bishop J[ohns], and as bright and agreeable in private as he is bold and dashing in the field. Our little cottage has many pleasant visitors, and I think we are as cheerful a family circle as the Confederacy can boast. We are very much occupied by our Sunday-schools—*white* in the morning and coloured in the afternoon. In the week we are often busy, like the "cotter's" wife, in making "auld claes look amaist as weel as new."[75] "*New claes*" are not attainable at present high prices; we are therefore likely to become very ingenious in fixing up "auld anes." My friend who lately arrived from Washington looked on very wonderingly when she saw us all ready for church. "Why, how genteel you look!" at last broke from her; "I had no idea of it. We all thought of you as suffering in every respect." I told her that the Southern women were as ingenious as the men were brave; and while we cared little for dress during such anxious times, yet when our husbands and sons returned from the field we preferred that their homes should be made attractive, and that they should not be pained by the indifferent appearance of their wives, sisters, and mothers. She was still more surprised by the neatly fitting, prettily made dresses of Southern manufacture. "Are they of Virginia cloth?" she asked. No, poor old Virginia has no time or opportunity for improving her manufactures, while almost her whole surface is scarred and furrowed by armies; but Georgia and North Carolina are doing much towards clothing the first ladies in the land. Sister M[ary] has just improved my wardrobe by sending me a black alpaca dress, bought from a Potomac blockade-runner. We, ever and anon, are assisted in that way: sometimes a pound of tea, sometimes a pair of gloves, is snugged away in a friendly pocket, and after many dangers reaches us, and meets a hearty welcome; and what is more important still, medicine is brought in the same way, having escaped the eagle eyes of Federal watchers. A lady in Richmond said laughingly to a friend who was about to make an effort to go to Baltimore, "Bring me a pound of tea and a hoop-skirt"; and after a very short absence, he appeared before her, with tea in one hand and the skirt in the other. It is pleasant to see how cheerfully the girls fall into habits of economy, and occupy themselves in a way of which we never dreamed before.

January 23—The gentlemen had their friend, General Lovell,[76] to spend last night with them. I was sorry not to be able to see more of him, as I was too sick to remain in the parlour, having been occupied night and day with my dear B[owyer], who has been again very dangerously ill, with erysipelas in his wound.[77] We are troubled about our son J[ames],[78] who has just been ordered to North Carolina; but we have no right to complain, as his health is good, and his position has hitherto been very pleasant.

31st—We are in *status quo*, and our armies quiet. The Northern army seems to be in commotion. Burnside has resigned, and "fighting Joe Hooker" has been put in his place.[79] Sumner and Franklin have also resigned their "grand divisions." *Pourquoi?* Won't the men advance? Perhaps the Stafford mud has been more than a match for them. Burnside had issued but a few days ago an address to his men, saying that they were about to "strike the final blow at the rebellion."[80] All was in readiness, and the "Grand Army" moved forward; just then the "rain descended and the floods came," and attempting to cross the Rappahannock ten miles above Fredericksburg, ambulances, wagons, big guns and all stuck in the mud; the order, "To your tents, O Israel,"[81] had to be given, and the "rebellion" still flourishes.

February 11—For ten days past I have been at the bedside of my patient in Richmond. The physicians for the third time despaired of his life; by the goodness of God he is again convalescent. Our wounded are suffering excessively for tonics, and I believe that many valuable lives are lost for the want of a few bottles of porter. One day a surgeon standing by B[owyer]'s bedside said to me, "He must sink in a day or two; he retains neither brandy nor milk, and his life is passing away for want of nourishment." In a state bordering on despair, I went out to houses and stores, to beg or buy porter; not a bottle was in town. At last a lady told me that a blockade-runner, it was said, had brought ale, and it was at the medical purveyor's. I went back to Mr. P[aine]'s instantly, and told my brother (B[owyer]'s father) of the rumour. To get a surgeon's requisition and go off to the purveyor's was the work of a moment. In a short time he returned, with a dozen bottles of India ale. It was administered cautiously at first, and when I found that he retained it, and feebly asked for more, tears of joy and thankfulness ran down my cheeks. "Give him as much as he will take during the night," was the order of the physician. The order was obeyed, and life seemed to return to his system; in twenty-four hours he had drank *four bottles;* he began then to take milk, and I never witnessed any thing like the reanimation of the whole man, physical and mental. The hospitals are now supplied with this life-giving beverage, and all have it who "absolutely require it," though great care is taken care of it, for the supply is limited. Oh, how cruel it is that the Northern Government should have made medicines, and the necessaries of life to the sick and wounded, contraband articles!

12th—We have lately had a little fight on the Blackwater.[82] The Yankees intended to take General Pryor by surprise, but he was wide awake, and ready to receive and repulse them handsomely. The late democratic majorities at the North seem to have given the people courage; denunciations are heard against the despotism of the Government. Gold has gone up to 160, causing a ferment. Oh that they would "bite and devour one another!" Since I have been so occupied in nursing B[owyer], I have not had as much time for the hospital, but go when I can. A few days ago, on going there in the morning, I found Miss T[ompkins] deeply interested about a soldier who had been brought in the evening before. The gentleman who accompanied him had found him in the pouring rain, wandering about the streets, shivering with cold, and utterly unable to tell his own story. The attendants quickly replaced his wet clothes by dry ones, and put him into a warm bed; rubbing and warm applications were resorted to, and a surgeon administered restoratives. Physical reaction took place, but no clearing of the mind. When soothingly asked about his name, his home, and his regiment, he would look up and speak incoherently, but no light was thrown on the questions. He was watched and nursed during the night. His pulse gradually weakened, and by the break of day he was no more. That morning I found the nameless, homeless boy on the couch which I had so often seen similarly occupied. The wind had raised one corner of the sheet, and as I approached to replace it a face was revealed which riveted me to the spot. It was young, almost boyish, and though disease and death had made sad ravages, they could not conceal delicately-carved features, a high, fair forehead, and light hair, which had been well cared for. He looked like one of gentle blood. All seemed so mysterious, my heart yearned over him, my tears fell fast. Father, mother, sisters, brothers—where are they? The morning papers represented the case, and called for information. He may have escaped in delirium from one of the hospitals! That evening, kind, gentle hands placed him in his soldier's coffin, and he had Christian burial at "Hollywood,"[83] with the lonely word "Stranger" carved upon the headboard. We trust that the sad story in the papers may meet some eye of which he had once been the light, for he was surely "Somebody's Darling." Sweet lines have been written, of which this sad case reminds me:

> Into a ward of the whitewashed walls,
> Where the dead and dying lay—
> Wounded by bayonets, shells, and balls—
> Somebody's darling was borne one day—
> Somebody's darling! so young and brace,
> Wearing yet on his sweet, pale face—
> Soon to be hid in the dust of the grave—
> The lingering light of his boyhood's grace.
>
> Matted and damp are the curls of gold,
> Kissing the snow of that fair young brow;

Pale are the lips of delicate mould—
Somebody's darling is dying now.
Back from the beautiful, blue-veined brow,
Brush his wandering waves of gold;
Cross his hand on his bosom now—
Somebody's darling is still and cold.

Kiss him once for somebody's sake;
Murmur a prayer soft and low;
One bright curl from its fair mates take—
They were somebody's pride, you know
Somebody's hand hath rested there;
Was it a mother's, soft and white?
Or have the lips of a sister fair
Been baptized in their waves of light?

God knows best! He has somebody's love
Somebody's heart enshrined him there;
Somebody wafted his name above,
Night and morn, on wings of prayer.
Somebody wept when he marched away,
Looking so handsome, brave, and grand!
Somebody's kiss on his forehead lay;
Somebody clung to his parting hand.

Somebody's watching and waiting for him,
Yearning to hold him again to her heart;
And there he lies with his blue eyes dim,
And the smiling, childlike lips apart.
Tenderly bury the fair young dead,
Pausing to drop on his grave a tear;
Carve on the wooden slab o'er his head—
"Somebody's darling slumbers here!"[84]

13th—Still in Richmond, nursing B[owyer]. He was wounded this day two months ago; but such fluctuations I have never witnessed in any case. We have more hope now, because his appetite has returned. I sent over to market this morning for partridges and eggs for him, and gave 75 cents apiece for the one, and $1.50 per dozen for the other. I am afraid that our currency is rapidly depreciating, and the time is approaching when, as in the old Revolution, a man had to give $300 for a breakfast. Mrs. P[aine] came in to scold me for my breach of good manners in *buying* any thing in her house. I confessed myself ashamed of it, but that I would be more ashamed to disturb her when-ever B[owyer]'s capricious appetite required indulgence. I have never seen more overflowing hospitality than that of this household. Many sick men are constantly refreshed from the bounties of the table; and supplies from the larder seem to be at the command of every soldier. One of the elegant parlours is still in the occupancy of the wounded soldier brought here with B[owyer]; his wound was considered slight, but he suffers excessively from nervous debility, and is still unfit for service. I did feel uncomfortable that we should give Mrs. P[aine] so much trouble, until she told me that, having no sons old enough for service,[85] and her husband being unable to serve the country personally, except as a member of the "Ambulance Committee,"[86] they had determined that their house should be at the service of the soldiers. Last summer, during the campaigns around Richmond, they took in seven wounded men, some of whom had to be nursed for months.

20th—A letter this morning from Sister M[ary], who has returned to her home on the Potomac. She gives me an account of many "excitements" to which they are exposed from the landing of Yankees, and the pleasures they take in receiving and entertaining Marylanders coming over to join us, and others who go to their house to "bide their time" for running the blockade for Maryland. "Among others," she says, "we have lately been honoured by two sprigs of English nobility, the Marquis of Hastings and Colonel Leslie of the British army.[87] The Marquis is the future Duke of Devonshire. They only spent the evening, as they hoped to cross the river last night. They are gentlemanly men, having no airs about them; but 'my lord' is excessively awkward. They don't compare at all in ease or elegance of manner or appear-ance with our educated men of the South. They wore travelling suits of very coarse cloth—a kind of pea-jacket, such as sailors wear. As it was raining, the boots of the Colonel were worn over his pantaloons. They were extremely tall, and might have passed very well at first sight for Western wagoners! We have also had the Rev. Dr. Joseph Wilmer[88] with us for some days. He is going to Europe, and came down with a party, the English included, to cross the river. The Doctor is too High Church for my views, but exceedingly agreeable, and an elegant gentleman. They crossed safely last night, and are now *en route* for New York, where they hope to take the steamer on Wednesday next." She does not finish her letter until the 17th, and gives an account of a pillaging raid through her neighbourhood. She writes on the 14th: "There had been rumours of Yankees for some days, and this morning they came in good earnest. They took our carriage horses, and two others, in spite of our remonstrances; demanded the key of the meat-house, and took as many of our sugar-cured hams as they wanted; to-night they broke open our barn, and fed their horses, and are even now prowling around the servants' houses in search of eggs, poultry, etc. They have taken many prisoners, and all the horses they could find in the neighbourhood. We have a rumour that an infantry force is coming up from Heathsville, where they landed yesterday.[89] We now see many camp-fires, and what we suppose to be a picket-fire, between this and the Rectory. My daughters, children and myself are here alone; not a man in the house. Our trust is in God. We pray not only that we may be delivered from our enemies, but from the fear of them. It requires much firmness to face the creatures, and to talk with them. The Eighth New York[90] is the regiment with which we are cursed. The officers are *polite* enough, but are determined to steal every thing they fancy." On the 15th she says: "This morning our enemies took their departure, promising to return in a few days. They visited our stable again, and took our little mare 'Virginia.' The servants behaved remarkably well, though they were told again and again that they were free." Again, on the 17th, she writes: "I saw many of the neighbours yesterday, and compared losses. We are all pretty severely pillaged. The infantry regiment from Heathsville took their departure on Sunday morning, in the '*Alice Price*,' stopped at Bushfield, and about twelve took breakfast there.[91] Mr. B.[92] says the vessel was loaded with plunder, and many negroes. They took off all the negroes from the Mantua estate; broke up the beautiful furniture at Summerfield, and committed depredations everywhere. A company of them came up as far as Cary's on Saturday evening and met the cavalry. They stole horses enough on their way to be pretty well mounted. They will blazon forth this invasion of a country of women, children, and old men, as a brilliant feat! Now that they are gone, we breathe more freely, but for how long a time?" We feel very anxious about our friends between the Rappahannock and the Potomac, both rivers filled with belligerent vessels; but they have not yet suffered at all, when compared with the lower Valley, the Piedmont country, poor old Fairfax, the country around Richmond, the Peninsula; and, indeed, wherever the Yankee army has been, it has left desolation behind it, and there is utter terror and dismay during its presence.

Ashland, February 22nd—A very deep snow this morning. The cars are moving slowly on the road, with two engines attached to each train. Our gentlemen could not go to Richmond to-day. Washington's birthday is forgotten, or only remembered with a sigh by his own Virginia. Had he been gifted with prophetic vision, in addition to his great powers, we would still remain a British colony; or, at least, he would never have fought and suffered for seven long years to have placed his native State in a situation far more humiliating than the colonies ever were towards the mother-country; or to have embroiled her in a war compared to which the old Revolution was but child's play.

26th—In the city again yesterday. B[owyer] improving. The morning paper reports firing upon Vicksburg.[93] Several steamers have arrived lately, laden for the Confederacy. Blockade-running seems to be attended with less danger than it was, though we have lately lost a most valuable cargo by the capture of the *Princess Royal*.[94] The *Alabama*[95] continues to perform the most miraculous feats, and the *Florida*[96] seems disposed to rival her in brilliant exploits. They "walk the water," capturing every thing in their way, and know no fear, though many vessels are in pursuit. I am grieved to hear that dear little J[efferson] P[age] has been ordered to Charleston. While he was on James River, I felt that I could be with him if he were wounded; but he is in God's hands:

> Be still, my heart; these anxious cares
> To thee are burdens, thorns, and snares.[97]

The papers full of the probable, or rather *hoped for,* intervention of France.[98] The proposition of the Emperor, contained in a letter from the Minister to Seward, and his artful, wily, Seward-like reply, are in a late paper. We pause to see what will be the next step of the Emperor. Oh that he would recognize us, and let fanatical England pursue her own cold, selfish course!

28th—To-day we are all at home. It is amusing to see, as each lady walks into the parlour, where we gather around the centre-table at night, that her work-basket is filled with *clothes to be repaired.* We are a cheerful set, notwithstanding. Our winding "*reel*," too, is generally busy. L.[99] has a very nice one, which is always in the hands of one or the other, preparing cotton for knitting. We are equal to German women in that line. Howitt says that throughout Germany, wherever you see a woman, you see the "everlasting knitting"; so it is with Confederate women. I only wish it was "everlasting," for our poor soldiers in their long marches strew the way with their wornout socks.

March 5th—Spent last night in Richmond with my friend Mrs. R.[100] This morning we attended Dr. Minnegerode's [101] prayer-meeting at seven o'clock. It is a blessed privilege enjoyed by people in town, that of attending religious services so often, particularly those social prayer-meetings, now that we feel our dependence on an Almighty arm, and our need of prayer more than we ever did in our lives. The President has issued another proclamation, setting aside the 27th of this month for fasting and prayer.

Again I have applied for an office, which seems necessary to the support of the family. If I fail, I shall try to think that it is not right for me to have it. Mr. [McGuire]'s salary is not much more than is necessary to pay our share of the expenses of the mess. Several of us are engaged in making soap,[102] and selling it, to buy things which seem essential to our wardrobe. A lady who has been perfectly independent in her circumstances, finding it necessary to do something of the kind for her support, has been very successful in making pickles and catsups for the restaurants. Another, like Mrs. Primrose,[103] rejoices in her success in making goose-berry wine, which sparkles like champagne, and is the best domestic wine I ever drank; this is designed for the highest bidder. The exercise of this kind of industry works two ways; it supplies our wants, and gives comfort to the public. Almost every girl plaits her own hat, and that of her father, brother, and lover, if she has the bad taste to have a lover out of the army, which no girl of spirit would do unless he is incapacitated by sickness or wounds. But these hats are beautifully plaited of rye straw, and the ladies' hats are shaped so becomingly, that though a Parisian milliner might pronounce them old-fashioned, and laugh them to scorn, yet our Confederate girls look fresh and lovely in them, with their gentle countenances and bright enthusiastic eyes; and what do we care for the

Parisian style, particularly as it would have to come to us through Yankee-land? The blockade has taught our people their own resources; but I often think that when the great veil is removed, and reveals us to the world, we will, in some respects, be a precious set of antiques. The ladies occasionally contrive to get a fashion-plate "direct from France," by way of Nassau; yet when one of them, with a laudable zeal for enhancing her own charms by embellishments from abroad, sends gold to Nassau, which should be kept in our own country, and receives in return a trunk of foreign fabrics, she will appear on the streets immediately afterwards in a costume which seems to us so new and fantastic, that we are forced to the opinion that we would appear to the world ludicrously *passé*.[104] A gentleman, lately from Columbia, tells me that the South Carolina girls pride themselves on their palmetto hats; and the belle of large fortune, who used to think no bonnet presentable but one made by the first New York or Parisian milliner, now glories in her palmetto. The balmoral, too, the product of our own spinning-wheel and loom, would show well with the prettiest imported ones. I have seen several, which the young wearers told me were "dyed in the wool, spun, and woven by the *poor* of our own neighbourhood. The dye-stuffs were from our own woods." These are little things, but, proving the independence of our people, I rejoice in them. The croakers are now indulging themselves with fears of famine; they elongate their gloomy visages, and tell us, in sad accents, that butter was $3.50 per pound in market this morning, and other things in proportion. I am sorry to say that it is true, and that it is evident we must have scarcity, particularly of such things as butter, for the cattle must go to feed the army. The soldiers must be fed; our gardens will give us vegetables; God will give us the fruits of the earth abundantly, as in days past, and if we are reduced, which I do not anticipate, to bread and water, we will bear it cheerfully, thank God and take courage:

Brought safely by his hand thus far,
Why should we now give place to fear?[105]

The *poor*, being well supplied with Government work, are better off than usual.

All quiet in the army. This may portend a storm. Several pieces of cannon passed this morning on the Fredericksburg train. Raids still continue in the Northern Neck, keeping us very uneasy about our friends there.

March 15th—Weather dark and cloudy. We had a good congregation in our little church. Mr. [McGuire] read the service. The Bishop preached on "Repentance." Richmond was greatly shocked on Friday, by the blowing up of the Laboratory,[106] in which women, girls, and boys were employed making cartridges; ten women and girls were killed on the spot, and many more will probably die from their wounds. May God have mercy upon them! Our dear friend Mrs. S[tuart] has just heard of the burning of her house, at beautiful Chantilly. The Yankee officers had occupied it as head-quarters, and on leaving it, set fire to every house on the land, except the overseer's house and one of the servants' quarters. Such ruthless Vandalism do they commit wherever they go! I expressed my surprise to Mrs. S[tuart] that she was enabled to bear it so well. She calmly replied, "God has spared my sons through so many battles, that I should be ungrateful indeed to complain of any thing else." This lovely spot has been her home from her marriage, and the native place of her many children, and when I remember it as I saw it two years ago, I feel that it is too hard for her to be thus deprived of it. An officer (Federal) quartered there last winter, describing it in a letter to the *New York Herald,* says the furniture had been "removed," except a large old-fashioned sideboard; he had been indulging his curiosity by reading the many private letters which he found scattered about the house; some of which, he says, were written by General Washington, "with whom the family seems to have been connected." In this last surmise he was right, and he must have read letters from which he derived the idea, or he may have gotten it from the servants, who are always proud of the aristocracy of their owners; but not a letter written by General Washington did he see, for Mrs. S[tuart] was always careful of them, and brought them away with her; they are now in this house. The officer took occasion to sneer at the pride and aristocracy of Virginia, and winds up by asserting that "this establishment belongs to the mother of General J. E. B. Stuart," to whom she is not at all related.

March 18th—This evening, when leaving Richmond, we were most unexpectedly joined at the cars by our friend N. P.[107] Dear child, we had not seen her since her father's family left their home, some weeks before we left ours. Well do I remember the feeling of misery which I experienced at seeing them go off. We have all suffered since that time, but none of us can compare with them in that respect. They are living in desolated Fauquier [County]. There they have buried their lovely little Kate, and N[annie]'s principal object in visiting this country now is to see the grave of her eldest brother, a victim of the war, and to see the lady at whose house he died, and who nursed him as though he had been her son. We enjoy her society exceedingly, and linger long over our reminiscences of the past, and of home scenes. Sadly enough do we talk, but there is a fascination about it which is irresistible. It seems marvellous that, in the chances and changes of war, so many of our "Seminary Hill" circle should be collected within the walls of this little cottage. Mrs. P[ackard] has once been, by permission of the military authorities, [able] to visit her old home; she found it *used as a bakery* for the troops stationed around it. After passing through rooms which she scarcely recognized, and seeing furniture once her own, broken and defaced, she found her way to her chamber. There was her wardrobe in its old place; she had left it packed with house-linen and other valuables, and advanced towards it, key in hand, for the purpose of removing some of its contents, when she was roughly told by a woman sitting in the room not to open that wardrobe, "there was nothing in it that belonged to her." Oh, how my blood would have boiled, and how I should have opened it, unless put aside by force of arms, just to have peeped in to see if my own things were still there, and to take them if they were! But Mrs. P[ackard], more prudently, used a gentle remonstrance, and finding that nothing could be effected, and that rudeness would ensue, quietly left the room. We bide our time.

19th—My birthday. While in Richmond, this morning, brother J.[108] and myself called on some friends, among others our relative Mrs. H.,[109] who has lately been celebrating the marriage of her only son, and took us into the next room for a lunch of wine and fruit-cake. We had never, during two years, thought of fruit-cake, and found it delightful. The fruit consisted of dried currants and cherries from her garden, at her elegant James River home, Brandon, now necessarily deserted. She fortunately was enabled to bring her furniture to Richmond, and is the only refugee that I know who is surrounded by home comforts.

March 20th—Severe snow-storm. This will retard the attack upon Fredericksburg, if the enemy designed it. We spent the morning in the parlour. N[ancy] P[ackard] read aloud the old-fashioned but amusing novel, *Pride and Prejudice*,[110] in very spirited style. The event of the day was the arrival from Alexandria of a bundle, filled with useful articles for a lady, who, not wanting them all herself, allowed us to help ourselves at the price which they cost her in Alexandria. It was amusing to see with what avidity the girls seized on a calico dress at only seventy-five cents per yard (Confederate money); every thing was in such demand, that I only got a tooth-brush, at one dollar; they are two dollars and fifty cents in Richmond.

27th—To-day was set apart by the President as a day of fasting and prayer. Some of us went to Richmond, and joined in the services at St. Paul's. The churches were all crowded with worshippers, who, I trust, felt their dependence on God in this great struggle. The President was in church, and, I believe, most of the dignitaries. One of the ladies of the hospital, seeing this morning two rough-looking convalescent soldiers sitting by the stove, exhorted them to observe the day by prayer and fasting. They seemed to have no objection to the praying, but could not see the "good of fasting," and doubted very much whether "Marse Jeff fasted all day himself—do you reckon he did?" The lady laughingly told him that she would inquire and let them know, but she *reckoned* that such was his habit. In the course of the morning she met with Mrs. Davis, and told her the anecdote. "Tell them from me," said Mrs. D[avis], "that Mr. Davis never eats on fast-day, and that as soon as he returns from church he shuts himself up in his study, and is never interrupted during the day, except on public business." Of course this was soon given as an example, not only to the two convalescents, but to the whole hospital.

March 28th—A letter from ——. She tells me that W. B. N[ewton] and E. C[olston] passed through the fierce fight at Kelly's Ford uninjured.[111] How can we be grateful enough for all our mercies? Letters also from B[ettie Smith], by underground railroad. That sweet child and her whole family surrounded and roughly treated by the Yankees; and so it will be as long as Millroy[112] is allowed to be the scourge of the Valley.

Sunday Night—Very sweet services in our little church to-day. The subject of the sermon was, "Woe to them who are at ease in Zion."[113] Mr. [McGuire] found a note on the pulpit from a Georgia soldier, asking the prayers of the congregation for himself and his family at home. The extemporaneous prayer after the service, offered by him, was most earnestly and tearfully joined by all.

April 1st—All quiet on the Rappahannock to-night, and we are almost as still as in days gone by. The girls got up a little merriment this morning by their "April fools." The remainder of the day passed in our usual way.

April 2d—We were shocked when the gentlemen returned, to hear of the riot which occurred in Richmond to-day.[114] A mob, principally of women, appeared in the streets, attacking the stores. Their object seemed to be to get any thing they could; dry goods, shoes, brooms, meat, glassware, jewelry, were caught up by them. The military was called out—the Governor dispersed them from one part of the town, telling them that unless they disappeared in five minutes, the soldiers would fire among them. This he said, holding his watch in his hand. Mr. [William P.] Munford, the President of the Young Men's Christian Association, quieted them on another street by inviting them to come to the rooms of the Association, and their wants should be supplied; many followed him—I suppose those who were really in want. Others there were, of the very worst class of women, and a great many who were not in want at all, which they proved by only supplying themselves with jewelry and other finery. The President was out speaking to them, and trying to secure order. The mayor [Joseph C. Mayo] made them a speech, and seemed to influence them, but I dare say that the bayonets of the soldiers produced the most decided effect. It is the first time such a thing has ever darkened the annals of Richmond. God grant that it may be the last. I fear that the poor suffer very much; meal was selling to-day at $16 per bushel. It has been bought up by speculators. Oh that these hard-hearted creatures could be made to suffer! Strange that men with human hearts can, in these dreadful times, thus grind the poor.

Good-Friday—The Bishop preached for us to-day most delightfully from the text: "Jesus Christ and Him crucified."[115] In the afternoon Mrs. S[tuart] had the inexpressible pleasure of welcoming her son, Mr. A. S.,[116] from the Western Army. He thinks that Vicksburg and Port Hudson are both impregnable. God grant that it may be so!

April 4th—Spent to-day in Richmond, attending on the wounded. The mob of women came out yesterday, but in smaller numbers, and was easily put down by military authority. To-day a repetition was expected, and the cannon was in place to rake the streets, but they thought discretion the better part of valour, and staid at home. I saw Rev. Mr. Peterkin,[117] who is perhaps more thoroughly acquainted with the state of the poor than any man in the city. He says that they are admirably attended to. Large sums of money are put into the hands of the clergy for their benefit; this money is disbursed by ladies, whose duty and pleasure it is to relieve the suffering. Our gentlemen gave as much as $5,000 last winter. Besides this, the industrious poor are supplied with work by the Government, and regularly paid for it.

The Bishop set off this morning for his spring visitations, which are becoming, alas! very circumscribed—so much of the diocese is in the hands of the enemy.

Mr. C., of Georgetown, Captain Norton, of New Orleans, and Mr. A[rthur] S[tuart] are with us.[118] The first of these gentlemen ran the blockade from his home some months ago, finding he was to be arrested for opinion's sake, and now holds a Confederate office in Richmond. He very rarely hears from his wife and children. Flag-of-truce letters seldom reach their destination, and when they do, letters of one page, written to be inspected by strangers, are very unsatisfactory. An occasional "underground" communication comes to him, like water in a thirsty land. I often look at his calm countenance with sympathy, knowing that there must be deep sorrow and anxiety underneath.

9th—On Monday saw B[owyer] removed from the bed of suffering, on which he had been lying four months, put on a stretcher, and carried to the canal-boat. His countenance was full of joyful anticipations of home. His arm, which should have been amputated on the field, hangs lifeless by his side; and yet he expects to return to his post, that of Major of artillery, as soon as he is strong enough. Poor fellow, it is well for him to amuse himself with the idea, but he will never again be fit for any duty but that at a post. He has been the recipient of kindnesses from Mr. and Mrs. P[aine] and others, which could only be experienced in this dear, warm-hearted Southern country of ours, and which he can never forget to his dying day. That night I spent with my kind friend Mrs. R[owland], and next morning made such purchases as were absolutely necessary for our comfort. I gave for bleached cotton, which used to be sold for 12½ cents $3.50 per yard; towelling $1.25 per yard; cotton 50 cents a spool, etc. Nothing reconciled me to this extravagance but that I had sold my soap for $1 per pound!!

The enemy has retired from Vicksburg, their canal having proved a failure.[119] Where they will reappear nobody knows. Another ineffectual at-tempt upon Charleston on the 7th and 8th.[120]

Sunday Night, April 12th—Mr. [McGuire] administered the Sacrament here to-day, the first time it was ever administered by Episcopalians in Ashland. There were fifty communicants, the large majority of them refugees. Our society here has been greatly improved by the refugees from Fredericksburg. The hotel is full. The G's have rented the last vacant cottage, and are board-ing others. The R's, with their three pretty young daughters and son, occupy the ball-room of the hotel. The dressing-room makes a pleasant chamber, and the long dancing-room, partitioned off into rooms by the suspension of their handsome crimson damask curtains, is very pretty, and, for spring and summer use, makes very comfortable apartments. They saved some of their furniture, and are nicely fixed for refugees, who must do the best they can, and be thankful it is no worse. The C's seem very happy in the old billiard-rooms; the large room answers the double purpose of dining-room and parlour, and the smaller rooms, which I am afraid were once used for card-playing when this place was a summer resort, are now put to a better use, as sleeping apartments and kitchen for three most agreeable families. One family in the opposite cottage has interested us very much. Mr. Ward (the husband) was an Englishman, who had been in office in Washington; he resigned and came south on the breaking out of the war, placed his family in Richmond, and joined our army; he was not young or healthy, and soon was broken down by the service; he was then made clerk in the Quartermaster's Department, and removed his family to Ashland for cheapness. He was very highly educated and gentlemanly, and his coming here seems to me very mysterious. Soon after his removal to this place he grew worse and died. His wife and five children were left penniless and friendless. They seemed to have no acquaintances, however slight. The villagers, from their limited resources, raised a sum for her present support, and after much difficulty procured her a situation in the Note-signing Department. She goes into the city every morning on the cars, as do several other ladies to the duties of their offices, leaving her children to the care of a faithful coloured nurse, whom she never saw until two months ago. We have taught her the art of making soap of concentrated lye, and often when she gets on the train, a basket may be seen in the freight-train filled with soap, which she sells to the grocers or commissaries. She is an interesting-looking woman, Northern born and educated. Her father, she says, is a Colonel in the Yankee army. She wrote to him again and again, and one of our gentlemen did the same, representing her case. After long silence he has written to her a short letter, which she showed me, inviting her, in rather an indifferent manner, to come to Georgetown, where her mother is now staying, but remits no money to pay her passage or to support her here. Our gentlemen have interested Mr. Lawley,[121] an Englishman of some note in Richmond, in her case; and her husband having been a British subject, he may be enabled to get her a passport and a free passage on the flag-of-truce boat.

15th—Spent yesterday in the hospital. I am particularly interested in two very ill men. One is a youth of seventeen years, who had been seventeen months in service.[122] Poor boy! He is now sinking with consumption, and has lately been brought to our hospital from another. His case elicits great sympathy and kindness. His name is Stansberry, and he is from Baltimore. We have reason to hope that he is prepared to meet his God.

Letters (underground) from the Valley to-day. Millroy is doing his worst among the dear people there. It is grievous to think how much of Virginia is down-trodden and lying in ruins. The old State has bared her breast to the destroyer, and borne the brunt of battle for the good of the Confederacy, and this too after long and vain efforts for peace. Her citizens, young and old, are doing what they can. Her sons have bled and died, and are still offering themselves willing sacrifices on the country's altar. Her daughters are striving in their vocation in this hallowed cause, all looking to God for his blessing upon our efforts.

17th—On going to the hospital yesterday, I found that young Stansberry had died, surrounded by sympathizing friends, and having a bright hope of a blessed immortality. We are anxious about our armies everywhere, from the Mississippi to the seaboard. Rumours are rife about General Longstreet having thrown his forces between Norfolk and the Yankee army at Suffolk.[123] In the mean time we must possess our souls in patience.

18th—A letter from our son J[ames] to-day; full of pleasant feeling at finding himself again in the Army of Northern Virginia. He is just established near General Jackson's head-quarters, as Surgeon of the First Virginia Battalion;

had just breakfasted with Stonewall and is filled with enthusiastic admiration for the great Christian soldier and patriot.

The enemy seems to have left Charleston.[124] The Northern papers, after much circumlocution, prevarication, and boasting of a successful reconnaissance, acknowledge that they were greatly injured by their last attack on it. "All quiet on the Rappahannock," continued to be reported. God grant that it may continue so!

Yesterday spent in the hospital; some of the men are very ill. I go back to-morrow.

Wednesday Night, April 29—On Saturday Mr. [McGuire] and myself went up to Cedar Hill,[125] and he attempted to go to Fredericksburg; when he reached Hamilton's Crossings he found it impossible to go on—conveyances were so scarce and the roads so terrible. He had the pleasure to dine, by invitation, with his old friend, Mr. M. Garnett.[126] Once having every luxury which could be desired, he now lives in his desolated house, surrounded by down-trodden fields, without fences, trees, or vegetation of any sort. His servants, except a few faithful ones, have deserted him; his horses and stock of all kinds have been swept away; his sons in the army; and he is cheerful and buoyed with hope, not for himself, but for the cause: good old patriot as he is, forgetting his own privations in zeal for his country. On Sunday Mr. [McGuire] heard an admirable sermon at head-quarters (General Jackson's) from the Rev. Mr. Lacy,[127] a Presbyterian chaplain, and returned home on Monday, having found it impossible to fulfill the object of his trip, that of preaching to the soldiers at Fredericksburg.

Saturday Night, May 9—So much has happened since I last wrote in my diary, that I can scarcely collect my thoughts to give a plain detail of facts as they occurred.[128]

Ten days ago, Mr. [McGuire] and myself went in to spend two days with our children who are living in Richmond. It soon became apparent that we could not return, as the Government had taken the cars for the purpose of transporting soldiers to Fredericksburg.

[Gen. Joseph] Hooker was making immense demonstrations and was crossing 159,000 men. They fought on Saturday, Sunday, and Monday, at different points, principally at Chancellorsville, and the enemy was repulsed at all points. Hooker and his host retired to the Rappahannock, and recrossed, I think, on Wednesday. It is said that General Lee would have followed him, but for the dreadful storm of Monday night and Tuesday. General Lee in his official report speaks of it as a "signal victory."[129] Our army was smaller than usual, as Longstreet was still near Suffolk, and could not get up in time. It is pretty certain that Hooker—fighting Joe!!—had two to Lee's one, and was defeated. But General Jackson was wounded severely. The great Stonewall is lost to us for a time; his left arm has been amputated, and there is a severe wound in his right hand.[130] Oh, I pray that God may raise him up to be a continued blessing to the country. His wife has gone to him. The best surgical skill of the army, the sympathy and anxiety of the whole South, and the prayers of the country, are his. General Paxton,[131] of the Stonewall Brigade, was killed, and many, ah, how many, valuable lives were lost! It is impossible for us yet to know, as the telegraphic wires are cut, and mail communication very uncertain. From my own family boys we have not heard, and we are willing to believe that "no news is good news." Two more of the dear ones over whose youth we so anxiously watched have fallen—Hill Carter, of Shirley, and Benjamin White, of Charlestown, Jefferson County.[132] Thank God, they were both Christians! My heart aches for their parents. The last was an only son, and justly the pride and joy of his household. His parents are in the enemy's lines. O Lord, uphold that tender mother when the withering stroke is known to her! Major Channing Price and Colonel Thomas Garnett are gone![133] God help our country! We can't afford to lose such men.

While our army was busily engaged last Sunday, the Yankees took occasion to send out a raiding party of their superfluous numbers.[134] A party of several hundred came here about three o'clock in the afternoon. They knew that the cars containing the wounded from the battle-field would be here. The cars arrived, and were immediately surrounded and the soldiers paroled. The ladies all the while were in the cars administering comfort to the wounded. They remained about three hours, took off every horse they could find, and every servant that they could induce to go, which was very few, and then rode off without burning the houses or offering other injury to the villagers. They belonged to [Gen. George] Stoneman's command. They went over this county, Goochland, Louisa, and a part of Fluvanna, without molestation. They became alarmed, however, and cut their career short. They went to Columbia for the purpose of destroying the [James River and Kanawha] canal, but in their haste did it very little injury. The injury to the railroads was slight, and easily repaired. To individuals they did some mischief; at W[estwood] they fed four hundred horses at my brother's barn, took his buggy horse, and rode off. His neighbours, and others in their route, fared very much in the same way. In Richmond the excitement was terrible.[135] The alarm-bell pealed out its startling notes; citizens were armed, and sent out to man the batteries; extemporaneous cavalry companies were formed and sent out; women were seen crying and wringing their hands on the streets; wild rumours were afloat; but it all ended in the raiders not attempting to get to the Richmond batteries, and the city in a few hours became perfectly quiet.

Sunday, May 10—Sad, sad tidings were brought to our cottage this morning! Washington, the youngest and darling son of our dear friend, Mrs. [Cornelia] Stuart, has fallen.[136] The mother and sisters are overwhelmed, while our whole household is shrouded in sorrow. He was young, brave, and a Christian. He fell while nobly fighting with his company, the famous Rockbridge Battery, on Marye's Hill. We have heard no other particulars. The brave boy had scarcely recovered from a most severe wound received last summer near Winchester. To God we commend his afflicted, though quietly submissive mother. He alone can soothe the sorrow which He has seen fit to permit.

Tuesday Evening, May 12th—How can I record the sorrow which has befallen our country! General T. J. Jackson is no more.[137] The good, the great, the glorious Stonewall Jackson is numbered with the dead! Humanly speaking, we cannot do without him; but the same God who raised him up, took him from us, and He who has so miraculously prospered our cause, can lead us on without him. Perhaps we have trusted too much to an arm of flesh; for he was the nation's idol. His soldiers almost worshipped him, and it may be that God has therefore removed him. We bow in meek submission to the great Ruler of events. May his blessed example be followed by officers and men, even to the gates of heaven! He died on Sunday the 10th, at a quarter past three P.M. His body was carried by yesterday, in a car, to Richmond. Almost every lady in Ashland visited the car, with a wreath or a cross of the most beautiful flowers, as a tribute to the illustrious dead. An immense concourse has assembled in Richmond, as the solitary car containing the body of the great soldier, accompanied by a suitable escort, slowly and solemnly approached the depot. The body lies in state to-day at the Capitol, wrapped in the Confederate flag, and literally covered with lilies of the valley and other beautiful Spring flowers. Tomorrow the sad *cortege* will wend its way to Lexington, where he will be buried, according to his dying request, in the "Valley of Virginia." As a warrior, we may appropriately quote from Byron:

> His spirit wraps the dusky mountain,
> His memory sparkles o'er the fountain,
> The meanest rill, the mightiest river,
> Rolls mingling with his fame forever.[138]

As a Christian, in the words of St. Paul, I thank God to be able to say, "He has fought the good fight, he has finished his course, he has kept the faith. Henceforth there is laid up for him a crown of righteousness, which the Lord, the righteous Judge, shall give him at the last day."[139]

Wednesday, 13th—I have just heard that my nephew, Will'by N[ewton][140] was wounded at Chancellorsville, and that his left leg has been amputated. He is at Mrs. Marye's, near Hamilton's Crossing, receiving the warm-hearted hospitality of that house, now so widely known. His mother has reached him, and he is doing well. I pray that God may have mercy upon him, and raise him up speedily for the Saviour's sake.

May 16th—We were aroused this morning before daylight, by reports that the Yankees were making a raid, and were very near this place. We all dressed hastily, and the gentlemen went out to devise means to stop the trains which were to pass through. Though within five miles of us, they became aware that notice had been given of their purpose, and they immediately turned their steps to some more private place, where they might rob and plunder without molestation. The miserable poltroons, when on one of their raids, will become frightened by the sudden rising of a covey of partridges, and be diverted from their course; then they will ride bravely to a house, where they know they will only find women and children; order meals to be prepared; search the house; take the valuables; feed their horses at the barns; take off the horses from the stables; shoot the pigs, sheep, and other stock, and leave them dead in the fields; rob the poultry-yards; then, after regaling themselves on the meals which have been prepared by force, with the threats of bayonets and pistols, they ride off, having pocketed the silver spoons and forks, which may have unwittingly been left in their way.[141]

I have been in Richmond for two days past, nursing the wounded of our little hospital. Some of them are very severely injured, yet they are the most cheerful invalids I ever saw. It is remarked in all the hospitals that the cheerfulness of the wounded in proportion to their suffering is much greater than that of the sick. Under my care, yesterday, was one poor fellow, with a ball embedded in his neck; another with an amputated leg; one with a hole in his breast, through which a bullet had passed; another with a shattered arm; and others with slighter wounds; yet all showed indomitable spirit; evinced a readiness to be amused or interested in every thing around them; asked that the morning papers might be read to them, and gloried in their late victory; and expressed an anxiety to get well, that they may have another "*chance at them fellows.*" The Yankees are said to have landed at West Point, and are thence sending out raiding parties over the country.[142] Colonel [Hasbrouck] Davis, who led the party here on the third, has been severely wounded by a scouting party, sent out by General [Henry] Wise towards Tunstall's Station. It is said he has lost his leg. So may it be!

Monday, May 18th—This morning we had the gratification of a short visit from General Lee.[143] He called and breakfasted with us, while the other passengers in the cars breakfasted at the hotel. We were very glad to see that great and good man look so well and so cheerful. His beard is very long, and painfully gray, which makes him appear much older than he really is. One of the ladies, at [the] table, with whom he is closely connected, rallied him on allowing his beard to grow, saying, "Cousin R[obert], it makes you look too venerable for your years." He was amused, and pleaded as his excuse the inconvenience of shaving in camp. "Well," she replied, "if I were in Cousin Mary's place (Mrs. L[ee]'s), I would allow it to remain now, but I would take it off as soon as the war is over." He answered, while a shade passed over his bright countenance, "When the war is over, my dear L., she may take my beard off, and my head with it, if she chooses." This he said as the whistle summoned him to his seat in the cars, not meaning to depress us, or imagining for an instant that we would think of it again; but it proved to us that he *knew* that the end was not yet, and disappointed us, for after every great victory we cannot help hoping that the Federal Government may be tired of war and bloodshed, rapine and murder, and withdraw its myriads to more innocent pursuits.

Yesterday evening we were agreeably surprised by a call from W. B. C.,[144] just recovered from his dreadful wound, received at Fredericksburg last

winter. He is an infantry captain of the Stonewall Brigade, and is just returning to his company. Alas! alas! his great Captain [Jackson] has passed away
during his absence, which makes his return very sad. He thinks that General
Ewell is the man of all others to put in his place, though no man can fill it.[145]
General Ewell, he says, is one of General Jackson's most enthusiastic admir-
ers, believing him to have been almost an inspired man. General E[well]
relates an incident of him, when on their victorious march through the Valley
last summer, which is beautifully characteristic of General J[ackson]. One
night, when it was evident that there must be a battle next day, he (General
E[well]) went to General Jackson for his plans. General J[ackson] replied that
he would give them to him next morning as they had not yet been formed.
General E[well] felt uneasy and restless, and could not sleep. About midnight
he arose, and, passing through the sleeping multitudes, he reached General
Jackson's tent, and was about to raise the curtain to enter it, when his attention
was arrested by the voice of prayer. General Jackson was praying fervently
for guidance through the coming day. General E[well] remarked to a friend
that he had never before heard a prayer so devout and beautiful; he then, for
the first time, felt the desire to be a Christian. He retired to his tent quietly,
without disturbing General J[ackson], feeling assured that all would be well.[146]
The next morning a fight came off, replete with victory. General Ewell was
subsequently wounded at the second battle of Manassas, and it is said that he
has since become a Christian. God grant that it may be so!

May 20th—I feel depressed to-night.[147] Army news from the South bad.
General Pemberton has been repulsed between Jackson and Vicksburg.[148]
General Johnston is there, I hope, by the mercy of God, he may be able to
keep the enemy out of Vicksburg. Besides the depressing news, the day has
been distressing in the hospital—so much suffering among the wounded.
One fine young man has the appearance and manner of imbecility, from
having been struck on the head by a piece of shell. No relief can be given
him, and the surgeons say that he must die.

Mr. [McGuire] staid in town to attend the Church "Council," as it is now
called. The new name may be more appropriate to an ecclesiastical meeting,
yet "Virginia Convention" has a sweet, hallowed sound to me.

23d—We tremble for Vicksburg; an immense army has been sent against it;
we await its fate with breathless anxiety.

25th—The enemy repulsed at Vicksburg, though it is still in a state of siege.[149] General Johnston is there, and we hope that the best means will be used to save that heroic little city; and we pray that God may bless the means used.

A friend called this morning and told us of the fall of another of those dear youths, over whose boyish sojourn with us memory loves to linger. Kennedy Groghan,[150] of Baltimore, who, in the very beginning of the war, came over to help us, fell in a skirmish in the Valley, a short time ago. The only account given us is, that the men were forced to retreat hastily, and were only able to place his loved body under the spreading branches of a tree. Oh! I trust that some kindly hand has put him beneath God's own earth, free from the din of war, from the strife of man, and from the curse of sin forever. I remember so well when, during our stay in Winchester, the first summer of the war, while General Johnston's army was stationed near there, how he, and so many others, would come in to see us, with their yet unfaded suits of gray—already sunburnt and soldier-like, but bright and cheerful. Alas! alas! how many now fill the graves of heroes—their young lives crushed out by the unscrupulous hand of an invading foe!

27th—The news from Vicksburg by the morning papers is very delightful, if authentic. We pause for confirmation of it. The young people among the villagers and refugees have been amusing themselves, during the past two evenings, with tableaux.[151] I am too old to enjoy such things in these troubled times, but one picture I regretted not seeing. It represented the young Confederacy. The whole bright galaxy was there—South Carolina in scarlet, restive and fiery; Virginia, grave and dignified, yet bright with hope, seemed to be beckoning Kentucky on, who stood beyond the threshold, her eyes cast down with shame and suffering; Maryland was at the threshold, but held back by a strong hand; all the rest of the fair sisters were there in their appropriate places, forming a beautiful picture.

I am amused to see how the Democrats of the North are speechifying and exciting themselves about the arrest of Vallandigham, and how Lincoln will soon make them *back down*.[152]

May 28th—Hospital day. The wounded cheerful and doing well. I read, distributed books, and talked with them. They are always ready to be amused, or to be instructed. I have never but in one instance had an unpleasant word or look from any whom I endeavoured to treat with kindness in any way. Bible reading is always kindly received.

J. J.[153] has returned home, as usual much interested in hospital work.

Notes

1. The full text of Lee's telegram to Davis is in Robert E. Lee, *The Wartime Papers of R. E. Lee,* ed. Clifford Dowdey (Boston: Little, Brown, 1961), 268.

2. It *was* too good to be true. Maj. Gen. Ambrose Burnside and his IX Corps were then attached to Gen. John Pope's Army of Virginia but saw no action at Second Manassas.

3. The campaign began with an August 28 attack by Jackson at Groveton and ended with Jackson's men charging through the rain on September 1 at Chantilly. Union casualties were 16,000; Confederate losses, 9,000 men. Among the Union dead was New Jersey's most distinguished soldier, Gen. Philip Kearny.

4. The letter writer was badly misinformed. By September 12, a huge Federal garrison at Harpers Ferry was blocking Lee's main retirement route, and McClellan's massive army was closing steadily on the Confederates. Lee stopped his advance before it got to Pennsylvania.

5. Benjamin Harrison McGuire enlisted in January 1862 in the Twenty-second Virginia Infantry Battalion. He received appointment as a lieutenant while home in Lynchburg on sick furlough. Thomas M. Rankin, *22nd Battalion Virginia Infantry* (Lynchburg, Va.: H. E. Howard, 1999), 92.

6. Rev. William H. Kinckle was rector of St. Paul's Episcopal Church in Lynchburg.

7. "And it came to pass, when Moses held up his hand, that Israel prevailed; and when he let down his hand, Amalek prevailed. But Moses' hands *were* heavy . . . and Aaron and Hur stayed up his hands . . . and his hands were steady until the going down of the sun. And Joshua discomfited Amalek and his people with the edge of the sword." *Exodus* 17:11–13.

8. On August 10, Gen. E. Kirby Smith's Confederates defeated a Union force at Richmond, Kentucky, thirty miles south of Lexington. This was the first engagement of Gen. Braxton Bragg's invasion of Kentucky. Although the victory was small, it was an impressive start.

9. Davis's proclamation appeared on September 4, the day that lead elements of Lee's army began crossing the Potomac River into Maryland.

10. After running afoul of "Stonewall" Jackson, Gen. William Wing Loring was sent to command forces in the Charleston, West Virginia, area. At this time

he was making a probe here and reconnaissance there, but no accomplishment of note resulted. See David L. Phillips and Rebecca L. Hill, *War Diaries: The 1861 Kanawha Valley Campaigns* (Leesburg, Va.: Gauley Mount, 1990), 393–95.

11. Coordination between the invading forces of Kirby Smith and Braxton Bragg was nonexistent from the start. The Southerners won minor successes in Kentucky, but the October 8 battle of Perryville marked the end of the invasion.

12. Capt. William Brockenbrough Colston of the Second Virginia would limp back to duty only to be severely wounded at the December battle of Fredericksburg. Dennis E. Frye, *2nd Virginia Infantry* (Lynchburg, Va.: H. E. Howard, 1984), 90.

13. "Stonewall" Jackson surrounded Harpers Ferry and, on the afternoon of September 14, began hammering the post with artillery fire as his infantry moved into position to attack. Jackson resumed the bombardment early the next morning. Col. Dixon S. Miles, the post commander, found himself outflanked and outgunned. Shortly after 8:00 A.M., Miles surrendered his force of 12,500 men—the largest number of captured Americans in history until World War II.

14. Mrs. McGuire is referring to the September 14 battle of South Mountain, Maryland, where Gen. Harvey Hill's lone Confederate division repulsed all-day assaults from two Union corps. Hill and what was left of his command retired down the west side of the mountain under cover of darkness. McClellan's army was not driven five miles from the field, as Mrs. McGuire believed.

15. A direct descendant of James Madison, graduate of the Virginia Military Institute, and prominent Lynchburg attorney, Garland led the Eleventh Virginia into war. He received promotion to brigadier general in May 1862. Garland was killed in the fighting at South Mountain while at the head of his brigade.

16. The September 1862 struggle at Antietam Creek, near Sharpsburg, Maryland, remains the bloodiest one-day battle in American history. In thirteen hours of fighting that Wednesday, some 6,000 men were killed or mortally wounded, while more than 17,000 others were reported injured or missing. For comparison, the American losses on D-Day in 1944 were one-fourth those numbers.

17. Mrs. McGuire's account of the September 20 engagement at Boteler's Ford reflects the exaggeration that continues to swirl around the fight. McClellan dispatched several artillery batteries and a single infantry brigade to probe the rear of Lee's retreating army. Jackson calmly detached three brigades under A. P. Hill to blunt the advance. Union cavalry officer Alfred Pleasonton was not involved in this action. Confederates easily drove the Federals into and across the Potomac River. Despite wild estimates, Union losses were 71 killed,

161 wounded, and 131 missing and presumed drowned. James I. Robertson Jr., *General A. P. Hill: The Story of a Confederate Warrior* (New York: Random House, 1987), 148–50.

18. Bettie Holmes McGuire was the oldest daughter of well-to-do Clarke County farmer and physician William D. McGuire. In February 1864, she married Mrs. McGuire's stepson James.

19. Misinterpretation has persisted about the Emancipation Proclamation. Lincoln declared that only slaves in those states "still in rebellion" on January 1, 1863, would be free. The presidential decree justified emancipation on the grounds of military necessity. A New England governor termed the proclamation "a poor document, but a mighty act." Allan Nevins, *The War for the Union* (New York: Scribner's, 1959–1971), 2:234.

20. What Mrs. McGuire heard was not exaggeration. At Antietam, Gen. Edwin V. Sumner's corps suffered 883 killed, 3,859 wounded, and 396 missing, for a total of 5,138 casualties. United States War Department, *War of the Rebellion: A Compilation of Official Records of the Union and Confederate Armies* (Washington, D.C.: Government Printing Office, 1880–1901), series I, vol. 19, pt. 2, 200 (hereafter cited as *OR*).

21. Son of a fourteen-term congressman from Norfolk, Virginia, John Newton graduated second in his West Point class. He enjoyed a distinguished engineering career prior to civil war. Newton remained loyal to the Union; he ultimately rose to major general and corps commander in the Army of the Potomac.

22. Donald Fairfax served as an officer in the U.S. navy and first achieved fame in the "Trent Affair," when Union officials arrested two Confederate emissaries on the high seas.

23. Socrates Maupin was a longtime stalwart on the University of Virginia faculty. He and his wife, Sally, had six children.

24. John Barbee Minor and Nannie C. Minor were another well-known faculty couple in Charlottesville.

25. Raleigh Thomas Colston began his army career as captain of a Berkeley County company in the Second Virginia. He temporarily commanded the regiment in the December 1862 expedition. Frye, *2nd Virginia Infantry,* 18, 90.

26. Albert Taylor Bledsoe attended West Point with Robert E. Lee and Jefferson Davis. He practiced law for a time with Abraham Lincoln. Colonel of the Thirty-sixth Virginia in 1861, Bledsoe was soon appointed chief of the Bureau of War.

27. James Ross Maupin served in the First Virginia Artillery and Fifty-sixth Virginia. His brother Chapman became a lieutenant in the First Confederate Engineer Troops.

186 Diary of a Southern Refugee

28. John Brockenbrough Newton was surgeon of the Fortieth Virginia and later Episcopal bishop of Virginia.

29. Lt. Edward Brockenbrough of the Fortieth Virginia was killed June 27 at Gaines' Mill.

30. The two sons of Dr. Ezekiel Talley served in the "Hanover Grays" of the Fifteenth Virginia. At Antietam, Pvt. Ezekiel Starke Talley was killed in action; his brother, John Abner Talley, fell mortally wounded. Their father traveled to Sharpsburg, Maryland, recovered the two bodies, and took them home to Hanover County for burial in the family cemetery. Louis H. Manarin, *15th Virginia Infantry* (Lynchburg, Va.: H. E. Howard, 1990), 29, 117.

31. On October 3, in ninety-degree weather, Confederates under Gen. Sterling Price and Gen. Earl Van Dorn assailed Union general William S. Rosecrans's lines at Corinth, Mississippi. They drove the Federals back two miles throughout a long day's fighting. Confederates resumed the attacks the next morning but soon succumbed to Union defense, heat, and thirst. A noon counterattack put Price and Van Dorn to flight. Union casualties were 2,520 men, while Confederate losses were 4,233 soldiers.

32. This is another reference to the oldest of Dr. W. S. R. Brockenbrough's children, Judith White Newton.

33. Kensey Johns was the elder son of the Episcopal bishop. The major spent the war in the Quartermaster Department and was in charge of river and canal transportation in the Richmond area.

34. In an October 8 fight primarily over control of water springs, a third of Bragg's army and two-thirds of Gen. Don Carlos Buell's forces fought throughout the day. Confederate losses were 3,000; Union casualties exceeded 6,000 men. Bragg retired after dark with the remainder of the Federal army approaching the field.

35. After eighteen months of war, with casualties soaring each month, a political backlash occurred in the autumn 1862 elections in the North. Democrats won governorships in New York and New Jersey, legislative majorities in Illinois and Indiana, plus an increase of thirty-four new members in the U.S. House of Representatives.

36. From August until well into December, Richmond was relatively quiet. The few military engagements were fifty or more miles away. The number treated at Chimborazo, the largest of the capital's military hospitals, never dropped below 4,300 men for any given month. Yet a surgeon at another facility wrote his wife at this time: "I have little to do . . . my hospital is almost clear of patients." Emory M. Thomas, *The Confederate State of Richmond* (Austin: University of Texas Press, 1971), 101–2.

37. The most influential figure in Halifax County, James Coles Bruce had been a member of the Virginia secession convention and became a staunch Confederate. His estate, Berry Hill, remains a landmark in Southside Virginia. Wirt Johnson Carrington, *A History of Halifax County (Virginia)* (Baltimore: Appeals, 1969), 122–24.

38. Sally Louisa Tompkins, from an old and cultured Tidewater family, became Richmond's most famous hospital superintendent during the war. In a converted private home at Main and Third streets, she oversaw the tender care of more than 1,300 sick and wounded soldiers. Mrs. McGuire and her son Dr. John P. McGuire Jr. were among many who served as volunteers at the Tompkins hospital.

39. McClellan's failure to move forward with superior numbers against Lee exhausted even the patience of Lincoln. On November 7, Gen. Ambrose E. Burnside was appointed to take command of the Army of the Potomac. Burnside did not consider himself qualified—an opinion he shortly demonstrated at Fredericksburg to be true.

40. Burnside knew that he was expected to take the offensive. He quickly devised a plan of shifting his army quickly and secretly from north-central Virginia to Fredericksburg. There he would cross the Rappahannock River and drive around Lee's flank toward Richmond. By November 17, two of Burnside's corps were at Falmouth, directly across the river from Fredericksburg. Failure to ensure that pontoon bridges were in place brought Burnside's movement to a month-long halt.

41. Mrs. McGuire made an understatement here, which is unusual. The shelling of a refugee train leaving Fredericksburg became widely publicized. No fatalities occurred, but the incident did provoke an even greater fear of Yankees. A similar shelling of a train in Fernandina, Florida, resulted in the deaths of two passengers. Mary Elizabeth Massey, *Refugee Life in the Confederacy* (Baton Rouge: Louisiana State University Press, 1964), 65.

42. For vivid pictures of these citizens forced from their homes, see George C. Rable, *Fredericksburg! Fredericksburg!* (Chapel Hill: University of North Carolina Press, 2002), 84–86.

43. Sallie Putnam noted that houses everywhere in Richmond were stretched to "India-rubber capacity." Another woman found the households to be "very heterogeneous." Sallie A. Brock Putnam, *In Richmond during the Confederacy: By a Lady of Richmond* (New York: R. M. McBride, 1961), 320; Eliza Frances Andrews, *The War-time Journal of a Georgia Girl* (New York: D. Appleton, 1908), 133.

44. Perhaps being welcomed so heartily by rural friends, and rebuffed so

sternly by Richmond residents, led Mrs. McGuire to conclude that country homes had "greater elasticity."

45. For other comments on high inflation at the time, see United Daughters of the Confederacy, South Carolina Division, *South Carolina Women in the Confederacy* (Columbia, S.C.: State Company, 1903), 1:172–73; Francis Warrington Dawson, *Our Women in the War: An Address by Francis W. Dawson, Delivered February 22, 1887, at the Fifth Annual Re-union of the Association of the Maryland Line, at the Academy of Music* (Baltimore and Charleston, S.C.: Walker, Evans and Cogswell, 1887), 356, 437; Elizabeth Preston Allan, *The Life and Letters of Margaret Junkin Preston* (Boston: Houghton, Mifflin, 1903), 134.

46. The 120,000 soldiers and thousands of horses comprising the Army of the Potomac remained stationary in Stafford County for the better part of a month. Naturally, the countryside would be stripped of anything usable.

47. This quotation is evidence that Mrs. McGuire reworked her diary prior to postwar publication. The person who called the Army of the Potomac "the finest army on the planet" was Union general Joseph Hooker, who succeeded Burnside a month after the battle of Fredericksburg. The boastful Hooker added in the same newspaper interview that he could "cross the Rapidan without losing a man and then take the rebs where the hair is short." Alexander K. McClure, *Recollections of Half a Century* (Salem, Mass.: Salem Press, 1902), 347.

48. Mrs. Sue Carrington was the widow of a prominent Richmond figure. Her home at Franklin and Twenty-eighth streets was one of the most fashionable residences in the capital. Robert Beverly Munford Jr., *Richmond Homes and Memories* (Richmond: Garrett and Massie, 1936), 61–62.

49. It is interesting that residents of Ashland, thirty-eight miles from the Fredericksburg battlefield, could hear the sound of cannon.

50. Burnside wasted a month waiting for pontoon bridges to span the Rappahannock. By the time they were in place, so was Lee's army on high ground behind the town. The resultant December 13 battle more resembled a massacre. Thirteen times Union soldiers made blind assaults against the heavily fortified Confederate lines; thirteen times the Federals were repulsed. Burnside suffered almost 12,700 casualties; Lee's losses were 5,300 soldiers.

51. Thomas Reade Rootes Cobb was commanding a Georgia brigade behind the now-famous "stone wall" at Fredericksburg when he received a bullet in the thigh. He bled to death before medical help could arrive. Maxcy Gregg and his South Carolinians were defending the portion of Jackson's lines that Federals momentarily punctured. Gregg fell mortally wounded in the action.

52. Whenever a troop train stopped at a town, individual women—and sometimes entire committees—would board the cars to assist the wounded

and provide whatever food and supplies they had. See United Daughters of the Confederacy, *South Carolina Women,* 1:147–48, 364.

53. Capt. John Bowyer Brockenbrough was temporarily commanding a battalion of five artillery batteries at Fredericksburg when he fell wounded "while gallantly discharging his duties." Although Brockenbrough was promoted to major, the lingering effect of his injuries forced him from field service at the end of 1863. *OR,* series 1, vol. 21, 367; vol. 29, pt. 2, 841. Capt. William Brockenbrough Colston fell from a shell wound that kept him from duty until the following summer. Frye, *2nd Virginia Infantry,* 90.

54. An auctioneer at Kent, Paine & Company in Richmond, William G. Paine lived with his wife, Elizabeth, and three small children on East Grace between Sixth and Seventh streets. Michael D. Gorman, Richmond, Virginia, to editor, June 10, 2004; 1860 Virginia Census—Henrico County.

55. Dr. James Bolton was one of the first surgeons in Richmond to use ether in an operation.

56. Every indication points to Dr. James Brown McCaw as the physician who attended Major Brockenbrough. Mr. Paine's company supplied commission merchants for Chimborazo Hospital, where Dr. McCaw was chief surgeon. In addition, McCaw lived less than a block away from the Paine residence. Michael D. Gorman, Richmond, Virginia, to editor, June 30, 2004.

57. In late April 1861, Charles Bell Gibson had been appointed surgeon general of the Virginia military department. His work in Richmond hospitals during the war won wide acclaim. Wyndham B. Blanton, *Medicine in Virginia in the Nineteenth Century* (Richmond: Garrett and Massie, 1933), 55, 273.

58. William Spencer Roane Brockenbrough was a Hanover County physician. At that time, Winder Hospital ("Camp Winder") on the west side of Richmond challenged Chimborazo Hospital on the east side of the capital as the largest military compound in the world.

59. Raleigh Edward Colston, a former professor at the Virginia Military Institute, commanded a brigade in Gen. "Stonewall" Jackson's corps.

60. A native of Alexandria, Randolph Cary Fairfax had graduated from Episcopal High School. He enlisted in the Rockbridge Artillery in 1861 and was wounded July 1, 1862, at Malvern Hill. In the December fighting at Fredericksburg, the twenty-year-old soldier was killed by a shell fragment. Mrs. McGuire's husband said of him: "Morally, I have not known his superior. God endowed him with a strange purity of mind and heart by nature, and then to this added the grace of true religion. . . . No nobler son was ever born within the grand old commonwealth." Philip Slaughter, *A Sketch of the Life of Randolph Fairfax* (Richmond: Enquirer Job Office, 1864), 46–47.

61. Heartbreak accompanying the death in battle of a loved one often shook the abiding faith of Southern women. While some turned away from God for failing to answer their prayers for the safety of kinsmen, others declared that it was impossible to fathom the ways of an inscrutable Providence. Yet Mrs. McGuire viewed losses differently. To her, God was taking the dead heroes to the eternal bliss of heaven.

62. David Rittenhouse Barton abandoned a teaching career to join the Rockbridge Artillery. In the summer of 1862 he had been promoted to lieutenant to replace his brother, Charles Marshall Barton, who was killed May 25 at Winchester.

63. Both of these passages are from William Knapp's hymn "Triumphant Sion, Lift Thy Head."

64. In the Union bombardment of Fredericksburg, more than twenty artillery shells struck the steeple of the town's Episcopal church. After the battle Federals used the sanctuary for a hospital. Rable, *Fredericksburg! Fredericksburg!* 427; Noel G. Harrison, *Fredericksburg Civil War Sites* (Lynchburg, Va.: H. E. Howard, 1995), 192–94.

65. Mrs. Harriet Keene's husband, Edward, was a lieutenant from Kentucky.

66. In the last week of December, Union general William S. Rosecrans moved south from Nashville with 43,000 troops. Confederate general Braxton Bragg had 38,000 soldiers posted along Stones River thirty miles away at Murfreesboro. The two hosts waged a bloody, confused fight that lasted four days (December 30, 1862–January 2, 1863), produced 25,000 casualties, and accomplished little for either side. Bragg withdrew to Tullahoma, Alabama; Rosecrans did not pursue.

67. Gen. William T. Sherman's late-December attempt to take Vicksburg via the Yazoo River proved a failure. Confederates heavily entrenched at Chickasaw Bluffs easily repulsed the Union advance and inflicted 1,700 casualties.

68. The Union ironclad *Monitor* was under tow en route to South Carolina when, near midnight on December 30–31, the vessel floundered in heavy seas off Cape Hatteras. Sixteen of sixty-three men on board drowned.

69. New Hampshire senator John Parker Hale was an outspoken champion of emancipation.

70. On the night of January 5, having returned from a long inspection of the western military theater, President Davis delivered a short address in Richmond. The long months of anxiety and many sacrifices endured, he stated, "has made us a band of brothers, and, I trust, we will be united forever." Jefferson Davis, *The Papers of Jefferson Davis,* vol. 9, ed. Lynda Lasswell Crist, Mary Seaton

Dix, and Kenneth H. Williams (Baton Rouge: Louisiana State University Press, 1997), 11–15.

71. For the benevolent labors of Mrs. James Harlan, see L. P. Brockett, *Woman's Work in the Civil War* (Philadelphia: R. H. Curran, 1867), 676–78.

72. After amassing troops and an improvised fleet of gunboats, Confederate general John B. Magruder on January 1 attacked Union-held Galveston, Texas, and its flotilla. Four hours of action brought the surrender of the city, the sinking of the gunboat *Harriet Lane,* and a temporary lifting of the blockade of the Texas coast.

73. In 1840 Jonathan Mayhew Wainwright had married Maria B. Page, the oldest of three daughters of Dr. Robert Powell Page of The Briars in Clarke County, Virginia. The couple had four children. Two sons were in Federal service. Richard Channing Moore Page, *Genealogy of the Page Family in Virginia* (Bridgewater, Va.: Carrier, 1965), 147. Union admiral David Farragut was furious over the Galveston defeat. Had not Wainwright been killed, Farragut reported, the *Harriet Lane* would have made it to safety. U.S. Naval War Records Office, ed., *Official Records of the Union and Confederate Navies in the War of the Rebellion* (Washington, D.C., 1894–1922), 19:440.

74. Bradley Tyler Johnson graduated from Princeton, became a prominent attorney in Maryland, and was a leader in the Democratic Party. He helped organize the First Maryland Infantry Regiment and ultimately rose to its colonelcy. Johnson was then on military court duties in Richmond.

75. "The mother, wi' her needles an' her shears / Gars auld claes look amaist as weel's the new" is from Robert Burns, "The Cotter's Saturday Night."

76. A high-ranking graduate of West Point and much-decorated hero of the Mexican War, Mansfield Lovell began the Civil War as a major general commanding the New Orleans military department. He then suffered the indignity of having to abandon the South's largest city because of lack of manpower, supplies, and support. The loss of New Orleans was not Lovell's fault, but no field commander wanted him thereafter. He had come to Richmond with the hope that a board of inquiry might clear his reputation.

77. Erysipelas is a virulent streptococcal infection that was much feared in the Civil War era. Physicians often referred to it as "pyemia" or "blood poisoning."

78. James M. G. McGuire spent January 1863 as surgeon of the Forty-fourth North Carolina. Louis H. Manarin, comp., *North Carolina Troops, 1861–1865: A Roster* (Raleigh, N.C.: State Department of Archives and History, 1966–2003), 10:397.

79. A month after his resounding defeat at Fredericksburg, Burnside started

his army upriver along the Rappahannock to turn Lee's flank and continue the advance on Richmond. The elements did not cooperate. Four consecutive days of rain converted the movement into a "Mud March" and another Union disaster. Burnside removed from command outspokenly critical Gen. William B. Franklin. Gen. Edwin V. Sumner, leading the other wing of the Army of the Potomac, resigned from service. Lincoln then replaced Burnside with the boastful but politically connected Gen. Joseph Hooker.

80. Burnside's General Orders No. 7, dated January 20, stated in part: "The late brilliant actions in North Carolina, Tennessee, and Arkansas divided and weakened the enemy on the Rappahannock, and the auspicious moment seems to have arrived to strike a great and mortal blow at the Rebellion." Benjamin Perley Poore, *The Life and Public Services of Ambrose E. Burnside, Soldier—Citizen—Statesman* (Providence, R.I.: J. A. and R. A. Reid, 1882), 198.

81. "So when all Israel saw that the king harkened not unto them, the people answered the king, saying, What portion have we in David? Neither *have we* inheritance in the son of Jesse; to your tents, O Israel: now see to thine own house, David. So Israel departed unto their own tents." I Kings 12:16.

82. Roger Atkinson Pryor, a native of Petersburg, was a successful prewar attorney, newspaper editor, and congressman. Although appointed a brigadier general for gallantry at the 1862 battle of Williamsburg, Pryor never fulfilled expectations in the field. Mrs. McGuire was referring to a January 10 foray by Pryor's brigade in the Blackwater region of Union-held Suffolk. The small affair was inconsequential.

83. Hollywood was Richmond's principal cemetery. Located west of town on a bluff overlooking the James River, it was long called President's Hill because of the number of chief executives buried there.

84. Marie Ravenal de la Coste, "Somebody's Darling."

85. According to the 1860 Henrico County census, William G. and Elizabeth F. Paine had three sons: John W., aged nine; James G., aged six; and Robert A., aged two.

86. One of the pioneering improvements in medical treatment during the Civil War was the creation of an ambulance network to convey wounded soldiers from the battlefield to a field hospital. In the spring of 1862, the Richmond Ambulance Committee came into existence to facilitate medical care. The committee consisted of almost a hundred well-to-do citizens who were exempt from military service. See H. H. Cunningham, *Doctors in Gray* (Baton Rouge: Louisiana State University Press, 1958), 121–22.

87. The Marquis of Hartington (not Hastings) and Col. William Leslie were both influential members of Parliament. For delightful descriptions of the

two Englishmen in Confederate camps, see Heros von Borcke, *Memoirs of the Confederate War for Independence* (Edinburgh: William Blackwood and Sons, 1866), 2:163–67.

88. Joseph Pere Bell Wilmer, the son of Bishop Richard Hooker Wilmer of Alabama, would eventually become bishop of the Episcopal Diocese of Louisiana.

89. Heathsville is the seat of Northumberland County, where the Potomac River empties into Chesapeake Bay.

90. This was one of the Union's several all-German regiments. It was originally under the command of Col. (later Gen.) Louis Blencker. The Eighth New York was so scarcely mentioned in the *Official Records* during this period that one has to assume it was on detached duty behind the lines.

91. During February 12–14, a Union foraging expedition advanced from Pratt's Landing to Heathsville. Some five hundred members of the Second and Sixth Wisconsin used the army steamer *Alice Price* for part of the journey. Bushfield was the home of John A. Washington, brother of George Washington. *OR,* series 1, vol. 25, pt. 1, 16–18; George H. Otis, *The Second Wisconsin Infantry* (Dayton, Ohio: Morningside, 1984), 75.

92. Mrs. McGuire identified this individual in the Dinkins Copy as "L. Berkeley." However, no resident by that name appears in the 1860 or 1870 censuses for Northumberland, Lancaster, or Richmond counties.

93. On February 24, four small Confederate vessels attacked the Union gunboat *Indianola.* The capture of the Union vessel was a serious blow to Federal naval operations against Vicksburg.

94. Loss of the blockade-runner *Princess Royal* was especially crippling to the Southern cause because the ship was carrying four highly accurate Whitworth cannon recently manufactured in England. Union forces seized the vessel near Morris Island, South Carolina.

95. The most famous of the Confederate raiders that preyed on Union merchant shipping, the *Alabama* captured and burned fifty-five vessels and bonded ten others. In all, Capt. Raphael Semmes's privateer inflicted more than $5 million in damages to the U.S. merchant marine.

96. Another of the wooden cruisers employed by the Confederate navy on the high seas was the *Florida,* under Capt. John N. Maffitt and Capt. Charles W. Read. It captured thirty-eight ships before its own illegal seizure in a Brazilian port by the USS *Wachusetts* in October 1864.

97. From John Newton's "Why Art Thou Cast Down?"

98. In February 1863, French ambassador to America Henri Mercier proposed to Union secretary of state William H. Seward that the Federal government

appoint commissioners to negotiate with the Confederacy for ending the war. Seward rejected the suggestion in a long, detailed paper. Glyndon G. Van Deusen, *William Henry Seward* (New York: Oxford University Press, 1967), 361–62.

99. Mrs. Cornelia Stuart of Fairfax County and two of her daughters were among those living at the Ashland cottage with the McGuires. Laura Stuart was then in her late twenties and unmarried. The "Howitt" mentioned appears to have been a printer's error, for another of Mrs. Stuart's daughters was Harriett Eugenia Stuart. She was in her mid-thirties. Edward T. Wenzel, Vienna, Virginia, to editor, July 22, 2004.

100. Catherine Armistead Mason Rowland was the wife of Alexandria resident Isaac S. Rowland and an aunt by marriage of Emily Mason (mentioned in this diary). Like the McGuires, the Rowlands had to abandon their home at the outset of the war and seek refuge in Richmond. Catherine Rowland was also a volunteer nurse in Richmond military hospitals. *Southern Historical Society Papers* 41 (1916): 113; 1860 Virginia Census—Henrico County.

101. Probably the most influential minister in wartime Richmond was Dr. Charles Frederic Ernest Minnigerode, rector of St. Paul's Episcopal Church on Capitol Square. Powerful and eloquent, with a Hessian accent, Minnigerode counted President Davis among his huge congregation.

102. Soap making was an art not usually known to the upper classes. During the war, Mrs. McGuire sold soap for $1 a pound and taught others in Ashland how to produce it. Twice a week she delivered soap to customers while proceeding to her regular work. The added income was useful.

103. Deborah Primrose was the wife of a minister and a main character in Oliver Goldsmith's novel *The Vicar of Wakefield.*

104. As clothing shortages increased in the wartime South, more and more women resorted to wearing men's attire such as trousers. This trend has continued to modern times. Drew Gilpin Faust, *Mothers of Invention: Women of the Slaveholding South in the American Civil War* (Chapel Hill: University of North Carolina Press, 1996), 221–28.

105. These lines are from John Newton's "Why Art Thou Cast Down?" cited in the February 26, 1863, entry.

106. On March 13, 1863, a "fearful explosion" occurred at the Richmond Laboratory. Sixty-nine people were killed or wounded, of whom sixty-two were young female employees. The head of Confederate ordnance noted in his journal: "It is terrible to think of—that so much suffering should arise from causes probably within our control." Josiah Gorgas, *The Civil War Diary of General Josiah Gorgas,* ed. Frank E. Vandiver (Tuscaloosa: University of Alabama Press, 1947), 25.

107. Nannie Packard was the daughter of Dr. Joseph Packard of the Episcopal Theological Seminary in Alexandria.

108. Judge John White Brockenbrough had been a Virginia delegate to the ill-fated 1861 Peace Convention in Washington.

109. Mrs. George Harrison, the former Gulielma Gordon of Savannah, Georgia, was living in the Linden Row section of Richmond. Mrs. Burton Harrison, *Recollections Grave and Gay* (New York: Scribner's, 1911), 155.

110. The reference is to Jane Austen's famous novel.

111. On March 17, probing Union cavalry crossed the Rappahannock River at Kelly's Ford and encountered a strong Confederate force of horsemen. Fighting was brief but intense before the Federals retired.

112. Union forces under Gen. Robert H. Milroy occupied Winchester at Christmastime 1862. Milroy's six-month tenure there has been likened to a reign of terror. "The most despised and hated of the Federal officers who ruled the Town during the war," Milroy seized homes and supplies, censored mail, and exiled citizens for any offense. Garland A. Quarles, *Occupied Winchester, 1861–1865* (Winchester, Va.: Winchester-Frederick Historical Society, 1955), 86–91.

113. Amos 6:1.

114. This was the famous "bread riot" in which a predominantly female crowd surged through downtown Richmond in search of food. All too quickly the assemblage became a mob looting every store in sight. President Davis and Mayor Joseph C. Mayo, as well as a large contingent of troops, finally quelled the disturbance. Confederate authorities sought hard to play down the incident for the sake of morale. Local newspapers helped by characterizing the participants as "prostitutes," "professional thieves," "Yankee hags," and "gallow birds." *Richmond Examiner*, April 4, 1863; *Richmond Sentinel*, April 7, 1863.

115. "For I am determined not to know any thing among you, save Jesus Christ, and him crucified." I Corinthians 2:2.

116. Arthur Lee Stuart was the third son of Mrs. McGuire's friend Cornelia Stuart. He served in the Fifth Tennessee Cavalry.

117. Richmond's second largest wartime Episcopal church was St. James, which stood at the corner of Fifth and Marshall streets. Its beloved rector was Joshua Peterkin. One source states that his "constant purpose in life was to walk humbly in the sight of God and to do good to his fellow men rather than to exhort them loudly." Munford, *Richmond Homes*, 147.

118. The Dinkins Copy identifies the first gentleman as "Capin." George Norton served for a time as captain and assistant adjutant and inspector general on the staff of Louisiana general Randall L. Gibson. "A. S." is Arthur Stuart, identified in note 116.

119. While President Davis was openly praising Vicksburg's defenders for repulsing every Union offensive—including the attempted construction of a bypassing canal—Gen. U. S. Grant was moving his forces downriver to cross the Mississippi and come at Vicksburg from the east.

120. Nine Union ironclads attacked Fort Sumter on April 7 in an effort to destroy Charleston's major defense. Confederate batteries disabled five of the ships and convinced flag officer Samuel Du Pont that Charleston could not be taken by naval vessels alone.

121. Francis Charles Lawley, a former member of Parliament, had replaced William Howard Russell as chief correspondent for the *London Times* in America. Lawley devoted almost all of his attention to the Confederate side.

122. Edward O. N. Stansbury was a member of the All-Maryland Chesapeake Artillery, which served as a Virginia unit under Capt. James Forrest. The battery served as part of Richmond's defensive forces until 1864.

123. In the lull following the battle of Fredericksburg, Lee grew short of supplies and became increasingly concerned about a possible Union threat on the Virginia Peninsula. He dispatched Longstreet and two divisions to secure Richmond and gather forage. Longstreet laid siege to the Federal-held city of Suffolk but failed to disengage quickly enough to join Lee in time for the May 1863 Chancellorsville campaign.

124. President Lincoln, anxious over the inability of Union ironclads to penetrate Charleston harbor, ordered the naval commander to withdraw the fleet to the opening of the harbor.

125. Cedar Hill, the home of the Harris family, was roughly midway between Richmond and Fredericksburg. Robert B. Lancaster, *Old Homes of Hanover County, Virginia* (Hanover, Va.: Hanover County Historical Society, 1983), 74.

126. This reference is likely to Muscoe Russell Hunter Garnett, who served two terms in the U.S. Congress before becoming a firebrand for Southern independence.

127. Presbyterian cleric Beverly Tucker Lacy became chief of chaplains for Gen. "Stonewall" Jackson's Second Corps as well as the general's personal pastor. See James I. Robertson Jr., *Stonewall Jackson: The Man, the Soldier, the Legend* (New York: Macmillan, 1997), 683–85.

128. Union general Joseph Hooker devised a sophisticated plan for the 1863 spring offensive in Virginia. While two Union corps fixed Lee at Fredericksburg, Hooker and five corps would advance wide around Lee's left flank and get behind the Confederate army. Lee would be trapped in the middle. In the ensuing Chancellorsville campaign, Lee unleashed Gen. "Stonewall" Jackson

on a counterflanking movement and achieved what many consider Lee's most brilliant victory.

129. In Lee's first battlefield telegram to President Davis, he states: "We have again to thank Almighty God for a great victory." Lee's official report, submitted four months later, states that "the conduct of the troops cannot be too highly praised. Attacking largely superior numbers in strongly entrenched positions, their heroic courage overcame every obstacle of nature and art, and achieved a triumph most honourable to our arms." Lee, *Wartime Papers,* 452, 469.

130. Three .69-caliber musket balls struck Jackson. One passed through his left forearm, a second struck his right palm and broke two fingers, and the third splintered the bone and tore tendons three inches below his left shoulder. That third injury necessitated the amputation of the limb.

131. Elisha Franklin Paxton of Lexington was commanding the Stonewall brigade when he was killed on May 3 at Chancellorsville. Confederate losses in the campaign were 1,581 dead and 9,700 wounded, which represented 22 percent of Lee's army. *OR,* series 1, vol., 25, pt. 1, 809.

132. Lt. Bernard Hill Carter Jr. of the Third Virginia Cavalry was killed in the initial fighting at Chancellorsville. Sgt. Benjamin S. White of the Second Virginia fell in the May 3 action.

133. On May 1, Richmond native Richard Channing Price was serving as an aide to his cousin, Gen. J. E. B. "Jeb" Stuart, when he was slain. The Forty-eighth Virginia's Thomas Stuart Garnett was mortally wounded two days later in an attack.

134. As Hooker began his flanking movement against Lee's army, Union cavalry under Gen. George Stoneman galloped southward to destroy Confederate communications and threaten Richmond. The contingent that struck Ashland on May 3 was the Twelfth Illinois Cavalry. Its commander, Col. Hasbrouck Davis, reported: "Words cannot describe the astonishment of the inhabitants at our appearance. I assured them no harm would be done their persons or property, and we soon became better acquainted." *OR,* series 1, vol. 25, pt. 1, 1086.

135. The unexpected approach of Union cavalry created pandemonium among the capital's citizenry. See Putnam, *Richmond,* 214–15. Yet Stoneman's raid was so tactically sterile that he was relieved of command shortly thereafter.

136. George Washington Custis Stuart had been badly wounded in the face at the May 1862 battle of Winchester. He returned to duty in January 1863, only to be killed May 3 in front of Fredericksburg. Lee stated: "I am deprived of one whom I loved and admired, and whose presence always brought me pleasure." Robert J. Driver, *The 1st and 2nd Rockbridge Artillery* (Lynchburg, Va.: H. E. Howard, 1987), 79.

137. "The death of Stonewall Jackson doubtless caused more grief among the women generally than any other single event of the war." Francis Butler Simkins and James Welch Patton, *The Women of the Confederacy* (Richmond: Garrett and Massie, 1936), 215.

138. Lord Byron, *The Siege of Corinth*.

139. II Timothy 4:7–8.

140. Lt. Willoughby Newton Jr., of the Fortieth Virginia, resigned from service in September 1863 as a result of the amputation. He was a brother of regimental surgeon John Brockenbrough Newton.

141. This description was obviously a composite, but a number of women's accounts point to the substantial accuracy of McGuire's statement.

142. In mid-May, Union troops under Gen. George H. Gordon briefly occupied the York River town of West Point. Foraging expeditions, notably by the Twelfth Illinois Cavalry, roamed the countryside. Col. Hasbrouck Davis of that unit was not wounded in any of the actions.

143. At the summons of the president, Lee left his headquarters near Fredericksburg and spent May 14–17 in Richmond. He conferred with Davis, the cabinet, and the secretary of war about a second Northern invasion.

144. Capt. William B. Colston of the Second Virginia never recovered fully from the shell wound received at Fredericksburg. He saw little action thereafter because of the leg impairment. Frye, *2nd Virginia Infantry*, 90.

145. Colorful Richard S. "Old Lady" Ewell succeeded Jackson as commander of the Second Corps in Lee's army. However, the loss of a leg in the 1862 Second Manassas campaign, plus a limited strategic sense, made Ewell an ineffective corps leader.

146. By inference, Mrs. McGuire received this story from Ewell himself. An enriched version is in J. William Jones, *Christ in the Camp* (Richmond: B. F. Johnson, 1888), 105–6. In reality, a close friend of the Ewell family, Rev. Moses Drury Hoge, took an active interest in Ewell's spiritual welfare and probably did more to turn the general into a reformed Christian than any other individual. Donald C. Pfanz, *Richard S. Ewell: A Soldier's Life* (Chapel Hill: University of North Carolina Press, 1998), 266.

147. The passing of weary months of uncertainty and anxiety produced in Mrs. McGuire and others a nagging despondency. As early as September 1862, Sarah Morgan of Baton Rouge, Louisiana, was writing in her journal: "If I dared to hope that next summer would bring us Peace! I always prophesy it just six months off; but do I believe it? Indeed, I don't know what will become of us if it is delayed much longer." Sarah Morgan Dawson, *A Confederate Girl's Diary*, ed. James I. Robertson Jr. (Bloomington: Indiana University Press, 1960), 210.

148. In the spring of 1863, U. S. Grant undertook one of the most daring and decisive campaigns of the war. Crossing the Mississippi below Vicksburg, he struck eastward toward the state capital, Jackson. Gen. Joseph E. Johnston, the Confederate departmental commander, could not concentrate enough troops to defend Jackson, and Gen. John C. Pemberton would not leave the Vicksburg fortress to fight in the open. Confederate defenses were in disarray. Grant moved swiftly and won victories at Raymond (May 12), Jackson (May 14), Champion's Hill (May 16), and Big Black River (May 17). Federals then enveloped Vicksburg.

149. Flushed with success, Grant on May 19 and 22 launched attacks on the Vicksburg defenses. Repulse and heavy casualties in both engagements convinced Grant to resort to conventional siege operations that would last forty-seven days.

150. A native of Clarke County, Virginia, Groghan served in the First Maryland prior to his June 1862 enlistment in the Thirty-fifth Virginia Cavalry Battalion. On April 23, 1863, Groghan fell mortally wounded in action at Greenland Gap. Robert J. Driver Jr., *First & Second Maryland Infantry, C.S.A.* (Bowie, Md.: Heritage, 2003), 427; John E. Divine, *35th Battalion Virginia Cavalry* (Lynchburg, Va.: H. E. Howard, 1985), 23–24, 93.

151. *Tableaux vivants* were highly popular staged representations of familiar (usually patriotic) themes. Costumed women posed as in still life during a short musical piece. See Faust, *Mothers of Invention*, 26–28, 227.

152. Peace Democrat leader Clement L. Vallandigham ran for governor of Ohio in the spring 1863 elections. An inflammatory speech against both the war and the Lincoln administration led to Vallandigham's arrest on charges of treason. A military commission sentenced the politician to life imprisonment. Cries of protest in the North became so loud that Lincoln commuted imprisonment to banishment to the South.

153. Julia Johns was the daughter of Episcopal bishop John Johns. See John Sumner Wood, *The Virginia Bishop: A Yankee Hero of the Confederacy* (Richmond: Garrett and Massie, 1961), 30–31.

Selected Bibliography

Allan, Elizabeth Preston. *The Life and Letters of Margaret Junkin Preston*. Boston: Houghton Mifflin, 1903.

Anderson, William T. "The Freedmen's Bureau and Negro Education in Virginia." *North Carolina Historical Review* 29 (January 1952).

Andrews, Eliza Frances. *The War-time Journal of a Georgia Girl*. New York: D. Appleton, 1908.

Andrews, J. Cutler. *The South Reports the Civil War*. Princeton, N.J.: Princeton University Press, 1970.

Andrews, Matthew Page, ed. *The Women of the South in War Times*. Baltimore: Norman, Remington, 1920.

Ash, Stephen V. *When the Yankees Came: Conflict and Chaos in the Occupied South, 1861–1865*. Chapel Hill: University of North Carolina Press, 1995.

Bacot, Ada W. *A Confederate Nurse: The Diary of Ada W. Bacot, 1860–1863*. Edited by Jean V. Berlin. Columbia: University of South Carolina Press, 1994.

Barton, William E. *Lincoln at Gettysburg: What He Intended to Say; What He Said; What He Was Reported to Have Said; What He Wished He Had Said*. New York: P. Smith, 1930.

Beecher, Catharine Esther, and Harriet Beecher Stowe. *American Woman's Home; or, Principles of Domestic Science; Being a Guide to the Formation and Maintenance of Economical, Healthful, Beautiful, and Christian Homes*. New York: J. B. Ford, 1869.

Berlin, Ira, Barbara J. Fields, Steven F. Miller, Joseph P. Reidy, and Leslie S. Rowland, eds. *Free at Last: A Documentary History of Slavery, Freedom, and the Civil War*. New York: New Press, 1992.

Bigelow, John, Jr. *The Campaign of Chancellorsville: A Strategic and Tactical Study*. New Haven, Conn.: Yale University Press, 1910.

Blair, William. *Virginia's Private War: Feeding Body and Soul in the Confederacy, 1861–1865*. New York: Oxford University Press, 1998.

Blanton, Wyndham B. *Medicine in Virginia in the Nineteenth Century*. Richmond: Garrett and Massie, 1933.

Borcke, Heros von. *Memoirs of the Confederate War for Independence*. Edinburgh: William Blackwood and Sons, 1866.

Breckinridge, Lucy. *Lucy Breckinridge of Grove Hill: The Journal of a Virginia Girl, 1862–1864*. Edited by Mary D. Robertson. Columbia: University of South Carolina Press, 1994.

Bremner, Robert H. *The Public Good: Philanthropy and Welfare in the Civil War Era*. New York: Knopf, 1980.

Brewer, James H. *The Confederate Negro: Virginia's Craftsmen and Military Laborers, 1861–1865*. Durham, N.C.: Duke University Press, 1969.

Bridges, Peter. *Pen of Fire: John Moncure Daniel*. Kent, Ohio: Kent State University Press, 2002.

Brockett, L. P. *Women's Work in the Civil War: A Record of Heroism, Patriotism, and Patience*. Philadelphia: R. H. Curran, 1867.

Brown, Kent Masterson. *Retreat from Gettysburg: Lee, Logistics, and the Pennsylvania Campaign*. Chapel Hill: University of North Carolina Press, 2005.

Butchart, Ronald E. *Northern Schools, Southern Blacks, and Reconstruction: Freedmen's Education, 1862–1875*. Westport, Conn.: Greenwood, 1980.

Butler, Benjamin F. *Private and Official Correspondence of Gen. Benjamin F. Butler, during the Period of the Civil War*. 5 vols. Norwood, Mass.: Plimpton, 1917.

Campbell, Edward D. C., Jr., and Kym S. Rice, eds. *A Woman's War: Southern Women, Civil War, and the Confederate Legacy*. Richmond and Charlottesville: Museum of the Confederacy and the University Press of Virginia, 1996.

Carrington, Virgil. *The Hatfields and the McCoys*. Chapel Hill: University of North Carolina Press, 1948.

Chambers, Lenoir. *Stonewall Jackson*. 2 vols. New York: W. Morrow, 1959.

Chancellor, Sue M. "Personal Recollections of the Battle of Chancellorsville." *Register of the Kentucky Historical Society* 66 (April 1968).

Chesnut, Mary Boykin Miller. *Mary Chesnut's Civil War*. Edited by C. Vann Woodward. New Haven, Conn.: Yale University Press, 1981.

Cimbala, Paul A., and Randall M. Miller, eds. *The Freedmen's Bureau and Reconstruction: Reconsiderations*. New York: Fordham University Press, 1999.

Clinton, Catherine, and Nina Silber, eds. *Divided Houses: Gender and the Civil War*. New York: Oxford University Press, 1992.

Cole, Scott C. *34th Battalion Virginia Cavalry*. Lynchburg, Va.: H. E. Howard, 1993.

Connelly, Thomas Lawrence. *Autumn of Glory: The Army of Tennessee, 1862–1865*. Baton Rouge: Louisiana State University Press, 1971.

Cormier, Steven A. *The Siege of Suffolk: The Forgotten Campaign, April 11–May 4, 1863.* Lynchburg, Va.: H. E. Howard, 1989.

Cunningham, H. H. *Doctors in Gray: The Confederate Medical Service.* Baton Rouge: Louisiana State University Press, 1958.

Davis, Jefferson. *The Papers of Jefferson Davis.* Vol. 9. Edited by Lynda Lasswell Crist, Mary Seaton Dix, and Kenneth H. Williams. Baton Rouge: Louisiana State University Press, 1997.

———. *The Papers of Jefferson Davis.* Vol. 10. Edited by Lynda Lasswell Crist, Kenneth H. Williams, and Peggy L. Dillard. Baton Rouge: Louisiana State University Press, 1999.

Dawson, Francis Warrington. *Our Women in the War: An Address by Francis W. Dawson, Delivered February 22, 1887, at the Fifth Annual Re-union of the Association of the Maryland Line, at the Academy of Music.* Baltimore and Charleston, S.C.: Walker, Evans and Cogswell, 1887.

Dawson, Sarah Morgan. *A Confederate Girl's Diary.* Edited by James I. Robertson Jr. Bloomington: Indiana University Press, 1960.

DeBoer, Clara Merritt. *His Truth Is Marching On: African Americans Who Taught the Freedmen for the American Missionary Association, 1861–1877.* New York: Garland, 1995.

Divine, John E. *35th Battalion Virginia Cavalry.* Lynchburg, Va.: H. E. Howard, 1985.

Driver, Robert J. *The 1st and 2nd Rockbridge Artillery.* Lynchburg, Va.: H. E. Howard, 1987.

Engs, Robert Francis. *Freedom's First Generation: Black Hampton, Virginia, 1861–1890.* Philadelphia: University of Pennsylvania Press, 1979.

Faust, Drew Gilpin. *The Creation of Confederate Nationalism: Ideology and Identity in the Civil War South.* Baton Rouge: Louisiana State University Press, 1988.

———. *Mothers of Invention: Women of the Slaveholding South in the American Civil War.* Chapel Hill: University of North Carolina Press, 1996.

Fen, Sing-Nan. "Notes on the Education of Negroes at Norfolk and Portsmouth, Virginia, during the Civil War." *Phylon* 28 (Summer 1967).

Fleet, Betsy, and John D. P. Fuller, eds. *Green Mount: A Virginia Plantation Family during the Civil War: Being the Journal of Benjamin Robert Fleet and Letters of His Family.* Lexington: University of Kentucky Press, 1962.

Freedmen and Southern Society Project. *Freedom: A Documentary History of Emancipation, 1861–1867.* 5 vols. New York: Cambridge University Press, 1985–2008.

Freeman, Douglas Southall. *Lee's Lieutenants: A Study in Command.* 3 vols. New York: Scribner's Sons, 1942–1944.

Frye, Dennis E. *2nd Virginia Infantry.* Lynchburg, Va.: H. E. Howard, 1984.

Furgurson, Ernest B. *Ashes of Glory: Richmond at War.* New York: Knopf, 1996.

———. *Chancellorsville, 1863: The Souls of the Brave.* New York: Knopf, 1992.

Gallagher, Gary W., ed. *Chancellorsville: The Battle and Its Aftermath.* Chapel Hill: University of North Carolina Press, 1996.

———. *The Fredericksburg Campaign: Decision on the Rappahannock.* Chapel Hill: University of North Carolina Press, 1995.

Garfield, James A. *The Wild Life of the Army: Civil War Letters of James A. Garfield.* Edited by Frederick D. Williams. East Lansing: Michigan State University Press, 1964.

Gatewood, Willard B., ed. *Free Man of Color: The Autobiography of Willis Augustus Hodges.* Knoxville: University of Tennessee Press, 1982.

Gorgas, Josiah. *The Civil War Diary of General Josiah Gorgas.* Edited by Frank E. Vandiver. Tuscaloosa: University of Alabama Press, 1947.

Grunder, Charles S., and Brandon H. Beck. *The Second Battle of Winchester, June 12–15, 1863.* Lynchburg, Va.: H. E. Howard, 1989.

Harris, Brayton. *Blue and Gray in Black and White: Newspapers in the Civil War.* Washington, D.C.: Brassey's, 1999.

Harris, F. S. "Noted Character of West Virginia." *Confederate Veteran Magazine* 8 (October 1900).

Harrison, Noel G. *Fredericksburg Civil War Sites.* Lynchburg, Va.: H. E. Howard, 1995.

Hatfield, G. Elliott. *The Hatfields.* Stanville, Ky.: Big Sandy Valley Historical Society, 1974.

Heidler, David S., and Jeanne T. Heidler, eds. *Encyclopedia of the American Civil War: A Political, Social, and Military History.* Santa Barbara, Calif.: ABC-CLIO, 2000.

Henderson, William D. *The Road to Bristoe Station: Campaigning with Lee and Meade, August 1–October 20, 1863.* Lynchburg, Va.: H. E. Howard, 1987.

Hopley, Catherine Cooper. *Life in the South; From the Commencement of the War. By a Blockaded British Subject. Being a Social History of Those Who Took Part in the Battles, from a Personal Acquaintance with Them in Their Own Homes. From the Spring of 1860 to August 1862.* 1863. Reprint, New York: Augustus M. Kelley, 1971.

James, Felix. "The Establishment of Freedman's Village in Arlington, Virginia." *Negro History Bulletin* 33 (1970).

Johnson, Ludwell H., III. "Blockade or Trade Monopoly? John A. Dix and the Union Occupation of Norfolk." *Virginia Magazine of History and Biography* 93 (January 1985).

———, ed. "The Horrible Butcheries of West Virginia: Dan Cunningham on the Hatfield-McCoy Feud." *West Virginia History* 46 (1985–1986).

Johnson, Thomas C. *The Life and Letters of Robert Lewis Dabney.* Richmond: Presbyterian Committee of Publication, 1903.

Jones, John B. *A Rebel War Clerk's Diary.* Edited by Earl Schenck Miers. New York: Sagamore, 1958.

———. *A Rebel War Clerk's Diary at the Confederate States Capital.* Philadelphia: Lippincott, 1866.

Jones, Virgil Carrington. *The Hatfields and the McCoys.* Chapel Hill: University of North Carolina Press, 1948.

Jordan, Ervin L., Jr. *Black Confederates and Afro-Yankees in Civil War Virginia.* Charlottesville: University Press of Virginia, 1995.

Lamon, Ward Hill. *Recollections of Abraham Lincoln, 1847–1865.* Edited by Dorothy Lamon Teillard. Washington, D.C.: The editor, 1911.

Lancaster, Robert B. *Old Homes of Hanover County, Virginia.* Hanover, Va.: Hanover County Historical Society, 1983.

Lee, Robert E. *The Wartime Papers of R. E. Lee.* Edited by Clifford Dowdey. Boston: Little, Brown, 1961.

Lincoln, Abraham. *The Collected Works of Abraham Lincoln.* 9 vols. Edited by Roy P. Basler, Marion Dolores Pratt, and Lloyd A. Dunlap. New Brunswick, N.J.: Rutgers University Press, 1953–1955.

Lincoln Sesquicentennial Commission. *Lincoln Day by Day: A Chronology, 1809–1865.* Edited by Earl Schenck Miers. Washington: Lincoln Sesquicentennial Commission, 1960.

Manarin, Louis H. *15th Virginia Infantry.* Lynchburg, Va.: H. E. Howard, 1990.

———, comp. *North Carolina Troops, 1861–1865: A Roster.* Raleigh, N.C.: State Department of Archives and History, 1966–2003.

Marmion, Annie P. *Under Fire: An Experience in the Civil War.* N.p., 1959.

Marten, James. *The Children's Civil War.* Chapel Hill: University of North Carolina Press, 1998.

Massey, Mary Elizabeth. *Refugee Life in the Confederacy.* Baton Rouge: Louisiana State University Press, 1964.

Maury, Betty Herndon. *The Confederate Diary of Betty Herndon Maury, 1861–1863.* Edited by Alica Maury Parmalee. Washington: Privately printed, 1938.

McClure, Alexander K. *Recollections of Half a Century.* Salem, Mass.: Salem Press, 1902.

McCoy, Hobert, and Orville McCoy. *Squirrel Huntin' Sam McCoy: His Memoir and Family Tree.* Pikeville, Ky.: Pikeville College Press, 1979.

McCoy, Truda Williams. *The McCoys: Their Story as Told to the Author by Eye Witnesses and Descendants.* Edited by Leonard Roberts. Pikeville, Ky.: Preservation Council Press of the Preservation Council of Pike County, 1976.

McDonald, Cornelia Peake. *A Woman's Civil War: A Diary, with Reminiscences of the War from March 1862.* Edited by Minrose C. Gwin. Madison: University of Wisconsin Press, 1992.

McFeely, William S. *Yankee Stepfather: General O. O. Howard and the Freedmen.* New York: Norton, 1970.

McGuire, Judith W. *Diary of a Southern Refugee during the War.* New York: E. J. Hale and Son, 1867.

McPherson, James M. *Battle Cry of Freedom: The Civil War Era.* New York: Oxford University Press, 1988.

Miller, Randal, Harry S. Stout, and Charles Reagan Wilson, eds. *Religion and the American Civil War.* New York: Oxford University Press, 1998.

Morris, Robert C. *Reading, 'Riting, and Reconstruction: The Education of Freedmen in the South, 1861–1870.* Chicago: University of Chicago Press, 1981.

Munford, Robert Beverly, Jr. *Richmond Homes and Memories.* Richmond, Va.: Garrett and Massie, 1936.

Nevins, Allan. *The War for the Union.* New York: Scribner's, 1959–1971.

O'Neill, Robert F., Jr. *The Cavalry Battles of Aldie, Middleburg and Upperville, June 10–27, 1863.* Lynchburg, Va.: H. E. Howard, 1993.

Osborne, Randall, and Jeffrey C. Weaver. *The Virginia State Rangers and State Line.* Lynchburg, Va.: H. E. Howard, 1994.

Pember, Phoebe Yates. *A Southern Woman's Story: Life in Confederate Richmond.* Edited by Bell Irvin Wiley. Jackson, Tenn.: McCowat-Mercer, 1959.

Perdue, Charles L., Jr., Thomas E. Barden, and Robert K. Phillips, eds. *Weevils in the Wheat: Interviews with Virginia Ex-Slaves.* Charlottesville: University Press of Virginia, 1976.

Pfanz, Donald C. *Richard S. Ewell: A Soldier's Life.* Chapel Hill: University of North Carolina Press, 1998.

Phillips, David L., and Rebecca L. Hill. *War Diaries: The 1861 Kanawha Valley Campaigns.* Leesburg, Va.: Gauley Mount, 1990.

Piston, William Garrett. *Carter's Raid: An Episode of the Civil War in East Tennessee.* Johnson City, Tenn.: Overmountain, 1989.

Poore, Benjamin Perley. *The Life and Public Services of Ambrose E. Burnside, Soldier—Citizen—Statesman.* Providence, R.I.: J. A. and R. A. Reid, 1882.

Putnam, Sallie A. Brock. *In Richmond during the Confederacy: By a Lady of Richmond.* New York: R. M. McBride, 1961.

———. *Richmond during the War: Four Years of Personal Observation; By a Richmond Lady.* New York: G. W. Carleton, 1867.

Quarles, Garland A. *Occupied Winchester, 1861–1865.* Winchester, Va.: Winchester-Frederick Historical Society, 1955.

Quarles, Garland A., et al., eds. *Diaries, Letters, and Recollections of the War between the States.* Winchester, Va.: Winchester-Frederick Historical Society, 1955.

Rable, George C. *Fredericksburg! Fredericksburg!* Chapel Hill: University of North Carolina Press, 2002.

Rankin, Thomas M. *22nd Battalion Virginia Infantry.* Lynchburg, Va.: H. E. Howard, 1999.

Rhodes, Robert Hunt, ed. *All for the Union: A History of the 2nd Rhode Island Volunteer Infantry in the War of the Great Rebellion as Told by the Diary and Letters of Elisha Hunt Rhodes, Who Enlisted as a Private in '61 and Rose to the Command of His Regiment.* Lincoln, R.I.: A. Mowbray, 1985.

Rice, Otis K. *The Hatfields and the McCoys.* Lexington: University Press of Kentucky, 1978.

Richardson, Joe M. *Christian Reconstruction: The American Missionary Association and Southern Blacks, 1861–1890.* Athens: University of Georgia Press, 1986.

Risely, Ford. "The Confederate Press Association: Cooperative News Reporting of the War." *Civil War History* 47 (2001).

Robertson, James I., Jr. *General A. P. Hill: The Story of a Confederate Warrior.* New York: Random House, 1987.

———. *Stonewall Jackson: The Man, the Soldier, the Legend.* New York: Macmillan, 1997.

Robinson, Armistead L. *Bitter Fruits of Bondage: The Demise of Slavery and the Collapse of the Confederacy, 1861–1865.* Charlottesville: University of Virginia Press, 2005.

Ruchames, Louis, ed. *John Brown: The Making of a Revolutionary.* New York: Grosset and Dunlap, 1969.

Ruffin, Edmund. *The Diary of Edmund Ruffin.* 3 vols. Edited by William Kauffman Scarborough. Baton Rouge: Louisiana State University Press, 1972–1989.

Sears, Stephen W. *Chancellorsville.* Boston: Houghton Mifflin, 1996.

Selby, John G. *Virginians at War: The Civil War Experience of Seven Young Confederates.* Wilmington, Del.: Scholarly Resources, 2002.

Siddali, Silvana R. *From Property to Person: Slavery and the Confiscation Acts, 1861–1862.* Baton Rouge: Louisiana State University Press, 2005.

Simkins, Francis Butler, and James Welch Patton. *The Women of the Confederacy.* Richmond: Garrett and Massie, 1936.

Simpson, Craig M. *A Good Southerner: The Life of Henry A. Wise of Virginia.* Chapel Hill: University of North Carolina Press, 1985.

Staton, Willis David. *Hatfields and McCoys: True Romance and Tragedies.* Huntington, W.Va.: Algina, 1993.

Stiles, Kenneth L. *4th Virginia Cavalry.* Lynchburg, Va.: H. E. Howard, 1985.

Stiles, Robert. *Four Years under Marse Robert.* New York: Neale, 1903.

Stowe, Catherine E., and Harriet Beecher Stowe. *American Woman's Home; or, Principles of Domestic Science.* 1869. Reprint, Hartford, Conn.: Stowe-Day Foundation, 1985.

Sutherland, Daniel E. *Fredericksburg and Chancellorsville: The Dark Mark Campaign.* Lincoln: University of Nebraska Press, 1998.

———. *Seasons of War: The Ordeal of a Confederate Community, 1861–1865.* New York: Free Press, 1995.

Swint, Henry Lee, ed. *Dear Ones at Home: Letters from Contraband Camps.* Nashville: Vanderbilt University Press, 1966.

———. *The Northern Teacher in the South, 1862–1870.* New York: Octagon, 1967.

Teamoh, George. *God Made Man, Man Made the Slave: The Autobiography of George Teamoh.* Edited by F. M. Boney, Richard L. Hume, and Rafia Zafar. Macon, Ga.: Mercer University Press, 1990.

Thomas, Emory M. *The Confederate State of Richmond: A Biography of the Capital.* Austin: University of Texas Press, 1971.

———. *Robert E. Lee: A Biography.* New York: Norton, 1995.

United Daughters of the Confederacy, South Carolina Division. *South Carolina Women in the Confederacy.* Columbia, S.C.: State Company, 1903.

United States Surgeon General's Office. *The Medical and Surgical History of the War of the Rebellion.* 6 vols. Washington, D.C.: Government Printing Office, 1870–1888.

United States War Department. *War of the Rebellion: A Compilation of Official Records of the Union and Confederate Armies.* 128 vols. Washington, D.C.: Government Printing Office, 1880–1901.

Van Deusen, Glyndon G. *Proceedings of the Virginia State Convention of 1861.* 4 vols. Richmond: Virginia State Library, 1965.

——. *William Henry Seward.* New York: Oxford University Press, 1967.

Wagner, Margaret E., Gary W. Gallagher, and Paul Finkelman, eds. *The Library of Congress Civil War Desk Reference.* New York: Simon and Schuster, 2002.

Waitt, Robert W. *Confederate Military Hospitals in Richmond.* Richmond: Richmond Civil War Centennial Committee, 1964.

Walker, Clarence E. *A Rock in a Weary Land: The African Methodist Episcopal Church during the Civil War and Reconstruction.* Baton Rouge: Louisiana State University Press, 1982.

Waller, Altina. *Feud: Hatfields, McCoys, and Social Change in Appalachia, 1860–1900.* Chapel Hill: University of North Carolina Press, 1988.

Ward, Evelyn D. *The Children of Bladensfield.* New York: Viking, 1978.

Warren, Louis Austin. *Lincoln's Gettysburg Declaration: "A New Birth of Freedom."* Fort Wayne, Ind.: Lincoln National Life Foundation, 1964.

Weaver, Jeffrey C. *The Civil War in Buchanan and Wise Counties: Bushwhackers' Paradise.* Lynchburg, Va.: H. E. Howard, 1994.

——. *45th Battalion Virginia Infantry, Smith and Count's Battalions of Partisan Rangers.* Lynchburg, Va.: H. E. Howard, 1994.

Werner, Emmy E. *Reluctant Witnesses: Children's Voices from the Civil War.* Boulder, Colo.: Westview, 1998.

Wert, Jeffry D. *The Sword of Lincoln: The Army of the Potomac.* New York: Simon and Schuster, 2005.

Whites, LeeAnn. *The Civil War as a Crisis in Gender: Augusta, Georgia, 1860–1890.* Athens: University of Georgia Press, 1995.

Wilkins, B. H. *"War Boy": A True Story of the Civil War and Re-construction Days.* Tullahoma, Tenn.: Wilson Brothers, 1990.

Wills, Brian Steel. *The War Hits Home: The Civil War in Southeastern Virginia.* Charlottesville: University Press of Virginia, 2001.

Wittenberg, Eric J. *The Union Cavalry Comes of Age: Hartwood Church to Brandy Station, 1863.* Washington, D.C.: Brassey's, 2003.

Wood, Sumner. *The Virginia Bishop: A Yankee Hero of the Confederacy.* Richmond: Garrett and Massie, 1961.

Woodworth, Steven E. *Six Armies in Tennessee: The Chickamauga and Chattanooga Campaigns.* Lincoln: University of Nebraska Press, 1998.

——. *While God Is Marching On: The Religious World of Civil War Soldiers.* Lawrence: University Press of Kansas, 2001.

Wyatt-Brown, Bertram. *Yankee Saints and Southern Sinners.* Baton Rouge: Louisiana State University Press, 1985.

Index